*B*y examining the structures of ego in the light of the Enneagram and the study of chaos in systems, Dr. Wolinsky opens up entire new ways of understanding the roadblocks to our psychological and spiritual growth. Anyone making use of his many anecdotes and exercises is sure to make significant personal breakthroughs.

Don Richard Riso & Russ Hudson,
Authors of the forthcoming
Working with the Enneagram and *Personality Types,*
Understanding the Enneagram, Discovering Your Personality Type,
and *Enneagram Transformation*

Quantum Consciousness: The Tao of Chaos is very timely in that it focuses on one of the major virtues of creative people—their ability to go on in spite of chaos and imperfections in their lives. Wolinsky masterfully develops therapy exercises to improve our ability to deal with chaos.

Amit Goswami Ph.D.,
author of *The Self-Aware Universe:*
How Consciousness Creates the Material World

QUANTUM CONSCIOUSNESS VOLUME II

THE TAO OF CHAOS

ESSENCE AND THE ENNEAGRAM

STEPHEN H. WOLINSKY

BRAMBLE❖BOOKS

Connecticut

For information write to:
Bramble Books, HC2, Box 8, Route 212, Bearsville, NY 12409

Library of Congress Cataloging-in-Publication Data

Wolinsky, Stephen
    The tao of chaos : essence and the enneagram / Stephen H.
Wolinsky.
        p.   cm.
    Includes bibliographical references and index.
    ISBN 1-883647-02-9 (pbk.)
    1. Psychology—Philosophy. 2. Personality. 3. Quantum
chaos. I. Title.
BF38.W768 1994
150.19'8—dc20   94-33697
                                                      CIP

First Printing 1994
1 3 5 7 9 10 8 6 4 2

Printed in the United States of America

The paper used in this publication meets the minimum requirements
of American National Standard for Information Sciences—
Permanence of Paper for Printed Library Materials,
ANSI Z39.48-1984.

DEDICATION

To the memory of Nisargadatta Maharaj, the ultimate de-programmer.

To the memory of Dr. David Bohm, the father of Energy, Space, Mass, and Time.

ACKNOWLEDGMENTS

Carl Ginsburg, Ph.D.
Jan Sultan
Kristi Kennen, M.S.W.
David Katzin, Ph.D., M.D.
Claudio Naranjo, Ph.D.
Idries Shah
Don Richard Riso
Helen Palmer
Susan Briley (word processing)
Jessie Page (copy edit)
Debra Ashton
Jerald H. Grimson (illustrator)

Special thanks and acknowledgment to Oscar Ichazo. At the time of the completion of this book, I had not seen the Arica materials. However, there is no doubt that the Arica Master Oscar Ichazo is the original source and father of the present day enneagram which he calls the enneagon.

To all my workshop participants and sponsors who were willing to explore their outer and inner chaos.

THE AUTHOR

Stephen H. Wolinsky, Ph.D., began his clinical practice in Los Angeles, California in 1974. A Gestalt and Reichian therapist and trainer, he led workshops in Southern California. He was also trained in Classical Hypnosis, Psychosynthesis, Psychodrama/Psychomotor, and Transactional Analysis. In 1977 he journeyed to India, where he lived for almost six years studying meditation. He moved to New Mexico in 1982 to resume a clinical practice. There he began to train therapists in Ericksonian Hypnosis, N.L.P. and family therapy. Dr. Wolinsky also conducted year-long trainings entitled: Integrating Hypnosis with Psychotherapy, and Integrating Hypnosis with Family Therapy. Dr. Wolinsky is also the author of *Trances People Live: Healing Approaches in Quantum Psychology*® (Bramble Books), *Quantum Consciousness: The Guide to Experiencing Quantum Psychology*® (Bramble Books), and *The Dark Side of the Inner Child: The Next Step* (Bramble Books). He is the co-developer of Quantum Seminars™ and the founder of Quantum Psychology®. Along with Kristi L. Kennen, M.S.W., he founded the first Quantum Psychology Institute®. For more information write: Quantum Psychology Institute®, c/o The Bramble Company, PO Box 209, Norfolk, CT 06058. To reach Dr. Stephen Wolinsky by phone: if you are using ATT dial 0 (700) 661-1993, for non-ATT dial 10288 0 (700) 661-1993.

TABLE OF CONTENTS

Section IV: Streams of Consciousness

Over the past 25 years of my life, I have explored in depth the field of psychology, the Yoga tradition of India, the Buddhist approach to self-realization, and Sufi Psychology, along with Quantum Physics. What became part of my study was a search for a *unified field theory* in Psychology.

For many years noted physicist Stephen Hawking has been writing about the search for a unified field theory in physics. When he says unified field theory, he means a *Theory of Everything*. Stephen Hawking believes that before the end of the century, there is a very high probability that there will be a unified field theory in physics which would describe the *movements of everything*.

This lead me to begin to look at a possibility of a unified field theory for the field of psychology or, better said, a theory of human behavior which describes the creation of personality. More simply put, an *organizing principle* that can explain the way personality is created, developed, and maintained—with the context not only being the individual, but including the entire universe. With this understanding in mind, Quantum Physics has demonstrated that everything is connected to everything else. In this way, behind all appearances of differences there exists a unified field of interconnected wholeness. Quantum Psychology holds this unified field or background as its context. The appearance of personality is space which has boundaries. For this reason and with this as my intention, I will offer an organizing principle of personality with its background being the underlying unity or unified field.

Most psychologies have offered this to varying degrees, as per the individual, but none have used the science of physics as its cornerstone, and none has included the unified field as its context. Psychology has organized and developed a system of human behavior based on the study of the individual. Family therapy made a leap as it expanded the context of human behavior to include the family unit. Social scientists and political frames from the Greeks to Karl Marx have expanded the nature of the context of human behavior to include the world and its economic and social orders. Quantum Psychology however, is asking us to take yet another leap; the development of a *Psychology of Everything* by expanding the context of the individual to include the entire universe.

In order to do this, we must stand on the shoulders of Quantum Physics and the emerging new Science of Chaos. In my former book *Quantum Consciousness: The Guide to Experiencing Quantum Psychology*, parallel universes and chaos theory were mentioned but were not explored in depth. One purpose of this book is to explore both of those in depth and use hard science as a jumping off point to create a unified field theory for psychology; a Psychology of Everything. Such a theory could be used to explain the organization of personality, and the creation of systems used by the personality which self-organize and maintain the limited and outdated psychic-apparatus of the individual mind.

The Tao of Chaos Made Simple

For example, let's imagine a child that has to face the uncertainty and chaos of an abusive father. To handle Dad, the child develops the false I-dentity called obedient son. Years later, the adult no longer needs this compliant obedient false self or I-dentity. However, the I-dentity develops a life of its own, and automatically organizes the adult's life years later. Stated more simply, the adult is organized by its earlier created I-dentity (obedient son to handle abusive Dad), rather than the obedient I-dentity being organized by the individual in present time.

Consequently, we have two important ideas. First, chaos seeks order by creating an obedient I-dentity, and second, to resist the chaos in the future, the obedient I-dentity is placed on automatic. Stated another way, chaos organizes the creation of an internal I-dentity and is maintained through a resistance to imagined future chaos. This creates and maintains the future subjective reality of the adult in present time.

The title *The Tao of Chaos* was chosen because understanding chaos in the physical universe and as it is mirrored in the individual psyche helps us to go beyond the resistance to chaos within ourselves. This, as will be demonstrated later, helps us to move through different and "higher" levels of order, rather than an attempt to freeze the chaos in order to manage it. What I have found to be most extraordinarily pervasive, in our society if not in all societies, is the *resistance to chaos*. People seem to *resist chaos* in their lives, people seem to *resist chaos* emotionally, people seem to *resist chaos* in their thought processes. There is a general and very powerful resistance to the experience of being out of control or chaotic in one's life.

Most religions, certainly the Buddhist religion, the Hindu religion, Christianity, the Sufi, Neo-Sufi, the esoteric traditions, and the *religion* of psychology, attempt to try and make sense out of and create belief structures that can order this chaos; this apparent randomness that we all find so intolerable and must resist. However, in order to be free one must be willing to ride the rapids of chaos. This allows the larger context or unified field to be included which connects us to the universe. In other words, by not resisting chaos, a more subtle form of order occurs. The way out of chaos is through it. This is the context of a psychology that chooses chaos as its organizing principle[1] and as the vehicle to reach a more universally integrated state, or what I call a no-state state. This no-state state is a more subtle form of order. Stated another way, it is the chaos which we resist that can lead us to a deeper order.

In *Quantum Consciousness* we talked of Dr. David Bohm's implicate order, which is the quantum field or emptiness. When the particles and waves and the field are seen as moving together and the same substance, Bohm calls this vision the second implicate order.

> "The first implicate order applies to the original field...
> And the second, or superimplicate order, applies to
> the "superfield" or information that organizes the
> original field.: (*Science, Order and Creativity* by
> David Bohm and F. David Peat, Bantam, 1987, p. 183)

This suggests that the second implicate order when the particles and space are seen as the same substance, contains the information that organizes the entire system. Simply stated, the chaos that the individual experiences, if the context is expanded, allows the emptiness of the unified quantum field or implicate order to become available. When the implicate (field) and explicate (chaos) are seen as the same, then the second implicate becomes available, and order is revealed. We all can feel that we resist chaos; we try to order chaos so

---

[1] See Chapter 20, The Organizing Principle, *Trances People Live: Healing Approaches in Quantum Psychology* by Stephen Wolinsky, Bramble Books, 1991.

that our lives make sense, our world makes sense, and the universe makes sense. But by attempting to manage the chaos, or apparent randomness of the world, we have created separate subjective structures and internal universes to explain such things. Unfortunately, creating structures to manage or explain chaos *continues* the chaos. It is through *allowing* chaos that higher orders can be revealed (Discussed in Section II).

Bell's Theorem

John Stuart Bell, who I mentioned at the end of *Quantum Consciousness Volume I*, created one of the most powerful theorems in Quantum Physics. Noted physicist Henry Stapp calls Bell's Theorem "The most important discovery in the field of science."[2] Bell's Theorem says that there is no local cause in the physical universe and that there is no location in the physical universe.

To look at this requires a very subtle inner vision. For if Bell's statement is correct—that there is no location in the universe—then there are no things you can point to as having causal relationship; *this causes that*. The universe and its actions are causeless and the ultimate cause, or better said the causeless cause, has order. This order, however, cannot be seen at the level of the individual, only at the level of the second implicate. At the level of the explicate this appears extraordinarily random. This promotes the feeling of chaos. Very few people would deny that they continually ask themselves, "*Why* did so and so get a promotion, and I not get a promotion? After all, I seem to deserve it, I worked harder." Questions like these continually pop into our minds because the world seems chaotic.

Some spiritual systems talk about the theory of karma to explain this discrepancy between action (what is done) and reaction (what is received). In Christianity it is said, "What

---

[2]*Einstein's Moon: Bell's Theorem and the Curious Quest for Quantum Reality* by F. David Peat, Contemporary Books, Chicago, 1990.

you sow so shall you reap." In Asia, reincarnation explains this discrepancy between sowing and reaping. For example, in a past life, I did this to so and so and my karma is coming back to me. It is related as cause and effect. This is a way of trying to *order chaos through explanation.* This *resists chaos* and keeps us stuck in chaos. What is important in this book is to look at what our *resistance to chaos* is and, as David Peat says in *The Philosophers Stone:*

> "possibly chaos is actually the natural order and in that chaos there might be islands of order. But chaos is the order." *The Philosophers Stone* by F. David Peat, Bantam Books, New York, 1991.

The *resistance* to chaos keeps the chaos there, makes life uncomfortable, but more importantly robs us of a higher order whereby interconnection and unity are revealed.

> "Order is actually being born out of chaos; rather than chaos out of order." *The Philosophers Stone* by F. David Peat, Bantam Books, New York, 1991, p. 199.

For example, if you could picture yourself as a very turbulent river. If you try to resist the flow of the river then you will experience more and more chaos. You will experience the water batting against your chest, your stomach; your whole self being knocked around. But if you become the water and flow with the water, then all of a sudden a new order comes out of the chaos. There was once a Zen teacher who said that the way he became enlightened is that he went down to the freeway and he saw that all the cars were going one way and he decided that all he would have to do is to go that way, to go in the direction the cars were already going.

So what we are going to explore is the notion that chaos has a natural order to it. That chaos, the thing we resist so much, actually has a beauty and an order to it. That when explored and discovered as an energy flow, chaos allows us, as David Bohm would say, "a deeper interconnectedness to ourselves as the universe."

Chronic Problem States and Chaos

The development of a diagnosis and treatment for the recognition of the order of chaos requires a reabsorption of frozen, stuck I-dentities or false selves that were created and whose purpose was to resist chaos. In the second two-thirds of the book, we will look at Essence as the second implicate order, and how by touching Essence, the personality can be reabsorbed. Stated another way, personality is the explicate order, Essence the second implicate, and the implicate is the quantum field. This will be discussed later in Section III, with exercises, and individual case studies.

Psychology

Psychology has a brief history. Although the early Greek philosophers searched to remedy the human condition, the world of psychology has been dominated by philosophies placed in action. By this I mean that each branch or school of psychology demonstrates a map or pathway to release the suffering of the human condition, and for the most part psychology is a soft science.

Although psychology has scored many successes in areas of human behavior from sexual dysfunction to family therapy, from phobic relief to chronic depression, the art of psychotherapy has left many questions unanswered and has left many dissatisfied customers.

The why of this will depend on the brand of therapy your therapist is offering, which will limit her/his ability to pierce through the uncharted waters of problem resolution. For example, few therapies can help all problems, although many claim to, and each form of therapy is limited by the model it represents.

This can best be understood by noted philosopher Alfred Korsybski's the "map is not the territory." This means that the therapist is offering a map of reality, which if the client puts it on like a pair of glasses, the client will view and, hence, experience life differently.

Time need not be spent here exploring all the different schools of psychotherapy, their belief systems, how they work, their development, application or position. This would only duplicate what has been written about over the last century and, I think, burden the reader with more and more maps and models of how reality is constructed.

A Unified Field Theory of Human Behavior

In the hard sciences, a *Theory of Everything* would be a monumental breakthrough. Unquestionably in the soft sciences of psychology and human behavior what is also needed is a *unified field theory*; a theory that can explain all the whys and wherefores of human behavior—why changes occur or do not occur and a view of reality that offers a scientific explanation of human interactions and behavior. This would include why change occurs or doesn't occur, and what is the "purpose," if any, of the discomfort and pain we all experience.

In order to broach such an enormous project, it becomes imperative to include the science of Quantum Physics, and more importantly, the most recent developments in the area of Chaos Theory.

It is by using these two approaches that we can hope to create a unified field theory in the area of human behavior, presently referred to as psychology. It is with this hope and intention that we can move toward an understanding of the nature of reality in general and, specifically, the nature of human behavior.

To do this will require the reader to delve into a layman's (which is mine) understanding of simple physics and Chaos

Theory. I beg the reader not to be scared of physics and science since I flunked Physics 101 in college, got a D in Biology, and failed Geology. Believe me when I say the explanation comes from a simple understanding of how reality occurs. So, please don't be put off by the science in the first 50 pages.

I will attempt to stand on the shoulders of the proven world of physics, to use their world and principles to propose a treatise of human behavior based on the movement of energy through the world.

This step can help to answer questions of what is God or supreme intelligence and finally you.

To do this we need to look at fundamental principles of Chaos theory and apply them to Psychology so that we can explain human interactions.

To do this we must look at CHAOS. As mentioned earlier, much of our lives are spent trying to manage chaos. For example, I feel overwhelmed at business, so to handle the "out of control," I have a business manager. I feel confused in my relationship with my spouse, so I hire a therapist to help me sort things out. I feel uncertain about myself, who I am, and my purpose, so I look for spiritual and philosophical answers to these questions. None of these steps is wrong, but it is the Chaos which we are resisting that pushes us to hire, or find an answer. This experience of chaos, which most of us resist, is so hard to handle that we seek professionals from all fields—from medical to spiritual to economic—to handle these feelings.

The Tao of Chaos

The fact is that life and the universe appear as chaos—an unexplainable and out-of-control dilemma—to the individual. The philosophies we seek to explain or "calm us down" are actually attempts to *resist* the fact that *chaos is the rule not the exception. Systems attempt to order chaos*, when what we need is a *TAO OF CHAOS*, or a way to not resist and allow chaos to order itself and reveal its true nature.

This book is divided into four sections. Section I explores basic understandings in Chaos Theory and Quantum Physics, and, if you find it *too much*, feel free to bypass it and move on to the more *experiential* sections. Section II utilizes these basic understandings with exercises so that *experiencing* Chaos Theory and Quantum Psychology can become more available. Section III moves into the diagnostic as well as the *Therapy of the Enneagram*. This section is in no way an attempt to *rewrite* the Enneagram. Rather, it looks for the first time, at a therapy that can be done with oneself and another to trance-end the enneagram fixations and their diagnostic counter part—character analysis—to enter into the essence of your real self. This section concludes with a summary called advanced attention training. This is a dramatic view taking the reader beyond the observer and it's fixations of attention. Finally, Section IV: Systems of Consciousness contains three articles; the first by myself on compassion. The second by Dr. Carl Ginsburg, an International Feldenkrais Trainer. The third article by Jan H. Sultan; senior member of the Rolf Institute of Structural Integration. These last two articles on Feldenkrais and Rolfing respectively were placed in the book to acquaint the reader, who maybe unfamiliar with them, with an integral part of my own self-discovery. I do not separate the mind and body, but rather see them as one unit. With this in mind, the work of Quantum Psychology has limitations. Feldenkrais and Rolfing fill those gaps, and, at every workshop I present around the country I always emphasize the importance of these two forms of hands-on somatic work in order to continue and deepen the work of Quantum Psychology.

What this book intends is to give us a way to allow chaos to be the rule rather than the exception. A process whereby chaos becomes our friend, a familiar experience, a welcome home or even a fuel to bring us back to our universal nature. All of our efforts to *order* chaos through resisting it by creating more and more systems to manage it have fallen short. It appears obvious that an individual born of chaos and resistance to chaos could only beget more chaos and resistance.[3]

The Tao of Chaos is about looking at our most resisted experience from several vantage points so that chaos is no longer an enemy but a friend. To do this will require the reader to participate in exercises which will ask you to experience your chaos. How else can you "get to know" this experience and yourself unless you're willing to "get to know" it?

Remember the old song:

"Getting to know you
Getting to know all about you.
When I am with you
Getting to know what to say. . . .

Then suddenly I am bright and breezy
Because of all the beautiful and new
Things I'm learning about you

day by day."

Hopefully when you finish doing the exercises in this book, you will be freer to welcome, not resist chaos and to use it as the pathway to your deepest nature.

With love
Your brother
Stephen

---

[3] This is discussed in my third book, *The Dark Side of the Inner Child: The Next Step* by Stephen Wolinsky, Ph.D., Bramble Books, 1993.

SECTION I
THE BEGINNING

I n 1987, I bought my first book on Chaos, appropriately called *Chaos* by James Gleick. What was intriguing me was a search for a theory in the hard science of Physics to explain human behavior. Also, human behavior for the individual, along with social, political, economic and religious systems must have some type of organizer. I was looking for something, some theory, some understanding, that could explain the emergence of psychological and religious systems as maps of reality. Why for example, did psychology emerge, what context caused the formation of spiritual understandings that created philosophies and systems? Here, as we stand at the beginning of the 21st century, it seemed paramount to find out the *bottom line* in the creation of systems. In the summer of 1989 I found my answer: **Chaos Theory.**

Let us begin by defining the word chaos.

Cha-os n. (1) Utter confusion or disorder wholly without organization or order. (2) The infinity of space or formless matter supposed to have preceded the existence of the ordered universe. (3) A chasm or abyss. (*The American College Dictionary*, Random House, New York, 1963, p. 201)

The first sections of this book will explore definition #1, the utter confusion or disorder wholly without organization or order. Much time has been spent however, in detailing this in my third book, *The Dark Side of the Inner Child: The Next Step.* The third section of the book will look at the perceived inner chaos or what we normally experience as an internal gnawing emptiness.

Let us begin by stating the basic principle of the *Tao of Chaos.*

Principle: All psychological systems are born out of resistance to chaos; or an attempt to organize chaos.

What does this mean? That, in order to resist the out-of-control, confused, overwhelmed feelings of life which are intolerable, we create elaborate psychological and spiritual systems in an attempt to *have it make sense.* In other words, we create internal explanations of external reality because we cannot have anything that doesn't make sense. Just a mere mention of the word chaos or craziness makes us all resist and shudder; not wanting to deal with either our own, or another's chaos.

To illustrate how psychological systems are created to handle and understand chaos, let us look at two contemporary theorists. First, *Wilhelm Reich, M.D.: The Father of Body Centered Psychotherapy.* The psychotherapy of Wilhelm Reich, M.D. is based on the biological process of energy being taken in the body and discharging out of the body. This natural vegetative biological process is illustrated in Reich's classic work, *The Function of the Orgasm.* Reich demonstrates that the orgasm has a regulatory function of discharging excess energy. Reich believed that when excess sexual energy (libido) was discharged in the orgasm, the person would be healthy. He believed that if the orgasm was "incomplete," the excess energy in the body would move up to the head creating thoughts, fantasies, and self-defeating intraphyic structures. Reich based psychological health on the ability to reach orgastic potency and discharge excess energy. Stated in a very simplistic and crude way; if you can have a good orgasm, you are healthy, if you can't have a good orgasm, you aren't healthy. The therapy was about the power of orgasm, and in a very systematic way Reich would help the client remove chronic "blocks" he called body armor which were inhibiting the natural charge and discharge of biological energy. What was the chaos within Reich that he was attempting to understand?

In the autobiography of Reich, it is quite clear that Reich as a small boy had several sexual encounters at approximately age four. We would certainly now call this sexual abuse. Reich came from a wealthy family and his father would often go away on business for months at a time. To tutor little Wilhelm, his parents hired a boy about age 20 to live with the family.

During one of his father's absences, Reich witnessed his mother making love with the tutor. Reich watched over many different nights and felt excited. Upon his return, Wilhelm's father sensed something had happened. He confronted Wilhelm's mother, and she denied that anything occurred. The father then went to little Wilhelm. Wilhelm told his father about the love affair his mother was having with the tutor. His father then confronted Wilhelm's mother and she committed suicide. Within two years, Wilhelm's father died from the pain of the experience.

It is easy to understand why Reich would create a therapy with the major focus on the power of orgasm, as an attempt to understand, "what happened."

Milton H. Erickson, M.D.

Milton H. Erickson, M.D. is arguably the most important contributor to the clinical use of hypnosis, certainly in recent years, if not in this century.

Milton Erickson suffered greatly from polio as a teenager, and later was bedridden; unable to move. Erickson had constant physical pain and also had several strokes.

In *Life Reframing in Hypnosis*; Erickson, being bedridden, had to face the chaos of the situation. He began to imagine times as a boy in Wisconsin picking up a pitch fork. He focused his attention on the image, and began to be able to move his hands. Eventually, Erickson was able to walk with crutches. Erickson also had to face the chaos of great physical pain.

What therapy and philosophy did Dr. Erickson adopt? First, he became a master of pain control, helping others and himself make tremendous progress in the field of hypnosis for pain control. It is said that Erickson would do self-hypnosis for pain control up to three hours a day so that he was able to then help others with their physical and psychological pain. Secondly, Erickson developed an application never before used in hypnosis, namely, the philosophy, "the resources a client needs lies in their personal history."

Advancing the field of hypnosis and psychotherapy to another level, Erickson began to use hypnosis to access resources which he had in the unconscious memory and were being unused, like his accessing the boy moving his hand (the resource) to grab the pitchfork. He used hypnosis to enable clients to bring unused resources from the past into present time situations.

Who else could become a master of pain control and develop the ability to handle their own chaos through resource retrieval, but one who had to do it to handle their own chaos.

At the thought or feeling of being chaotic or out of control, there is an immediate reaction to clamp down, hold on, and tighten our muscles or make sense out of it. "Let's put this craziness out of our mind." This meager attempt to control our own and another's craziness (chaos) or certainly to understand it and have it go away has been the origin of Psychology and Philosophy. Certainly most people experience another's craziness as something they wish *to run away from*, and our own as something to *get rid of*. The question is, why does there seem to be such a "strict" automatic reaction to avoid or run away from craziness? Perhaps it is programming, a social stigma, perhaps a decision that this discomfort is not okay.

But what's wrong with craziness or chaos? What is wrong with feeling surges of energy and sensations running through out our body? And what, if anything, is its purpose?

What is wrong with craziness (chaos)? Well, obviously when I say the word crazy, people have associations of a mad woman/man with hair thrown in ten directions, yelling four-letter words, dressed in rags, or in a straight jacket. Our society doesn't seem to like chaos and individually our efforts are to stay "cool," "get control over it," and avoid it at all costs.

Chaos Theory, a recent (last 20 years) discovery in Physics has provoked much interest lately because of the unpredictable pattern of weather. This craziness has created a new science in trying to find out if there is order in chaos. The answer has come up with a *yes*.

Why do people resist surges of energy and feeling out of control? Once again, we have all been conditioned to control our feelings (anger), control this energy.

The free flow of energy occurs constantly, be it as a thought, a feeling, a look (energy) from one person to another. Yet so much time is spent trying to hold in or not allow the energy flow from self-to-self, or from self-to-other.

There are taboos to just allowing the flow of energy. If I say, "I like you" to someone (which is a flow of energy) the person might have an experience (which is made of energy) of feeling uneasy. For example, they might have a thought (which is made of energy) "What does that mean?" "Does he like me? Want to sleep with me?" etc. More often than not the energy from self to other is blocked by self or the energy once received is dissipated or thwarted upon receipt of the energy. In case of the former, the "I love you" energy is blocked, solidified, and the energy becomes a thought like, "Well, I'm not sure, should I or shouldn't I say it." This makes the individual feel a little crazy. The individual might dissipate the energy by saying to herself, "He really doesn't mean it" or "Why me, I'm not attractive," etc. All these are attempts to organize the flow of energy from one individual system into another. At an individual level, when energy is in the form of another person, and enters into your system, momentarily your system feels chaotic. To resist this chaos the system attempts to organize or order the chaos through blocking it out, tightening muscles and dissipating it. In short, the system, i.e. you, resists the extra energy of another person by organizing what their behavior means, or solidifying the natural flow of the energy of one person adding energy into your system. It is in the energy flow that chaos is experienced, and the resistance to this extra energy by us denies us a deeper order which might become available.

Why we do this will be described later, for now however, suffice it to say that as energy moves from self-to-self or self-to-other, the energy disrupts the stable system making the person feel a little uneasy, crazy, out of control, or chaotic. Rather than allowing the chaos, which will lead us to a higher order, we resist it, leading us into a separate self-organizing individual universe, which most of us experience as painful, lonely, isolated, alienated, etc.

The third question; "Why?" This can best be summed up as follows. Recently, I was giving a workshop on Quantum Psychology; the workshop was mostly about experiencing *Quantum Consciousness*.

When I began talking about Chaos Theory, one of the participants, Carl Ginsburg, a Feldenkrais trainer and also former President of the Feldenkrais Guild, commented that years ago he was working directly with Moshe Feldenkrais. Feldenkrais asked a group of his trainees, "What is the function of the nervous system?" After coming up with many ideas Feldenkrais said, "The function of the nervous system is to organize chaos."

This is precisely what Chaos Theory suggests, that energy (feeling) comes into your system from "another system," you feel a little chaotic about it, and you attempt to *order* the chaos so that you feel comfortable, actually familiar. The problem arises in that we always seem to order the energy in the *same way*, or we might say we organize the energy (feelings) coming in in such a way as to always get the same outcome. For example, recently Dr. Ginsburg and I were conducting a workshop on the west coast. A man in the training had a memory of having eczema as a child and that his parents had tied him up so he could not scratch himself. Two points need to be made to appreciate how he and his nervous system ordered chaos. First, he made himself as comfortable as possible given his situation. This, of course, was not very comfortable. The second, and more important point, is that the position that was found, which was still uncomfortable by most standards, became his *reference point* for comfort. In other words, he organized the chaos so as to be as comfortable as he could, and then this *position* became his *reference point or standard for comfort*. This rigid pathway of what energy is let in and what energy is let out is a pattern or habit of behavior. This habit is an attempt to organize chaos. Chaos therefore is often perceived as anything which disrupts a psychological system. In the above mentioned case; even if it is uncomfortable, he would use this *discomfort as his new standard for comfort*.

In another way, if I see myself as unattractive and someone says "I'm attracted to you," the energy disrupts my system and I begin to feel nervous and fearful and maybe will even avoid seeing a person or having further contact. The energy that comes in from the statement from the person saying, "I'm attracted to you," feels chaotic to the individual who has a frozen internal image of themselves as being unattractive. If the outcome is painful enough, you'll see a therapist or family counselor. Noted Fourth Way teacher G.I. Gurdjieff often said that people have a limited number of positions both physical and psychological. This means that there is a rigidity in the system that doesn't allow many experiences to be experienced subjectively. For example, few people would deny that anger or fear are not allowed or are resisted inside their bodies. Dr. William Reich said that the body is an energy system that needs to charge (take on energy) and discharge (release energy) as a self-organizing biological system. Psychological problems, according to Reich, would occur because the body would develop chronic body armor to resist experiences. This means that on every level (psychological, emotional, physical, and spiritual), energy as emotions internally described as chaos are resisted and, hence, limit individual experience. The father of Bioenergetics, Dr. Alexander Lowen, termed this energy, bio-energy. Hence his therapy works with the bioenergy, and the chronic interruptions in the flow of energy or emotions.

According to Chaos Theory however, if you expand the context out far enough you will find order in chaos. Quantum Psychology states that if you cannot allow the energy to flow, it will yield chaos; but if you let it be, it will reorder or reorganize itself at a higher, deeper, and more connected universal level. To picture this, imagine a lake. If a large rock was thrown in the lake it would cause a big ripple. If we resist the ripple by placing a circular wall around the ripple to contain it, the chaotic ripple will gain strength. If we expand the context of the ripple to include the entire lake, the chaotic ripple will reach a deeper connection to the rest of the lake. In the same way, the appearance of chaos within an individual system, if allowed, ultimately will take you to the entire lake (the implicate order). The *Tao of Chaos* suggests that by *including, allowing,* and *expanding* the context of individual chaos, infinitely if necessary, a new order is revealed. This means that emotions must be experienced and allowed "as energy"—the chaos must be allowed as energy. This nonresistance to chaos helps the person to reorganize themselves at a new level.[1] Stated another way, if you allow chaos, the underlying unity or united field that connects us will be revealed.

This is the *Tao of Chaos*, the willingness to *allow chaos*, so that the experience of Quantum Consciousness can become even more available. More simply put; allow chaos to order itself.

To say it another way, let it (the chaos) be and it will let you *BE*!

---

[1] *See* Quantum Consciousness: The Guide to Experiencing Quantum Psychology, *Chapter 4, The Energy of Emotions. Stephen H. Wolinsky, Ph.D.*

TWO · QUANTUM PSYCHOLOGY AND CHAOS THEORY

Quantum Psychology is an outgrowth of my desire to know myself. My Indian teacher Nisargadatta Maharaj used to say that

> "You cannot give up anything unless you know what it is, and that to discover who you are you must first discover who you are not."

In the same vein, before one can give up or let go of a behavior pattern, which is actually an energy pattern, we must first know what it is. This book praises psychology in its attempts to know exactly what is there. Modern psychology has taken *step one,* the discovery of what is there within the individual, and then offered a new behavior pattern in the form of a new belief; but it has not explored the following four major steps.

Step two is the ordering or organizing of chaos. A comprehensive energetic explanation of the movement of energy or consciousness. *Step three* is a technology to offer individuals so they can develop the ability to recognize their own order within chaos, and *step four* is the discovery of *who one is.*

The first step which Psychology has offered is to learn about oneself. Steps 2 through step 4 however, have been neglected, and in our search for the answer to step 2 through step 4 we are journeying toward the development of a unified field theory of human behavior.

The Ordering of Chaos

As mentioned in Chapter 1 the personal experience of chaos and the recognition of its order must be *allowed* to shift the *attraction* from one energy pattern to another.

In chaos theory the term *attractor* is used to denote the movement of energy within the system to particular states within the system.

> "An attractor is a region of phase space which exerts a "magnetic" appeal for a system, seemingly pulling the system toward it...Systems in nature are attracted to energy valleys and move away from energy hills." (*The Turbulent Mirror*, F. David Peat and John Briggs, Harper and Row, 1989, p.36)

In psychological terms, energy is seeking order and is attracted to valleys rather than hills. For example, a child might learn to control her anger energy and turn it into a smile (valley) to order the chaos of an abusive parent, rather than yell at the mother which would appear as a hill. This attraction to order causes repetitive patterns which later in life move us further away from ourselves rather than closer. In other words, our chronic habit of hiding our feelings behind a smile moves us further away from our true self rather than closer to our true self.

In the above example, the child organizes and orders the anger energy into a smile to get closer to Mom. In the future, this attempt becomes habitual and rather than the chaos of anger being used to bring us closer to connection, we feel habitually more disconnected because we have to hide our true feelings behind a smile.

In order to do this it becomes the task of the energy package called therapist to offer ways and means for the client to recognize their own energy pattern or to teach the energy package of client to realize their own order in chaos so as to develop a better understanding of who they are. This allows the client (condensed energy packet) to discover by themselves who and what they are about.

Observation and Awareness as the Agent of Recognition

What then becomes the agent or ingredient that enables the order within chaos to be seen? First, let's examine exactly what we mean by energy.

To do this we must go back to one of the basic tenets developed by Albert Einstein in Quantum Physics. Einstein states, "Everything is made of emptiness and form is condensed emptiness." From this emptiness, the emptiness which is undifferentiated consciousness condenses forming what we might call differentiated consciousness. When we say undifferentiated we mean just that; there is no subject or object, no observer or observed. Hence no experience or experiencer.

This undifferentiated consciousness contracts further forming differential consciousness, i.e. an observer and observed. When consciousness condenses further, consciousness creates the concept of space, the concept of time, the concept of solidness or mass, and the concept of energy.

The observer, although it is made of the same material as that which is observed, creates several ideas. First that space has different positions and phases or parts (this is why in Chaos Theory it is called *phase space)*. Furthermore, the observer differentiates time into past, present, and future (phase time). The observer then differentiates solidness or mass into phases, more solid less solid (phase mass), and finally differentiates energy into various intensities from very intense to no energy (phase energy).

What is fascinating is that although everything is made of consciousness which is condensed emptiness, to the observer there is an appearance of differences where there are no differences. Once an observer arises so do differences. The observer and observed are consciousness, yet to the observer they appear as separate. This concept of separateness causes suffering. In East Indian philosophy it would be said that although consciousness appears to be an object or an observer, consciousness can never lose its true nature of being consciousness. Consciousness can, however, *pretend* to be separate from itself and thus experience separation. This in the sanskrit is called Chitshaki Vilas; The Play of Consciousness. The *Tao of Chaos* is asking us to begin to discover this play of consciousness by going into chaos. Stated more simply, the random arising and subsiding shifting and turning of consciousness appears chaotic. Being willing to allow and ride that experience of out-of-control and chaos allows the individual to move into a state of Essence which is prior to consciousness, and hence the second implicate order (this will be discussed in the second section).

Once while I was with Nisargadatta Maharaj he emphasized that, "prior to your last thought arising *stay there.*" He was saying that the thought is consciousness and hence, appears chaotic. Prior to its arising is emptiness, and the second implicate. People often want to escape this random movement of thought, but if you sit for a minute, eyes closed, you will notice many thoughts arising unconnected to one another and random. At first this appears as chaos—but looking deeper we *can* find the underlying order.

The *Tao of Chaos*, along with the companion volume *Quantum Consciousness*, contains many exercises to help make these understandings more experiential and less intellectual. With this in mind, let us explore an experience of *The Tao of Chaos*.

Tao of Chaos Exercise #1

The randomness of thought.
Eyes closed.

Step I   Watch your thoughts coming and going.
Step II   Focus your attention on the *lack* of connec-
            tion between thoughts.

Some people are surprised to discover that their thoughts are not connected at all. For example you might have a memory from the past, a picture of a romance, a pizza, and an idea of making money or a vacation all in a span of just a few minutes.

This appears as random chaos. This is riding the waves of chaos or the *Tao of Chaos*. If, however, we look more deeply, we discover the space between thoughts. This is the order within the chaos. (See Chapter 3, *Quantum Consciousness: Volume I*, Quantum exercise number 1.)

The Observer and Observed

As discussed in *Quantum Consciousness*, *Volume I*, the observer and observed, such as observer of an emotion and the emotion, are *connected* but appear to be separate from other observers and emotions.

This permits consciousness to split-off into what appears as separate universes, each with an observer, creating observables. This is what parallel universe theory is about in Quantum Psychology.

Each observer and observed appears to live in its own individual universe. Now each individual or parallel universe (since they are side by side) continues to create realities within itself which are *self-organizing*. For example, let's say we have a belief such as, "all men are bad." The observer we call observer A will then organize all behaviors around this energy pattern.

Imagine the solar system; the observer being the sun, and the planets which surround it the belief structures. The observer is stable and held together by a Quantum force (to be discussed later).

Or let's imagine an atom with an electron swirling around a nucleus. The nucleus would be the observer and the electron the belief system.

This energy packet* or system appears stable. But as we know, other energies can, at any moment, enter into your system causing your beliefs (electrons) to speed up making you (the nucleus) feel out of control and chaotic.

In the psychotherapeutic setting, the energy of the therapist enters into the energy system of a couple. For example, the therapist intends to help organize or order the two nuclei (husband and wife) so they don't get too chaotic and the electrons don't make a quantum jump out of the relationship and into another energy system.

This explains why, when you as an energy system see a therapist (energy system), your system speeds up as the therapist's energy is added to your energy. This understanding explains why often in the presence of a therapist, guru, teacher or guide, you have experiential changes. But once you return to your home, job, or relationship, your energy system goes back to the way it was. Why? The change was made because the therapist's energy was added to yours; the learning was *context dependent*. Essentially, it is not your energy. This is why while in the presence of another, or a group, change and new decisions occur—but once we leave the group or therapist the changes don't stabilize. The *Tao of Chaos* asks us all to become our own *energetic generators* at the level of Essence. Essence is prior to personality and is what personality organizes around, the source of our nature, the second implicate (discussed in Section III).

---

*Quantum, which comes from the word Quanta means energy packet.

How this is done has been explained in many different schools. But few could deny that every school of therapy or spirituality is a belief structure that attempts to order or organize chaos.

Recognizing the Order in Chaos

Ordering of Energy

In order to recognize the order in chaos Quantum Psychology offers another view. It asks the observer to see what is observed as made of energy.[1]

This delabeling allows the order in chaos to be revealed. How do you know when the order is recognized in the chaos? The problem recedes back into the quantum field or emptiness prior to the problem arising.

At this point let us review the spiral or hierarchy that consciousness goes through in its attempt to order itself.

The I called you

First, let us look at any I-dentity or pair of opposing identities, I-dentity #1, *life-is-hard* and I-dentity #2, *let's try to make life easy.* By stepping back we can see that *life-is-hard* is an energy pattern that can contain any or all of the cognitive distortions[2] and trances.

Each cognitive distortion and trance can be viewed as a way the I-dentity called *life-is-hard* can organize itself so that the *life-is-hard* experience keeps being repeated subjectively.

Ways of Organization

If the I-dentity chooses to be more stable and rigid it can adapt many different psycho-spiritual strategies that enable the energy pattern to solidify and create a more rigid charac-

---

[1] This is discussed in detail in Chapter 4 of my former book, Quantum Consciousness.

[2] Cognitive distortion is a term developed by Dr. Albert Ellis, the father of Cognitive Therapy.

ter structure. For example, when Magic Johnson reported having tested positive for the AIDS virus, an associate of mine, like myself, went into a confusion (chaos). Instead of being with the confusion (chaos) or chaotic feelings, he adapted his spiritual or metaphysical reorganization strategy, "I wonder why he chose to get AIDS, and what lessons is he trying to learn." Magic Johnson and others reorganized their confusion (chaos) by saying, "God chose Magic for a special mission." It imagines that God said to Magic, "sleep with 2500 women without a condom—because I have a special mission for you." This spiritualization is a subtle form of denial, which provides a way to organize chaos.[3]

Although this reorganization made him feel better, it actually helped him to resist the confusion and chaos which was there. Adapting this strategy, his system *created a system* which appeared to stabilize the energy, but actually *solidified and rigidified it*, robbing him of the chaos and hence an experience of the second implicate or a deeper understanding.

Recently I had a conversation with a therapist who is an expert in the treatment of Post-Traumatic Stress Disorder, dissociative disorders, and incest; Kristi L. Kennen, M.S.W. We were discussing how many of the new forms of therapy suggest that the client suffering from these traumas did not have to know what happened. Furthermore, many *new* philosophies of therapy believe there is an unconscious mind separate from them, which can decide what needs to be known in order to heal. Ms. Kennen said,

> "People will develop any form of philosophy or therapy that makes it okay to not have to know or feel the pain (chaos) of those traumas. It is interesting how these forms of therapy continue to re-enforce how it is not okay to "talk about" the rape or the incest."

[3] See Chapter 14 *The Dark Side of the Inner Child: The Next Step* by Stephen H. Wolinsky, Ph.D., Bramble Books, CT. 1993.

System Breakdown

In order to reorganize a system, it must first be allowed. This is why in the psychological application of Chaos Theory, *being* and *allowing* the chaos to be experienced as energy shifts the system. This allows the order in chaos to be revealed. To do this, the system must feel as though it is breaking down. Actually, the system is allowed to move and have *motion*, where movement was frozen when the chaos was resisted. Chaos therefore can be viewed as the messenger which lets you know *change* is about to occur. Better said, internal chaos lets you know that one of your rigidfied structures is being challenged.

For this reason, internal chaos needs to be cherished as the indicator that an underlying assumption, world view or self view needs to be brought into question. Once, the limiting structure is seen and released, more space becomes available. In this way, chaos can be seen as the fuel or energy which can guide us back to Quantum Consciousness.

The Self-Organizing Universe

Most people who have explored psychology know that each person's subjective universe is self-organizing. This means that our beliefs will organize how we interpret and then experience our experiences and actually what we will experience. Noted Biologists Varela and Maturana set biology on its head when they suggested that an amoeba acts toward a food particle, not in a stimulus response (to surround and eat it). Rather, they suggest that the amoeba is self-organizing. That the amoeba surrounds and eats the food to maintain its own set of internal relations. In psychological terms, once a belief is ridigfied, individuals again, will limit themselves *only* to the experiences that validate their belief. For example, a man might have a belief that all he deserves is to be treated poorly by women. The internal universe or underlying state might be melancholy. To maintain that state, he will self-organize and get involved only with women that treat him poorly. The underlying melancholy becomes the standard to be maintained.

For example, subjectively speaking, if we believe "life is hard," we will experience "life is hard". Also, we will make something that is very simple and easy feel subjectively extremely difficult and painful. As an example, I have a belief that filling out insurance forms is hard. As long as I have held this belief, I resist ad nauseam filling out insurance forms. Filling out insurance forms then becomes hard and painful regardless of the fact that it only takes a few minutes. The fact is that insurance forms are insurance forms, but I create, via my belief structure, my *subjective* experience of filling out insurance forms thus re-enforcing and self-organizing my universe around that underlying state.

Interactionally between two people, if I believe getting together to go to dinner with you is difficult, I will experience it *subjectively* that way whether it is true or not. I had a friend who believed she would always be late for her appointments. Even if she tried to be early, at the last minute she would find things that would take up her time so that she would be late. Hence her beliefs, as mentioned in *Quantum Consciousness: Volume I*, help to self-organize and order her experience. In other words the energy got organized the same way each time. This, in Chaos Theory, is called *infinite nesting* which is the natural phenomena whereby structures tend to replicate themselves.

It might be said that belief structures act as control parameters for the outcome of behavior. In other words, the limitations placed on an individual by their beliefs create certain boundaries or parameters of experience that will occur within their subjective psyche. This idea in Chaos Theory gives a hard science explanation as to "why" patterns repeat. For example, the above situation, my friend who believed she would always be late, contained a belief underneath it called "people get mad at me" which contained a belief underneath that of "nobody wants to be with me," which contained a belief underneath that of "I'm no good." This belief within belief is a pattern within a pattern. This is talked about in Chaos Theory as self-similarly.

"The notion of self-similarity strikes ancient cords in our culture...beliefs that a drop of water contained a whole teeming universe, containing in turn, water drops and new universes within. "To see the world in a grain of sand." Blake wrote, and often scientists were predisposed to see it." (*Chaos: Making a New Science*, James Gleick, Penguin Books, p. 115.)

Let's use a physics explanation. Let's say there is an atom. This atom has a nucleus (self) and two electrons (beliefs) spinning around it. This single atom is surrounded by empty space.

The self (nucleus) is self-organizing in that it only allows into the self (nucleus) other electrons (beliefs) and atoms which agree with or are compatible with its basic structure. If an atom with different electrons enters its path, it creates *chaos*, because the two systems don't match in that they are not compatible. At a sub-atomic level, the atoms join together forming a molecule. For example, an atom of oxygen and atom of hydrogen when they meet form H_2O (water).

At a more experiential level, let's take the example of a fundamentalist Christian who believes that following Jesus is the only way to salvation, and that any other form is bad and of the devil. Along comes a Buddhist, who believes everything is everything else. When these two interact the right-wing Christian feels *chaos*, she/he feels jumbled. The energy starts moving through her/his body and the central belief structure or subatomic structure gets rattled. Now she/he could *allow* the chaos to enter the structure which might perhaps bring her/him into a deeper understanding of the world, but instead she/he is *attracted to or drawn down a pathway* of closing down, saying to herself/himself, "she's/he's of the devil and will go to hell," and closes herself/himself down. The belief structure and interactional energic pattern is called a dynamical system. In other words, the energy that is experienced as the fundamentalist Christian meets the Buddhist creates an interaction of energy. This interaction based on the control parameters of the individual, or how the individuals' belief organize their reactions, is a dynamical system.

The way the Christian organizes his chaos is to be *attracted* to the path of shut-down which self-organizes herself/himself and leaves her/him with the same certainty: Buddhists are bad. He probably might even see a devilish look in the Buddhist's eyes and *mind-read*[1], image and project some evil intent upon this Buddhist, and then react to the Buddhist as if the *mind-read* is true.

This self-organizing of our internal universe in order to maintain its equilibrium causes major psycho-emotional limitations. This is because psycho-emotionally we have an underlying state which is maintained unknowingly through how we self-organize. Generally speaking, we will reject all disruptions to this underlying state and self-organizing, and accept only those which maintain our view of ourself and the world. For example, if your underlying state is "I am going to be rejected," all incoming information is internally experienced as rejection. To explain further; if you have, "I am going to be rejected," as your reference point to be maintained, and I say, "I like you," internally you might not allow that information in because it *disrupts* your self-organizing reference point. To combat this *chaotic* disruption of your self-organizing reference point, you might *reject* me first, so that I feel stand-offish toward you, thus re-enforcing and maintaining your self-organizing reference point of "I am going to be rejected." For this reason, to continue our internal work of taking apart self-organizing I-dentities to discover who we are, we might consider the disruptions as information coming in to help us look at our internal structures.

---

[1] Mind-reading is a cognitive distortion developed in cognitive therapy by Dr. Albert Ellis.

In Journey With A Sufi Master[2], the author H.B.M. Dervish wonders how he can learn from the Sufi Master Idries Shah. A student of Shah says to him,

> "the best of approach is to remember that when a teaching strikes you as correct you need not think much about it. Most people dwell on things of which they approve. But when something, in Sufi circles, strikes you as strange or even unacceptable, you should give it special attention; because it almost always means that a real teaching aspect has struck against your prejudices, which are trying to *reject* it, trying to keep you in narrow servitude. Sufi teachers sometimes provoke highly dramatic "incidents" to help bring psychological insights to people who are deeply conditioned. Even so, the very superficial will still fail to get the message.[3]

Let's take another example. A thought (which is made of energy) goes through your mind, "I don't want to be in this marriage." The energy that passes from husband to wife and from wife to husband is called a trajectory. The trajectory of energy is the dynamical system. In each interaction, the control parameters (beliefs) are the same, hence, both people are attracted to the same stable outcome. This thought trajectory is like an electron orbiting around a central *self*, which is made of condensed energy we are calling the *nucleus*. When the wife says, "Can you pick up the kids?"—a question from self (nucleus) to other nucleus—it adds energy to the system. These two energies, "I want out of this marriage," and "Can you pick up the kids," meet forming *chaos*.

The central self or condensed energy of the nucleus then becomes attracted to the energy of anger out of the collision

---

[2] *Journey With A Sufi Master,* H.B.M. Dervish. Octagon Press, London, England, 1982.
[3] *Journey with a Sufi Master,* H.B.M. Dervish, Octagon Press, London, 1982, p. 12-13.

between the two energy forces. This creates a fight. The couple then decides to expand the control parameters by seeing a psychotherapist. This creates a crisis point, or what is called a bifurcation point. For example, in structural family therapy, the therapist often *intensifies* the problem, making it appear even worse than it is to create a *crisis* point or what is called Chaos Theory a bifurcation point so that the couple might have to expand their beliefs and interactions, (control parameters) and hence their *attractor* patterns which are frozen might move to another level.

For example, I once was watching noted Structural Family therapist Braulio Montalvo supervising a case. The girl, age 15, was cutting school and the parents were in the same interactional attractor pattern of being passive and not doing anything about it. Braulio Montalvo came in to the room and *intensified* the situation by creating a bifurcation point so that the frozen *attractor* pattern would change. Knowing that the research demonstrated the correlation between cutting school, drugs, and teen pregnancy, Montalvo began to *intensify* the situation to the parents suggesting that in a few years she would be pregnant and using drugs. This created a bifurcation point by intensifying the energy. The parents then began to change their interactions between themselves and self-organized; changing their own interactions and their interactions with their daughter.

These two energies combined which created chaos, forcing the feeling of uneasiness. When the two energies (parents) joined, like two atoms forming a new substance or molecule, the family unit (molecule) reorganized.

Inner Bifurcation

Now, if the condensed energy or nucleus shifts its attention around and becomes aware of itself as energy, then the *attraction* to create the molecule of anger is shifted. To explain further. The condensed energy of the nucleus or self, when attention is turned around, creates a new energy called the observer. This new energy of the observer creates an added *new* energy to the package of husband and wife energy. The chaos from the collision of the wife/husband energy is reorganized into another system. The recognition of the order out of the chaos of the family occurs by adding energy of *awareness*, which acts as a bifurcation point. This allows a new order to occur out of the chaos. The added ingredient is the energy of awareness. Stated another way awareness is the energy that is needed to allow chaos to order itself. The Tao of Chaos therefore sees one of therapy's primary functions as teaching and developing awareness within individuals so that they can become their own energetic generator.

What becomes interesting about this movement of energy is that the attraction of two energies forms the same pattern again and again, but by adding the energy of awareness through intensification or by asking the client to exaggerate their experience as in Gestalt Therapy, the pattern reorders. Without adding the energy of the awareness of the observer, this attraction could be called a *fatal attraction* because it always yields the same limited result.

> "Whenever the various parts of a system work together collectively to produce stability or repetitive motion, then somewhere an attractor is to be found..In this case the disturbed system always falls back to a limit point." (*Philosopher's Stone* by F. David Peat, Bantam Books, New York, p. 181-182)

In Chaos Theory the attractor is a force which keeps the self- organizing system stable and rigidfied. Hence it is a *fatal attraction*.

Attractors

It seems that somehow, everything tends to order chaos, and that chaos becomes ordered by being attracted to particular energy systems that are self-similar. Here the old saying, "birds of a feather flock together" applies. This organizes us in our old patterns and old belief systems. This attraction to one, two, or maybe three options as how to organize chaos accounts for our repetitive patterns.

We appear to be somehow bound and attracted to a particular energy. In psychotherapy, therapists somehow try to get the client aware of how she/he is attracted to particular reactions (energy patterns) and tries to get us to "complete" this pattern someway, or change the meaning of what is occurring (reframe), or possibly to accentuate the positive and hence create a new habit. The purpose being that the attraction to one universe of pain is lessened and the attraction to another universe of pleasure is enhanced. This is re-ordering the presenting problem (chaos in someone's life) in a psychological sense to shift the energy's structure.

The problem is that the therapist has a preference which is for "good energy" rather than "bad" (energy), or stated another way, the therapist adds his/her energy through questions, models or belief systems, techniques, and approaches to re-order or change the existing energy structure. This can work.

Therapists remain perplexed, as mentioned earlier, as to why a client can "change" their opinion (energy) about a spouse or phobia or painful issue in the office, but will return the next week saying something like, "I felt better for a day or so but then my wife/husband said _____ and we got into a huge fight."

This occurs because the therapist is adding their energy to a system that feels chaotic. In the office, the energy of the therapist is enough to shift the person from "bad" pattern to "good" pattern. When clients return back to their own energy unit (the family), they are once again *strangely attracted* to the same energy (fight). This phenomena of strange attractions, whereby interactions seem random, are strangely attracted to the same endpoint. Few therapists would deny that to make a major and lasting *change* in the energy pattern takes time. Hopefully, over time, clients become more aware of this pattern, and by *adding their own energy of awareness* to their *own* system, eventually they might leave the relationship, find a new job, or maybe stop reacting.

Why does it take so long to shift this energy pattern? Why does this re-ordering take so long? This is the essence of integrating Quantum Physics with chaos in developing a unified field theory of human behavior. It is working with oneself or with another to wake up the observer and *instill the generator of awareness*, which leads us to expanding our context that a problem occurs in. This leads us to see the underlying order in the chaos.

Unfortunately, as will be discussed later, to I-dentities and false selves this order or Essence seems like chaos, hence an I-dentity or false self resists it out of a fear of death or disappearance.

SECTION II

THE TAO OF ENERGY, SPACE, MASS, AND TIME

FOUR • PARALLEL UNIVERSES

Parallel: lying in the same plane but never meeting no matter how far extended.[1]

The concept of parallel universes or different *places* which exist simultaneously has intrigued science fiction writers as well as mystics, shamans, and metaphysicians. One of the most curious and yet well-accepted ideas in Quantum Physics is the many world interpretation developed by DeWitt in 1964. Simply stated, universes exist side-by-side and simultaneously with other universes.

The physics of it, not to mention the mathematics, scares people like myself into closing the book quickly, with pain in the frontal lobes along with a feeling of frustration. But when the many worlds interpretation of the universe, or more popularly called Parallel Universe Theory[2], is explained with its psychological implication and application, soft scientists like myself can appreciate its enormous application in creating a unified field theory of Psychology.

---

[1] Webster, page 878
[2] For illustrations see *Quantum Consciousness*, Vol. 1, Chapter 8.

Simply put, universes exist side-by-side surrounded by emptiness. If we were to look into the sky on a bright night we can see the moons, stars and even planets. Each of these represents a different world. Each planet has different oxygen content, different food supplies, and probably different values. Like the planets in the sky, each of us has a boundary, surrounded by space with different needs, wants, values and perceptions. Yet we all exist in parallel worlds, with a skin boundary surrounded by space. This can be experienced in our physical world by shifting our perception.

"This would suggest that the different universes are simply spatially separated and one could possibly interact with them by sending signals, one to the other.

But the parallel universes are absolutely separate, from the perspective of normal physical interactions. Each universe has its own associated space-time and the "space" of one universe does not "flow" or "join" to the space of any other. To compare different universes to different stars in the sky is not therefore a good image—for it suggests entities which share in some common way and are simply spatially separated or surrounded by a spatial boundary.

But parallel universes may exhibit different structures, the forms within such universes—the ones that separated very early in time will be different. With respect to us, another universe is like a ghost that moves with ease through our doors and walls—yet that ghost lives in a solid universe of its own. So one could imagine an infinity of rooms that overlay your own, some containing a Stephen Wolinsky, and some containing an alien Stepen, a ssepthen, a Szzuuuaaen, and some not containing a Stephen at all. All coexist yet without any physical means of communicating— so in that sense their separation is more subtle than a spatial separation." (Commentary by F. David Peat submitted in a letter to the author dated October 4, 1993)

Noted Sufi Teacher J.G. Bennett says:

"Most people see things simply as flat projections. I propose that in the course of various things you may do today, you set yourself to remember to look at things in depth ... you have the power of seeing the depth of the field of your visual image." (*How We Do Things*, John G. Bennett, Claymont Communications, Charles Town, West Virginia, 1974, p. 14.)

Here Bennett is telling us to focus on the depth of an object. What occurs when we attempt this experiment is that the space which objects are in becomes foreground, and the objects background.

Bennett says it this way:

"There is one thing that you do get a glimpse of with this experiment, and that is seeing emptiness. You begin to be aware that what feels to be empty is not empty because it is how everything is connected."

To illustrate this experientially:

Tao of Chaos Exercise #2

(eyes open)

Step I Look at objects in the room noticing their depth.

Step II Notice how the empty space connects all the solid objects. All objects are connected by the empty space.

Step III Notice how all objects are floating in the empty space.

Step IV See the objects as condensed empty space.

Tao of Chaos Exercise #3

Step I Close your eyes and see the emptiness in front of your eyes.

Step II As a thought goes by see it as a bubble.*

Step III Next as you open your eyes and see your furniture in your house, the "I don't get it" world may seem not real, but check to see if you still might carry the energy of the "I don't get it" planet in your chest, jaw, arms, or as a feeling of despair.

*For example, let's say a thought goes by that says, "I don't understand." Feel the thought as you might see a star appearing in a clear and dark evening sky. Let's say this star or particle contains within it a universe of "I don't get it." As we begin to move closer and closer to this bubble we can hear it's beliefs, feel the feelings of the bubble, etc. until we become the bubble.

As we approach the "I don't get it bubble," a voice enters of your mother saying, "How could you spill your milk again," implying you were a jerk by not understanding how to drink milk at the table. As we approach the "I don't get it" bubble, memories, voices, pictures, which are all made of energy "pop-up" until eventually you become smaller and fuse or merge with the "I don't get it" world.

Now you can be in this world and experience all possible events and feelings and ideas of the "I don't get it" world.

All of the parts of this bubble are made of condensed emptiness, and what we have described as energy systems within energy systems, within energy systems or, in psychological terminology, beliefs within beliefs are glued together by past experiences and associations. In chaos terminology we called it *self-similarity* or *intensive nesting*. In another view you could say it was worlds within worlds within worlds, each one that has similar energy ordering itself within and organizing the other or being *attracted* to one another forming a universe or place that initially, as we started this journey, appears as just a thought passing through the dark emptiness behind your eyelids.

Tao of Chaos Exercise #4

Step I   Close your eyes again and notice the emptiness again. This time allow a thought of a pleasant vacation passing by; see it as a bubble and approach slowly, noting the energy of the memory of a beach or a mountain within the bubble.

Step II   As you approach the beach notice how you become more solid.

As we enter into the bubble "vacation," memories of past beaches collapse with other beaches (universes) or mountains (universes), possibly a love interest. Notice how by merging with the planet (bubble) you experience excitement at merging with memories (energy worlds) collapsed with memories (energy worlds). Once again notice how this chain of events or similar energies are attracted and collapsed in our vacation world with similar vacation worlds. When you open your eyes, you can probably even experience directly a feeling in that body of yours of relaxation or excitement. Freud said it this way; "traumas are connected in chains of earlier similar events." Not only traumas, but all similar events attract one another and form an *associational network* or chain of similar events.

What you have experienced is parallel worlds: the "I don't get it" planet, which contains energy within condensed energy in the form of memories or sensations forming one world; and right next to it, side-by-side, with planet "vacation" and its world.

All of us can consider that in the emptiness there are many worlds side-by-side floating in space.

As "you" enter into each world you can experience its effects and that they all exist in parallel worlds. You might say that, like a wire plugs into a socket, you experience the energy of a world that you plug into.

Parallel Worlds and Internal Reality

Appreciating that in the sky we have boundaries around planets and stars separated by space, so, too, parallel worlds inside of us possess the same phenomena. From the point of view of a personality, it can be said that we are all composed of parallel worlds or, in psychology jargon, parts of ourselves. Each world which some people call roles, parts, sub-personalities, I-dentities, false selves, ego states, or schemas. Different schools of psychology have different names for these parallel worlds.

What we are adding here is the unifying aspect of emptiness. Each part of our "personality" has different feelings, thoughts, memories, etc. For example, when you are at work, the world of independence and decision making is the one you operate from. In this world view, you take charge and get and react according to what business decision needs to be made. In the world of spouse you feel vulnerable, dependent, and indecisive about what to do in your relationship. Both of these parallel worlds exist inside of us, and at one point we become the world of work at another time the world of relationship. Each one is boundaried and surrounded by emptiness.

Fractals and Chaos

The question emerges, then, how can we get to the underlying order or Bohm's second implicate order? Fractals might be our way in. Normally most of us think about expansion as a moving out. For example, if you look at an object and expand your awareness you notice other objects. Perhaps, however, fractals or moving our awareness *in* might lead us to the infinite order.

What are fractals? Fractals can be thought of as fractions of dimensions. Let us think of fractals in terms of measuring something specific like the size of a room. What seems to occur is that the more specific we break down, let's say 10 feet x 12 feet, by using smaller and smaller units of measurement, the larger the parameter of the room seems to get. Not only does the room get bigger but there is a specific pattern or underlying order that goes on infinitely as you keep getting smaller and smaller fractions.

This process is called iteration (repetition). Mandelbrot discovered that as we multiply a fraction by itself it gets smaller and smaller and the universe gets bigger and bigger.

In other words, by making things smaller and smaller, the entire universe and its exquisite order is revealed.

The answer therefore seems to be; to reach the second implicate order, go inside and get smaller to find the nothing which when condensed contains the everything.

If we start, for example, with a fraction and repeat it by multiplying it by itself, we get a *generative order*.

"In the fractual case, a generation which proceeds by repeated application of a similar shape, but on a decreasing scale."

The Organizing Self

In many ways of understanding ourselves we look to an

organizer, one observer which moves from one parallel world to another hopefully in some kind of order. What is interesting is that we define (put boundaries around) emptiness and become one or the other world many times a day without noticing any problem. *Who we are at any given moment is defined by the parallel world we are living in!!!* In reality there is no organizing *I* or self, just a movement from one world and definition of ourself to another. There is, however, an illusion of time (see Chapter 7: Time), that makes it appear as though we are always present. This illusion of connection from one world to another without the space is an *appearance*. The fact is we appear and disappear and define ourselves in an ever changing view, *who we are is how we have defined (boundaried) ourselves and our not-self at any given moment*. There is not one observer, but an infinite number (discussed in Chapter 23: Advanced Attention Training).

Emptiness and Parallel Worlds

It can be said that each parallel world is made of a condensation of emptiness (See Chapter 5: Space). This means that how we define ourself as ourself is a parallel world composed of condensed emptiness. This condensed emptiness appears as though it is always present when it actually condenses and is thinned out. This means *we are the condensation and thinning out of space as a pulsation*. In the Taoist philosophy of China, energy is termed ch'i: condensed emptiness which forms a parallel world and then returns to emptiness.

> "When the ch'i condenses its visibility becomes apparent so that there are then the shapes of individual things. When it disperses, its visibility is no longer apparent and there are no shapes." (Quoted in Fung Yu-lan, a *Short History of Chinese Philosophy*, p. 279)

"The great void cannot but consist of ch'i; this ch'i cannot but condense to form all things; and these things cannot but become dispersed so as to form once more the Great Void." (Quoted in Fung Yu-lan, a *Short History of Chinese Philosophy*, p. 280)

Tao of Chaos Exercise #5

Step I   Allow your eyes to close and notice the emptiness.

Step II Now when a thought goes by see it as condensed emptiness or made of the same substance as the emptiness.

Step III Notice that the emptiness pulsates condensing down becoming a thought feeling sensation, or association, and then thins out becoming emptiness.

This means that who you think you are appears and disappears yet we don't notice it. Why? Because the emptiness disappears. This means as emptiness condenses into a thought called "I like myself," at some point the condensed emptiness will thin out and become emptiness. Then out of emptiness another condensation of emptiness will occur which we call a thought called "I don't like myself." At the moment when "I don't like myself" is present, "I like myself" has disappeared. In reality, the "I like myself" does not exist at that moment.

Let us look at this in the light of fractals. We notice, for example, that thoughts appear and disappear. If we slow down that process, a thought which seems chaotic can be seen to have an underlying order of emptiness.

The Riddle

"All things must past ...,
All things must away."

George Harrison

The answer to the riddle is in the fact that the pulsation of emptiness to condensed emptiness continues on its own. How to live then?

Principle: *Whatever experience you are having, keep the understanding; I wonder how long this condensed emptiness will remain before it becomes emptiness.*

The problem is that when an uncomfortable feeling occurs we think it will last forever. By holding the understanding that form will become emptiness and emptiness will become form shifts your relationship to the experience.

In the *Spanda Karikas*, a sanskrit text, this process is described as umesa (the emergence) becomes the nimesa (submergence). As in physics, "everything is emptiness and form is condensed emptiness," so in the Tantric Yoga of Kashmier, the Chinese Philosophy of Ch'i and the Heart Sutra of Buddhism, "Form is none other than emptiness, emptiness is none other than form."

Chaos and Parallel Worlds

With each of us possessing so many I-dentities or parallel universes by which we define ourselves, and with each part as a parallel world unto itself, where does chaos come from? To best understand this we need only to look at any one boundaried world. For example, a world called, "I have to please others to survive." The terror is disappearance or no-survival. Each world has a *survival extinct* which beckons us, begging to survive with a tenacity of epic proportions. The disappearance of a world (condensed emptiness) by the world is seen as the worst form of chaos...a journey into no-thingness. So strong is the terror each parallel world experiences, that even this natural process of change—which is moving from condensed emptiness to emptiness—is resisted and fought bringing up myriads of philosophies, stories, and religions to try to quell and explain this natural pulsation process.

This process of pulsation from condensed emptiness to emptiness becomes the only way we know the world and ourselves. As the condensed emptiness thins out what we call our world and ourself thins out. We label this natural disappearance *Chaos* or *DEATH* and fight it tooth and nail. The universe is in a constant flux, a constant movement and change and yet we act as if this most basic change is like looking into the Jaws of Death. To learn to flow and follow this natural pulsation is the *Tao of Chaos*. To no longer see the change as chaos makes it feel more like the Joy of Chaos. To resist is to fear and create philosophies and religions to deny this natural pulsation.

Interestingly enough whether you resist or not, the *change will occur*. The *Tao of Chaos* is about learning that chaos is not disruption but the *Way of Things*. The "how to" allows us to recognize the order in the chaos and the chaos in the order. This understanding is the cornerstone of the deepest re-education we must go through; seeing disappearance and chaos as *what is* and order as a possibility *not yet known*. More paradoxically put, to see chaos as order and order as a brief gap between chaos. To do this requires unlearning and questioning of what we have held so dear, *Our Concept of Self*, which is merely an arising and subsiding, condensation/thinning-out, appearance/disappearance of emptiness fused with the illusion of the permanency called *Time*.

FIVE • SPACE

David Bohm demonstrated, as early as 1950, in his classic text *Quantum Theory*, that the universe is an unfolding and enfolding of energy, space, mass, and time. In *Quantum Consciousness: Volume I*, I discuss that the universe, according to Bohm, contains energy, space, mass, and time. Nothing can exist in the physical universe, or better said, in order for something to exist in the physical universe it has to have energy in it, it has to occupy space, it has to have a solidness, or mass and it has to have a beginning, middle and end, or time. For example, we are in a problem state, a thought, a feeling of anger or sadness; the emotion has energy to it that we all can feel. The anger has a subtle solidness to it, a shape so to speak. It has a duration, a beginning, a middle, and an end. And it has a space that it occupies.

Space

In Chaos Theory what is discussed in detail is the idea of *phase space*.

> "Any state of a system at a moment frozen in time was represented as a point in phase space; all the information about its position or velocity is contained in the coordinates of that

point. As the system changes in some way, the point would move to a new portion in phase space. (*Chaos*, James Gleick, p. 49-50)

What *phase space* means for our purposes is that if we have a rocket that is travelling from earth to the moon, then the rocket occupies a particular space. In other words, as the rocket takes off from earth and goes to the moon the first ten seconds might occupy a *phase of space* of one hundred feet and the next ten seconds might occupy a *phase* or part of *space* that is one thousand feet. In the next ten seconds it might occupy a *phase of space* or a part of space that is ten thousand feet. So in order to measure a rocket, you would measure the phase of space or the part of space that it occupied at any given moment. Let's take as an example, a thought called "I feel bad." That thought has a phase of space that it occupies. If you could watch the thought, it would arise, it would occupy a *phase of space* in different points of space, and then it would subside. Now in the Yoga tradition, they would say that a thought like "I feel bad" would be created, and would occupy a phase of space called creation; where it came out of. The thought would be sustained for a while and occupy a different phase of space; and then it would be dissolved or destroyed and so would no longer occupy that particular phase of space. This means that each thought, feeling, association, etc. that you experience can only exist in a very specific *phase of space*.

F. David Peat says it this way. Phase space is a well-defined term, and is used in many branches of physics including chaos theory—as when a strange attractor is defined not in space but in phase space.

Phase space is many dimensional and is not made out of joining together "phases" or ordinary space. It would be best to think of it as a form of "behavior

space". One is used to pictures in terms of temperature and time, or interest rates and GNP, etc. Phase
space is a bit like that.

You can pin down an object by giving its location in
space but that won't tell you how fast its going and in
which direction. In Newtonian physics, however, a
particle can be exhaustively pinned down by giving
six coordinates—three spatial coordinates and three
momentum coordinates (its momentum in each of the
three directions). If you are given all six coordinates,
then you can predict the future movement of the particle forever. If you have two particles, then you need
2 x 6 = 12 coordinates to predict all movements, col-
lisions, etc. of the two particles.

With n particles you need n x 6 coordinates. Knowing those 6 n coordinates enables you to predict everything that will ever happen in that system. But
knowing only the location of each particle in our ordinary space will never be sufficient to tell you what
will happen to the system in the future.

Now suppose you want to picture all this on a graph.
For one particle you will need a phase space of 6 dimensions. The system is then defined by a point in
this 6 dimensional PHASE SPACE. Likewise two
particles are defined by ONE POINT in a 12 dimensional space. i.e., if you know the location of that point,
then you can define the entire future of both particles.

For n-particles you need a 6n dimensional phase
space—the entire system is defined by a single point
in a 6n dimensional phase space—knowing the location of this point enables you to predict the entire future of the system. Likewise a strange attractor is not
in space but in phase space—and knowing the attractor

helps you know not simply where a system is in space but how a chaotic system is moving, i.e., its momentum as well. Even though such a system may be chaotic, we know that its chaos is contained within a certain region of phase space—i.e., it may be unpredictable in its details, but at least we know that its chaos falls within a particular range of all possible behaviors. i.e., it's not true to say the rocket occupies different "phases" of a three dimensional space. Rather it occupies points in a 6 dimensional phase space. (Commentary by F. David Peat—from a personal letter.)

While working with clients or myself, I thought, what would happen if I could move those thoughts or feelings to a different phase of space? In other words, since a thought can only exist as long as it is in a very particular *specific* space, then if you change the space the thought is occupying then the thought will disappear. The same goes for feelings. Why is this true? Because the thought can *only* occupy a specific area of space; change the phase of space and the thought disappears.

Noted Sufi Master Idries Shah says it this way; that in the sufi tradition, it is very important to note that there is a space and time for everything.

Here, Shah is stating that if the space or time is changed, the property of the system, both internal and external loses its power. This will be discussed in greater depth in Chapter 9 on Time. For now, however, let us explore what happens experientially to our internal state as we change the space that thoughts or feelings exist in.

The Tao of Chaos Exercise #6

Eyes Closed.

Step I   Notice your inner space.

Step II   Notice a thought or feeling you are having.

Step III   Notice the phase of space the thought or feeling is occupying.

Step IV   Move the thought or feeling to another phase of inner space.

Step V   Notice what happens.

If you recall in Quantum Consciousness what Einstein had demonstrated, that "everything is made of emptiness and that form is condensed emptiness," then the thought would only be able to occupy a particular space. Why? Because it is made of that space. If you move it to another space, the space would not be able to hold it. Therefore the thought or feeling would disappear. Why? Because the thought or feeling is condensed emptiness and can only exist in a very specific phase of space. Since the space and the thought or feeling are one, separating the thought or feeling from the space dismantles it and hence it has no space to exist in.

> *Space*: the unlimited or indefinitely great receptacle of things, commonly conceived as an expanse extending in all directions (or having three dimensions), in which, or occupying portions of which, all material objects are located.[1]

Space has been, and will probably continue to be, one of the most intriguing areas of human existence. Our individual mind finds it incomprehensible to imagine space going on forever, not to mention having no beginning, middle or end. Space, as with energy, gets *defined* and limited. For example, I say, "This is my space, or that is your space" referring to either the space the body occupies or what you define as your psychological space. When we look at your homes, certain areas of space are defined as used in only a specific way. The kitchen and the stove is the *space* you cook in, not the *space*

---

[1] pg. 1156, Webster

you read in. This definition of space leaves us with boundaries.

Why does this cause chaos? Because created boundaries define and hence limit what can occur there. For example, in your skin boundary you may decide anger is not allowed; this causes chaos when another person is angry in your presence.

Definitions and Chaos

Definitions are markers which define and separate one thing from another. For example, we define "our" body by the skin boundary. We determine who we are by where the skin ends. Yet, Quantum Physics has demonstrated to us that matter (the skin boundary) is made of space. Furthermore, the boundaries are created by us. If physics is correct and as David Bohm suggests "everything overlaps and interpenetrates everything else," then where do we begin or end? Definitions provide us with the answers.

Inside is generally accepted as "inside the skin boundaries." Outside, "outside the skin boundaries." "My space" is the space "my" body occupies; "your space" is the space your body occupies. When does chaos occur? When the defined boundary we call us is somehow invaded or violated. For example, if you punch my face, "I" being the space the body occupies and the body occupies feels invaded. This is easy to appreciate. Let's imagine your car gets broken into; you feel invaded. Why? Because you have defined the car as "your space" and as you. If I am strongly pro-choice and the government passes a law saying no-choice, I feel invaded. Why? Because I have defined myself and the space of the thought and feeling as me. From this we can see that sectioning off undifferentiated space by defining it as mine or yours, "my thought" and "your thought," makes us all feel a bit crazy (chaotic). What puts us into a double bind is that when we define undifferentiated space we create boundaries which creates chaos. Physics suggests that there is an underlying order, however, where order emerges.

"Systems return to the same peculiar pattern of irregularity as before. It is locally unpredictable globally stable." (*Chaos*, James Gleick, p. 48)

Therefore, moving a thought or experience from one phase of space to a different phase of space shows us the underlying order.

Disappearance and Chaos

We disappear if there are no boundaries. Because without making undifferentiated space into boundaried space we do not exist as separate individuals. Simply put, everything without definitions or boundaries runs into or interpenetrates everything else. For example, imagine a glass jar. Notice there is a space inside the jar and a space outside the jar. If we break the jar (boundaries), the space runs into itself and there is no longer an inside space (called you) and an outside space (called outside).

What, then, are these boundaries of the glass? Condensed space. Therefore, in order to feel "connected" to everything, we must first examine our *imaginary* boundary and, second, experience *non-boundaried* existence.

Tao of Chaos Exercise #7

Eyes Closed

Step I   Experience your skin as a solid.

Step II Designate the space inside the solid skin as you; and the space outside as not you.

Step III Experience the skin boundary as made of condensed space.

Step IV Experience "inside" space, "outside" space, and the "condensed" space of the skin as the same substance, *space*.

Step V　　Notice the only thing that separates the "inner space" called you from the outer space called "not you," is the condensed space or our defined boundary.

This experience can open the doorway for us to look at the boundary. In *Quantum Consciousness* Einstein was quoted as saying, "Everything is made of emptiness and form is condensed emptiness." In terms of the skin boundary then, the boundary is condensed space.

Tao of Chaos Exercise #8

Eyes Closed

Step I　　Experience your skin as a solid.

Step II　　Notice the space inside the solid skin as you; and the space outside as not you.

Step III　　Experience the space as the same substance, space.

Step IV　　Notice the only thing that separates the "inner space" called you from the outer space called "not you," is the solid defined boundary.

Step V　　Now experience the skin boundary as made of condensed space.

Step VI　　Allow the undifferentiated space; (inner, skin, outer) to merge.

Tao of Chaos Exercise #9

Step I　　Experience yourself a solid.

Step II　　Experience another's solidness.

Tao of Chaos Exercise #10

Step I   Experience yourself as space.

Step II   Experience another as space.

Step III Notice the connection from your space to their space.

Step IV Feel the difference as you explore no boundaries in this exercise to boundaries of the last exercise.

Fear of Disappearance

Once space is designated and defined as "me" and "not me" the me now called "inside" fears the loss of the *contrived* boundary. We resist this fear of merging and losing ourselves in every facet of life. For example, we resist the disappearance in a relationship. It is this resistance to disappearance which is seen as the greatest chaos of all, one which must be avoided at all costs!

Tao of Chaos Exercise #11

Step I   Experience the fear of disappearance.

Step II   Experience the fear as condensed space.

Step III Experience the space as condensed emptiness.

Step IV Notice your experience.

In this exercise we are finding the condensed space that the fear is made of. By allowing the fear to just be condensed space, and the space to be condensed emptiness, we no longer resist the chaos of disappearance.

Emotions and Space

Since all emotions and thoughts are made of condensed space, take a few moments to look at the thoughts and emotions that are occurring. See the thoughts and emotions as condensed space.

Tao of Chaos Exercise #12

Step I   Notice a thought or feeling you are having.

Step II   Notice the empty space which surrounds the thought or feeling.

Step III See the thought or feeling as condensed space.

Distance and Location

One of the most chaotic and disturbing ideas in Quantum Psychology is the understanding that there is no distance between anything and anything else. Why? Because since everything is connected to everything else there can be no distance. Why? Because, *distance is relative to position.*

Location

Bell's Theorem Reviewed

John Stuart Bell in 1964 proved two things which changed the course of human understanding: (1) there is no location, and (2) there were no local causes. In the former there can be no location because there is no separation and boundary. In the later, there is no local cause which means you cannot say this particular thing or event caused this or that to occur because everything is made of the same substance; hence everything causes everything else.

"John Stuart Bell showed that distant Quantum objects remain actively correlated without any need for some intermediary field or mechanical connection. One way this can be pictured is for Quantum forms to unfold out of a deeper implicite order. Two electrons would therefore be in contact at the implicate level but well separated at the explicate level. (*Philosophers Stone*, F. David Peat, Bantam Books, New York, p. 185).

In a personal letter to me noted physicist F. David Peat said,

"There was no location and there are no local causes." In a way this is perfectly correct. But it could confuse general readers who have read other science books. It's a very difficult point to explain and get right.

Yes, Einstein had believed in "independent elements of reality", but Bell had shown that this is not possible. Nevertheless, quantum theory does assume the existence of space—and points in space. It is not even possible to formulate quantum theory without assuming the existence of localizable space. Yet once the theory has been formulated, it does allow that the descriptions (the wave function) of quantum systems cannot be spatially separated into independent localized parts—rather they are *one whole*. So in a way, this is confusing and paradoxical, but this is really a reflection of the incompleteness of the theory itself.

Think of the experimental verification of Bell's Theorem itself. It depends upon doing measurements far apart on two physically isolated systems and then discovering that they remain correlated, i.e. designing the experiment. It is based on the notion that physical distance has meaning but then the interpretation of the results says that in some mysterious fashion quantum systems are correlated in ways that transcend this classical concept of distance.

I suppose the best I can do is to say that certain concepts like localization and distance work perfectly well in our large scale world but at the quantum level, we are forced to face the limitations of such notions. (Personal commentary by F. David Peat, in a personal letter.)

Cause and Effect

If everything is everything else, then everything not only is the *cause* of everything else but everything is the effect of everything else. This means that the cause is made of the same substance as the effect. Therefore, the cause is the effect, and the effect is the cause.

In 1982 I returned from India and went to hear a lecture about Mahatma Gandhi. Gandhi's doctrine of nonviolence, which became a model for Martin Luther King, was based on this understanding. Gandhi understood that the cause was the effect. How did he apply this and how could we apply this?

People often believe in the idea that the end justifies the means. This gives us license to do things (the means) because the goal (end) is "good." What Gandhi understood was that the means *is* the end and the end *is* the means. This understanding of Gandhi demonstrates the unity of cause and effect and the unity of end and means.

Chaos, Distance and Location

Simply stated, there are two types of chaos.

Chaos #1 Confusion, overwhelm, out of control, craziness, uncertainty, and not knowing.

Chaos #2 The empty space, and the fear of disappearance and annihilation.

Chaos #1

Chaos #1 is our futile attempt to explain events through causality; i.e., this caused that. Thoughts are linear and limit us by their very nature. In our attempt to use thoughts to find explanations, chaos emerges when the thought or *map* does not fully explain what occurred; the *territory*. The map can never explain the territory, and the cognitive dissonance that comes of this discrepancy creates uneasiness and confusion. There is such a resistance to *not knowing* that numerous schools of thought and psychologies and religions have been created to avoid this chaos of "not knowing." The fact is that we don't know why. *Explanations* are the way we resist the "chaos" of *NOT-KNOWING* because thoughts are linear and as we explained in Level #1 of *Quantum Consciousness*, we are beyond thought.

Tao of Chaos Exercise #13

Step I Recall a problem or situation in your life about which you could never figure out the why. For example, why person A did that to person B.

Step II Feel the discomfort of *not knowing* why.

Step III Be willing to feel the discomfort.

Step IV Notice the substance of the feeling and the space that surrounds the feeling.

Step V Notice the tiny spaces contained within the substance.

Step VI Notice that the discomfort and the space which surrounds the discomfort is made of the same space.

Step VII Intentionally watch and choose the condensed space, called discomfort, and allow it to be there, with no label, just allow it to float in space.

The key is to *be willing to not know* without placing judgments, evaluations, or significances as to what that means.

Furthermore, to see the order in chaos we must see the underlying unity of substance, i.e., *the emptiness*. To do this we simply have to be willing to *not know* and experience *not knowing*. This allows the "chaos" of *not knowing* to not have resistance to it. This allows the not knowing to be and guide us to the underlying unity or order.

Principle: The underlying unity or emptiness is the order.

Chaos #2 The fear of disappearance and the empty-space. This will be taken apart in depth in the last section of this book entitled *The Therapy of Chaos.*

It seems that most clients I see and most people I know have this terror of disappearance which is viewed as annihilation.

Disappearance from what? The I-dentities which were formed out of the resistance to chaos, also resisted their disappearance. Often times clients have called this annihilation. To be free to disappear and free not to disappear; to be free to be in chaos and free not to; allows us to experience the ease of *no preference* for a particular state of consciousness or a particular position or point of view.

Tao of Chaos Exercise #14

Step I   Notice a point of view you are defending.

Step II   Feel like your life depends on it.

Step III   Notice the fear that if you give up this position you'll disappear or won't be.

Step IV   Experience the fear as condensed space.

Step V   Be willing to experience the disappearance of the position.

Step VI   Notice the position, and feel the position and the emptiness as being made of the same substance.

Disappearance is often associated with the idea of death. The problem, what we call death, is the emptiness and what we call life is the condensed emptiness. To enjoy freedom the *Tao of Chaos* suggests we be *willing to disappear.*

The Understanding

In *Quantum Consciousness* we discussed the parallel between Albert Einstein's "Everything is emptiness and form is condensed emptiness" and the Heart Sutra of Buddhism, "Emptiness is none other than form, form is none other than emptiness."

The precursor to working with oneself, or prior to the final understanding of form being the same as emptiness, is that emptiness being the same as form comprises a more comprehensible level of understanding.

Principle: Everything that is form will eventually become emptiness and disappear.

Principle: Everything that is emptiness will eventually become a form and re-appear.

Let's look at this in a practical way. The wooden chair in your room will some day disintegrate, be trashed, be burned and disappear. The energy that is released will reappear in a different form at some point in time.

The feeling of confusion will eventually become something else and will eventually disappear as another state appears. The problem is that when a state of discomfort occurs, it is experienced as more painful than it needs to be because while we are in any state, whether it be love or hate, we think it will last forever, rather than having the understanding that it will disappear and eventually another state will appear out of the emptiness. For example, remember the last time you fell in love. Didn't you think it would last forever? Suddenly, the *in love* turned to *in hate*, which we also thought would last forever. In this scenario, we resisted both the loss of *in love* by trying to hold onto it, and we resisted the *in hate* by trying to get rid of it. In both cases, we experience pain and chaos. Why? Because everything changes, it is the resistance to this natural change process, i.e., form changing to emptiness, emptiness changing into another form that creates a feeling of inner chaos. To illustrate this:

Tao of Chaos Exercise #15

Eyes closed.

Step I   See the emptiness in front of you.

Step II   Notice that a thought or feeling emerges from the emptiness.

Step III Notice that eventually the feeling or thought goes back to emptiness.

Tao of Chaos Exercise #16

Eyes closed.

Step I   Notice the empty space in front of you.

Step II   Condense down emptiness and organize it into a problem state you have been resisting.

Step III Be willing to have the problem state as condensed emptiness—hold the understanding, *"I wonder how long the state will last?"*

Step IV Notice what occurred.

This approach pulls us out of the time-locked feeling of uncomfortable states, or comfortable states which feel like they will last forever.

In that disappearance back into emptiness, location, separation, distance, and resistance are no longer. Here is where the no-experience experience or no-state state of the non-being shines through. In the perception of the nervous system, which Francisco Varela calls the *Embodied Mind*, we see only the explicate order, or appearance and distance. With no perception or nervous system present; everything is seen as the same substance. To see with no-mind is the important point.

(See *Quantum Consciousness, Volume I*). To see with no-mind all we know disappears briefly to reappear *later*. If we do not resist this natural process of disappear and reappearance, we do not suffer. If we fear disappearance as a permanent state, then we suffer. Likewise, if we resist appearance as a permanent state we suffer. No states are permanent, they are just appearances and disappearance of emptiness, or emptiness becoming form and form becoming emptiness. This is the way of the universe and the *Tao of Chaos*. To paraphrase, my teacher Nisargadatta Maharaj summed it up this way:

> "Before you were born there was Nothing absolutely. Then Nothing condensed and became a consciousness called "I am" and what you call *You* arose. At some point this consciousness will become nothing again. This that you call *you* is a sample of this universal consciousness which is the absolute nothing."

The *Tao of Chaos* is not to resist the appearance or disappearance of any state; none are permanent, they are really phenomenological occurrences with no cause, effect, or location. The nothing appears and disappears randomly and is ordered in emptiness. This allowing and understanding is the *Tao of Chaos*.

Tao of Chaos Exercise #17

Eyes closed.

Step I   Notice the emptiness that surrounds you.

Step II   Experience yourself as condensed emptiness.

Step III   Experience all the objects in the room as condensed emptiness.

Step IV   Experience yourself and all objects in the room as being made of the same condensed emptiness.

Conclusion

The underlying unity or the implicate order orders chaos. Chaos is merely a *description* of the explicate order becoming the implicate order.

SIX • ENERGY

Everything in the universe from thoughts to chairs, from skin to emotions, has a certain amount of energy. Let's say for example I have a thought called "I feel bad." That thought has a particular amount of energy. In fact everything, to be the thing it is, must have a certain amount of energy in it. In Sanskrit even depression is defined in terms of a lack of energy. We all know how it feels to be depressed and energyless. If we add energy to that state of depression the state changes. This is why the Psychotherapy of Milton H. Erickson, M.D. had a prescription for depression—*get the person active*, get the energy moving.

Since each thought or emotion contains a certain amount of energy, I call this *phase energy*, or the amount of energy a thing or experience possess at any given moment of time. The approach asks the person to add energy to, or take energy away from a thought, emotion, or state of consciousness. This, in Chaos Theory is called bifurcation.

> "Bifurcation is a word which means the place of branching or forking. A Bifurcation in a system is a vital instant when something as small as a single photon of energy, a slight fluctuation

in external temperature, a change in density or the flapping of the butterfly's wings in Hong Kong (The Butterfly Effect) is swelled by iteration to a size so great that a fork is created and the system takes off in a new direction....At the bifurcation point the system underlying a flux is, in effect, being offered a *choice* of orders..... Bifurcation points are milestones in the systems evolution; they crystalize the system's history." (*The Turbulent Mirror*, John Briggs and F. David Peat, Harper & Row, New York, 1989. p. 143-144)

When I am working with somebody or myself, if I get them to add energy to the thought, it creates a bifurcation point and new choices appear. This can cause reabsorption (to be discussed later) of an experience into essence or underlying order. Since the thought only can contain a certain amount of energy, by adding energy to a thought a bifurcation point, or intensity develops, which, when allowed, takes a person to a deeper level of ordering and understanding. Stated another way, by adding energy to the critical point of intensity, a bifurcation point is created which reveals new options and understanding.

This way of looking and working with oneself or another has been done for decades. The Gestalt Therapy of Fritz Perls, M.D. asked clients to "exaggerate" what they were feeling, and then "stay with it." What occurred was a bifurcation point which revealed a new order of understanding. For example, one of my favorite movies *Lawrence of Arabia*, demonstrates this bifurcation point. Lawrence, about 45 minutes into the film, faces a problem. The Arabs are to either retreat and become part of the British army, or to cross an uncrossable desert and attack the Turkish Army from behind. Everyone says that the desert cannot be crossed. Lawrence is in pain (chaos) and suffering. He goes into the desert and *focuses* on the pain all night. As the sun rises, the chaos shifts, and Lawrence not only *knows* what to do, he has a *vision* as he enters the second implicate order of a future time when he will be in the Turkish city of Acaba. He continually says, "I will be in Acaba, it is written in here" (pointing to his head). He can see as the chaos shifts into the second implicate order which is outside of time to an event, which has already occurred in the future. Entering into the second implicate is like entering into a no-time space where future and past time can be viewed. This is the power of entering into chaos and the utilization of the bifurcation point.

In Gestalt therapy, asking the client to exaggerate an experience and then to *stay with* the bifurcation point often leads to the second implicate order. For example, I have seen hundreds of clients, when asked to exaggerate and stay with their feelings, have memories emerge from the past. These memories are part of the chain of self-similarity and reveal the content of what occurred in the past.

This is saying that by intensification and by exaggerating the feeling of chaos, the second implicate order reveals the origin, and hopefully the resolution of the chaos, or, better said, the order prior to the chaos.

This process is also used in structural family therapy, intensifying the problem when parents deny the chaos of a teenager who is *acting out*. This approach forces the parents into a bifurcation point with the hope of getting them to shift and organize around the child and recognize the Chaos.

The Movement of Energy

Energy in its colloquial sense usually brings up the idea of movement. In the land of psychology, energy usually means something of a transfer of energy from one person to another or one person to a situation. For example, it is widely accepted that if I talk with you, there is a transfer of an unseen substance called energy from me to you or from you to me. This transfer of energy comes in the form of words, or it could be said that energy is the medium and the words and sounds are the message. Actually, words or sounds are solidified energy, and so are you. For example, at a very basic level if I say, "I like you," the energy is solidified and translated by you into a feeling of well-being, or maybe a picture or impression in your mind of something pleasant like feeling appreciated. On the other hand, if "I like you" has meant something negative such as Mom saying "I like you" in order to get you to behave a certain way, then the energy gets solidified and a different impression (solidified energy) "pops-up" in your mind of being used or a betrayal of trust. Simply stated, when energy gets solidified, it forms impressions in the psyche. Through interactions it seems that energy gets solidified and develops meanings. Each meaning creates similar meanings because, as mentioned earlier, universes are self-similar and strongly attracted to one another. This is how associations cling to one another. For example, Freud said "all traumas are organized in chains of earlier, similar events." In this case, if someone hurt you in 1992 it will cling to all similar events and look like a chain. It seems that there is a strange *attraction* of similar associations, as Freud said, which occurs and looks like a chain.

Once this self-organized chain of energy gets solidified it develops a life of its own, and an energy of its own, arising and subsiding in a person's consciousness by its own will. This appears subjectively to someone observing their mind as chaos. Actually, as will be discussed later, this chaos is ordered in a "chain of earlier similar associations."

Chaos and Energy

It is the definition placed on energy which gives it boundaries.[1] Energy when undefined does what it does, but when we define ourselves as separate from other energy giving it a meaning, a significance, we place boundaries around ourself

---

[1] See *Quantum Consciousness*, Chapters 4 and 5

and others. What then is this self? *As will be discussed later, it is the accumulation or chain of associations of events in a self-similar organization of universes held within consciousness.* This is parallel universes that arise and subside in emptiness with its own order and which subjectively appears as chaos. In short, it can be said that what you call your psyche is an accumulation of energy which is solidified. This solidified energy organizes itself into networks of similar associations and experiences. This accumulation of solidified energy forms I-dentities and structures. These I-dentities and structures form patterns. These patterns are then used to explain the world and its movement. For this reason, since the solidified energy creates structures and patterns which explain the external world, and since all of these structures are based on past solidified energy, now called memory, the human individual psyche can only see present-time reality in terms of the past solidified energy.

The feeling of chaos occurs because we place arbitrary boundaries around ourself and others defining energy clusters of associations as mine and yours. The feelings of chaos bring up feelings and memories of out-of-control, confusion, craziness, which arise out of the terror of disappearance.

In order to learn the *Tao of Chaos*, we must do as was talked about in *Quantum Consciousness, Volume I*, Chapter 4; namely, *de-*label. Taking the label off, as we saw in the previous book, helps us to shift our subjective experience into its true nature; namely energy. At this point, for the reader who does not feel fluent in Chapter 4 of *Quantum Consciousness, Volume I*; please review the exercises until they feel like second nature.

Assuming that the work is clear, let's move on in the *Tao of Chaos* and how it relates to energy.

Tao of Chaos Exercises #18

Step I   Allow a memory to come into your mind that brings forth an unwanted emotion like anger, sadness, hatred, etc.

Step II   Notice where in your body this energy is being experienced.

Step III   See the emotion as made of energy.

Step IV   Experience the memory as made of energy.

Step V   Any voices or internal dialogues that are occurring; see them as energy.

Step VI   Any experience that occurs; a voice, feeling, memory, etc, allow the experience; experiencing them as energy. Allowing experiences as energy subjectively will shift and allow us to have any experience without judgment, evaluation, or significance.

Interaction with Others
Verbal

Now that we have mastered the *de*-labeling of subjective experience, it becomes time to move into the interactive realm. Few of us can doubt the upsetting and chaotic feelings that arise when an intimate partner says something, does something, or gives a certain look that sends us into *chaos*. To do the next two exercises, pair up with a partner.

Tao of Chaos Exercise #19

Step I   Ask your partner to say something to you that might be upsetting (I don't like you," "I hate you," etc.).

Step II See your partner as solid, the words as solid, yourself as solid and your reactions as solid.

Step III Switch rolls and give each other feedback.

Tao of Chaos Exercise #20

Step I As in the previous exercise ask your partner to say something that might be upsetting.

Step II See your partner as solid, the words as solid and your reactions as solid.

Step III Repeat Step I except see your partner as energy, the words as energy, and your reactions as energy.

Step IV Notice the shift, and practice using both positive (I love you) and negative (I hate you) suggestions until you are able to de-label and see your partner as energy, the words as energy, yourself as energy and your reactions as energy.

Tao of Chaos Exercise #21

Touching: With a partner.

Step I Allow your partner to touch your body.

Step II Experience your partner as solid, the touch as solid and your reactions as solid.

Tao of Chaos Exercise #22

Touching: With a partner.

Step I Allow your partner to touch your body.

> *Step II*   Experience your partner as energy, their touch as energy and your reactions as energy.
>
> *Step III*   Notice the difference and give each other feedback.

Getting Your Button Pushed

Few of us could deny the automatic reactions we get when someone "pushes our button." All too often there is an old part of oneself that is a reaction. This old reactionary *I-dentity* is causing us pain and chaos even though we know it's outdated nature.

To handle this, we must de-label and undefine.

Period Doubling

A Princeton physicist named Robert May discovered a way to get to chaos, which would later yield order.

> "A period is the amount of time it takes a system to return to its original state. But mathematically at least, that's not the end of the story. Scientists have learned that the period doubling route to chaos contains a whole circus of previously unimaginable orders." (*Turbulent Mirror*, F. David Peat & John Briggs, Harper & Row, New York, 1989, p. 60)

Psychologically speaking, if we create a bifurcation point by adding energy to a system and then period double the loop in a problem state, changes and reordering naturally become available.

Tao of Chaos Exercise #23

Step I　　Notice an I-dentity which seems to react to someone else's words or actions. For example, let's say every time someone says, "I don't agree," you react with anger.

Step II　　Notice where in your body this reactive I-dentity lives. For example, you might notice your stomach tightens or your throat closes down.

Step III　　Notice the reaction that you "fire-back" on the person who said, "I don't agree with you." For example, "I don't like you." This will give you a clear understanding of the looping motion; the person says something, and I-dentity reacts and "fires back," the person reacts and "fires back." Notice this creates an energy loop.

Step IV　　Intentionally create the trigger person saying something as an energy coming at you.

Step V　　See the I-dentity as energy and its reaction as energy.

Step VI　　Notice the trigger person as energy reacting to you as energy.

Step VII　　See the loop as energy.

Step VIII　　Allow and watch the energy loop to continue to go on its own.

Step IX　　Allow the energy loop to make a design or energy pattern.

ILLUSTRATION # 1

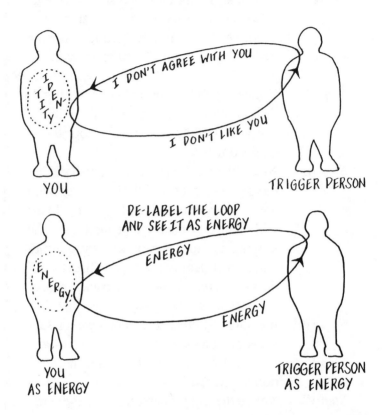

What chaos has demonstrated to us is that our resistance to feeling chaotic energy causes a reaction (anger) or a thought process to occur. In the former example, seeing the emotional loop as energy allows it to go back to its nature. Whereas when we resist the chaos, the energy moves up creating thoughts and systems to justify and defend us from the chaos.

For example, let's imagine some trigger person saying, "I don't agree with you." Since it is not okay with you to "get angry," the energy freezes causing you to feel rigid and distant, or you have the energy move up to your head creating thoughts that justify you rigidifying and distancing yourself.

Repetitive Psychological Patterns: Iteration

"Iteration: Multiplying a factor by itself produces feedback or iteration"... (*Turbulent Mirror*, p. 57)

"Robert May, a Princeton physicist turned biologist is one of the key figures in the story of how scientists learned about what is now called the period-doubling rout to chaos." A period is the amount of time it takes for a system to return to it's original state." (*Turbulent Mirror*, p. 58)

In Chaos theory, there is a particular idea of mathematics whereby things are repeated again and again, as in the idea of a *pattern* in psychology. What Mandelbrot demonstrated was that if you use this iteration process of repeating a pattern, which is multiplying a number by itself again and again and again, that the pattern that emerges is chaotic, and yet reveals a *mandala* like order. This chaotic pattern is an energy pattern which is generally considered uncomfortable and hence is called a symptom or a problem state.

When you apply Chaos Theory, of periodic doubling, creating a bifurcation point, with *intention* the psychology yields a beautiful order. This means that if you keep on repeating (iterating) a problem it creates extra tension or energy which reveals order. How do you relate this to psychology? Well, let's take the example of a compulsion, or an obsessive thought. Let's say the obsessive thought is, "Things don't work for me things don't work for me, things don't work for me." This is a particular energy pattern that continues on its own volition repeating (iterating) itself, again and again. It might occur in an energetic interaction with another person. For example, Barbara, a woman I was working with recently, said that whenever she saw her lover she would give up her power and feel very weak. What I asked her to do was to repeat or *iterate* the energetic pattern that happens with her husband *intentionally* adding energy to the circular loop.

In this case I had her create an image of her husband in the room, visualizing her husband in the room, which is an energy flow. Then have the energy flowing from him in a looping fashion to her feeling of powerlessness. I asked her to create this loop again and again in a looping fashion. What occurred as I had her do this was that she added to the loop the energy of awareness. This process created a new order as she got more and more detached and she observed with the energetic pattern which seemed to have an energy circle or cycle or loop of its own. See Illustration #2.

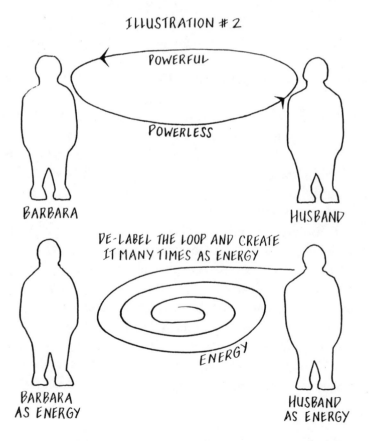

ILLUSTRATION # 2

POWERFUL

POWERLESS

BARBARA

HUSBAND

DE-LABEL THE LOOP AND CREATE IT MANY TIMES AS ENERGY

ENERGY

BARBARA AS ENERGY

HUSBAND AS ENERGY

I asked her if she would then allow this circle pattern to do whatever it wanted to do, to make whatever design it wanted to make.

And it did, it made the design of Mandebrot's Mandala.

"The plot is a graphic display of the underlying structure of chaos" (*Turbulent Mirror*, F. David Peat & John Briggs, Harper & Row, New York, 1989, p. 60)

This pattern has a cycle to it and hence is called a cyclic attractor since it oscillates from one person to another. This is the interactional loop. When the client first came to me, she was in an intrapersonal (self to self) loop. This means that she thought she was interacting with her lover when she was actually only relating to herself. Moving her from her intrapersonal (self to self) loop to an interpersonal (self to other) loop, creating the trajectory of energy from lover to herself, freed the pattern.

The Tao of Energy

The way of energy has countless systems to describe what occurs when chaos is resisted. For now let us look at several healing traditions in brief. It is suggested that the reader look at other books, which will be included in the bibliography to explore these topics further.

Bioenergetics

Bioenergetics, created by Alexander Lowen, M.D., focuses on the movement of energy within the physical body. Lowen calls this energic movement, bio-energy, and, like his mentor Wilhelm Reich, M.D. looks at the body as a system with a natural energic movement. According to Lowen or Reich, the movement of energy becomes blocked during trauma, and the natural flow of bioenergy is inhibited. This natural flow of bio-energy when habitedly inhibited causes chronic body armor to prevent the e-motions (outward-motion) of energy. The chronic inhibition of the natural flow of energy can cause dis-ease, or in psychological terms, neurotic psycho-emotional behavior patterns. In the brilliant work of Reich and Lowen, the chronic body armor is removed, trauma released, and the bio-energy restored to its natural flow. This experience of the natural whole body flow of bio-energy, Lowen calls streaming.

Alexander Lowen made major advances in Bioenergetics by including the arms and legs as well as the rest of the body in the process of releasing the chronic inhibitors to the flow of bio-energy. Furthermore, Lowen creates specific body postures, which he called *stress postures*, that create a bifurcation point by forcing energy to areas where the bioenergetic flow is being stopped. This is also used in the Oriental system of Chi Kung and Acupuncture.

Acupuncture

Acupuncture, an ancient healing system, views the physical body as containing energy meridians. These meridians can be viewed as wires that pass vertically through the body. Diseases in acupuncture are caused by an inability, an inhibition, or a blocking in the energy flow. Each meridian connects to several organs of the body, and stimulating the acupuncture point (bifurcation point), intensifies the energy and causes energy to move through a wire of meridian, thus adding energy to an area where energy is needed.

In Einstein's famous Special Theory of Relativity, he demonstrated that $E = Mc^2$, or in our terms, mass is condensed energy. In this system, when there is a physical mass which causes dis-ease, energy is added to the mass, which through the bifurcation points (acupuncture points) disperses the physical mass. For example, I have a tendency to get stiff necks and little "pain lumps" along my trapezia muscle. The most effective treatment I have found is acupuncture. In this system, the muscles are ruled by the liver meridian (wire). By adding energy to this bifurcation point, the energy moves through this meridian adding energy to the pain lump. Amazingly, the lump is dispersed.

In the same way as Lowen's Bioenergetics, the body armor is a mass. When energy is added to this mass through Bioenergetics techniques, not only does the blockage dissipate, but the trauma which created the blockage is often revealed.

Ch'i Kung or Qi Gong

In China, many forms of energy movement are correlated to martial arts. The most famous, Tai Chi, works with physical movement, breath, and energy to enhance health, strength, and well-being. Less known, but more directly powerful, is Chi Kung. Translated, Chi Kung means the cultivation of energy. Chi is the chinese word for energy, and Chi Kung, like Lowen's bioenergy, uses particular physical body positions to enhance the flow of energy and hence shift dis-ease. Earlier I commented that in Sanskrit depression is defined as a lack of energy. Chi Kung, like Lowen's Bioenergetics, uses posture and breath, with a focus on bifurcation points (acupuncture points) in the body to facilitate the flow of energy.

All of these systems are the way energy is blocked which causes dis-ease.

The Chakras

In the Yoga traditions, bifurcation points are called Chakras. Chakras, which translated means "spinning wheel," are major energy points. In the Yoga traditions, the energy is called Kundalini. It is said that the Kundalini lies at the bifurcation point called the root Chakra at the base of the spine. When this energy begins to move, i.e., awakes, it pierces the seven major bifurcation points which connect to an elaborate system of 72,000 smaller bifurcation points called nadies. Within each Chakra are intense points or packets of energy. Within each Chakra are layers upon layers of "past impressions", but which is actually solidified energy. Each Chakra contains quanta (energy packets) or energy patterns pertaining to a different level of consciousness. For example, the second Chakra just below the naval is a quanta of sexual energy. The third Chakra at the solar plexus is the quata of emotions. The fourth Chakra at the heart is the quanta of love.

Volumes of books have been written discussing ways and means to open up these bifurcation points and how to liberate the condensed energy of each Chakra. It can be said that as each Chakra is opened and the condensed energy packet of past impressions is released, the individual feels freer and gains more energy. This occurs because the energy is no longer contracted and can move onto other levels of consciousness. Nadis are smaller energy packets that also, in this system, contain impressions to be released.

In this way, the bifurcation points occur in many systems of healing and spirituality. Like chaos, the description of the bifurcation points is a description of the movement of energy, and the movement of the chaos of energy to the underlying order of chaos. These are however descriptions and hence the *map*, not the *territory*.

Each system has trajectories of energy which form a picture of the dynamic movement of energy. In Chaos Theory, this picture is called a *phase portrait*, and denotes how energy is moved in a pattern (in a self-similar pattern), which always attracts the same outcome. Adding energy to the system causes a shift or chaotic attraction. This adding of energy to a self-similar dynamic system causes the cyclic attractor to become chaotically attracted to another dynamic system. This is where change and healing take place; the energetic jump from one self-similar system which is disrupted by adding energy. What must be past through, however, is the *chaos* as the system reorganizes into another pattern, and hence another phase portrait.

Basic Premises of The Tao of Chaos

Resistance to chaos is the cornerstone of most of our lives. We all resist chaos. A feeling that comes up that feels chaotic might cause us to resist. We might binge on chocolate to resist feeling overwhelmed. We might all of a sudden have a love affair which we don't want to have or to avoid feeling out of control. We might create fantasies. In other words, if we have *chaos* around not having enough money we might begin to develop a fantasy about having money. If we have *chaos* in our marriage we might fantasize ourselves in to being with somebody else. If we have *chaos* in an illness we might create a fantasy of ourself being healthy. In all of its forms out-of-control, overwhelmed, emptiness, feeling crazy, etc., there is an attempt to order the chaos.

Fantasies can enable or help us to go to a doctor or to work hard or maybe to leave a relationship and find another one. But all of these are attempts to order chaos. There is an extraordinary resistance to experiencing just pure chaos.

So what are the basic premises that we are going to use?

Premise 1: *Allowing and Acknowledging.*

Allowing chaos to be seen as energy dissipates the structure and allows the "chaos" just to be there.

Premise 2: *Everything is made of energy.*

Rather than labeling chaos or craziness in our life as something to get rid of, something to reframe, something to relabel, something to change, one has to begin by seeing it and experiencing it as made of energy.

Premise 3: *Change is Resistance.*

Chaos must be allowed to be there as energy with no intention or goal of getting rid of the chaos. If you are trying to get rid of chaos then you have a judgment that chaos is something you wish to get rid of...which is again *resistance*.

Any time you try to get rid of something you are resisting its natural order and the natural way it is. Instead of trying to get rid of dis-ease, add energy to it at a strategic bifurcation point. This is what Fourth Way teacher G.I. Gurdjieff called the *first conscious shock*; adding the energy of awareness to a habitual pattern reorders the pattern.

Review Summary

Step I   Acknowledge there is chaos and allow it to be there.

Step II   See the chaos as energy.

Step III   Don't resist it by trying to get rid of the chaos... observe it as it is.

Tao of Chaos Exercise #24

Step I   Imagine a trigger person saying, "I don't agree with you."

Step II   Resist the words and create distance.

Step III   Allow the energy to move upward into a thought process and *justify* your reactions.

Notice how the habitual pattern of resisting chaos forms a system to justify you "freezing" the trigger person out.

Tao of Chaos Exercise #25

Step I   Imagine a trigger person saying, "I don't agree with you."

Step II   Resist the words and create distance.

Step III   Allow the energy to move upward to *justify* your reactions.

NOW

Step IV   See the person as energy.

Step V   See the words as energy.

Step VI   See the freezing of energy as energy.

Step VII   See the thoughts of justifying your reactions as energy.

Step VIII Allow the internal energy loop to do whatever it wants, once again removing the labels. Notice how not defining allows us to experience the energy of the interaction, without judgment, evaluation, or significance.

Tao of Chaos Exercise #26

Eyes Closed

Step I   Feel the energy that surrounds your body.

Step II   Experience your skin boundary as condensed energy.

Step III   Experience the "you" inside the body as energy.

Step IV   Experience all objects in the room as condensed energy.

Conclusion

In the final analysis, it is by the process of defining energy or space that boundaries are created. By labeling energy bad, good, anger or love, we define the undefinable and hence desire or resist. Why does this occur? Because underlying all resistance is the resistance to nothingness or disappearance. When you de-label and see things as energy, things and ourselves reorganize. This is experienced by the I-dentity, (condensed energy) as death when actually it is a natural process. Chaos is viewed as the space pre-existing before consciousness. Consciousness is that which knows differences and boundaries. With the resistance to chaos there, we as individuals exist; because of the resistance to chaos. This is why we, which is defined and labeled energy, label others (which is defined and labeled energy). Without the labeling and defining there would be no us. This is seen by the I-dentity as chaos. Emptiness in a pulsation organizes and reorganizes into different energy patterns. Simply put, *to resist is to exist*; to *de-label is to reorganize*. Ultimately, however, existence is nonexistence and nonexistence is existence since they are made of the same substance. To allow this appearance and disappearance is the *Tao of Chaos*.

Let's look at this experientially.

Tao of Chaos Exercise #27

Step I	Notice a person that pushes your buttons.
Step II	Notice the observer that is looking at the person, and explaining why this person "pushes your button."
Step III	Experience the person who pushes your button, and the observer who is explaining why this person "pushes your button" as being made of the same energy.
Step IV	Notice what happens.

To conclude this section is to include the experience, that all "external" energy and "internal" energy are made of the same energy. This understanding of the unification of energy eliminates boundaries and unifies consciousness. This is the *Tao of Chaos*.

SEVEN • TIME

All things must pass...
All things must pass away...
George Harrison

Time generally is considered to be a given, an automatic. Past is followed by present is followed by future. With each coming of an event, however, we somehow enter into one of time's great illusions. Time has a great illusion which is when an experience, such as an emotion, or thought, or state of consciousness is present, *we feel it will last forever*. For example, when you are "in love" you feel it will *last forever*, when you are depressed you feel it will *last forever*, when you are anxious or angry you feel it will last forever. Objectively speaking, however, we "know" it will pass, but while we are *identified* with an experience we assume that it will never end. This is time's great illusion, which is contained within experiences. Because of this illusion, we resist experiences. For example, when you are angry or sad, you might resist experiencing these because intrinsic to their nature is the appearance that they will never leave. On the opposite side, love, we resist losing the feeling, try to keep it, check it, get it back, or work at bringing it back which is a way to *resist* its time-bound nature. What we continue to presuppose and never question is that states of consciousness are time bound.

Chaotic Contemplation

> Contemplate that everything that is perceivable or conceivable will disappear.

Chaotic Contemplation

> Contemplate the transience of everything in your universe.

Chaotic Contemplation

> Contemplate that the perceiver is transient.

Chaotic Contemplation

> Without using your memory, mind, or associations...who were you before you were born?

Obviously, these are not contemplations for the faint of heart. Because upon contemplation, the world can be seen to ebb and flow and you can get a sense of that being the case. In the last contemplation there is justness because without memory or mind there is no past, present and future—you just are, or you are just *awareness with no object*.

Working with Time

If we watch a thought, it has a time duration of seconds. This is what I call *phase time*, or the *time* that a particular experience occupies the space in your consciousness. For example, the thought called "I feel bad" has a phase time. If we speed up the phase time or slow down the phase time and have it take 1 second or have it take 50 seconds, you are changing the time component. Here you are adding a bifurcation point (intensity) to an existing system. By changing the time component, the experience cannot exist. Why? Because all experiences have a specific amount of time and have a specific amount of mass, a specific amount of space, and a specific amount of energy. Once any aspect of that combination is altered it alters the ingredients of the experience. Thus the experience cannot remain the same or exist as it was.

Let's say it this way; there is a rigidity that time, space, the thought and the energy of the thought called "I feel bad" all have to have in order for that thought to exist. Otherwise, it can no longer be there. Think in terms of a chocolate cake; it needs a certain amount of flour, water, salt, sugar, etc; to be a chocolate cake. In the same way, experiences like anger must have a certain amount of energy, space, mass, and time. If, for example, the anger moved very slowly you might feel it even more. Anger moving very quickly might be experienced as a 3-second rush through the system, barely identifiable as anger.

Tao of Chaos Exercise #28

Eyes closed.

Step I	Notice the emptiness in front of you.
Step II	Allow the emptiness to condense and become a thought.
Step III	Slow the thought down.
Step IV	Notice what happens.

Tao of Chaos Exercise #29

Step I	Notice the emptiness in front of you.
Step II	Allow the emptiness to condense and become a thought.
Step III	Speed the thought up.
Step IV	Notice what happens.

Tao of Chaos Exercise #28

Step I   Notice the emptiness in front of you.
Step II   Allow it to organize into an emotion.
Step III   Slow the duration of the emotion down.
Step IV   Notice what happens.

Tao of Chaos Exercise #31

Step I   Notice the emptiness in front of you.
Step II   Allow it to organize into an emotion.
Step III   Speed up the duration of the emotion.
Step IV   Notice what happens.

Time: The system or those relations which any event has to any other as past, present and future; the period necessary for or occupied by something.[1]

Time in Asia has been called the Great Illusion. What is the Great Illusion of Time; that we are here in a continuous manner. For example, as you look at a table, your mind tells you that the table was there a few seconds ago, and that the table will be there a moment from now. Time gives us the illusion of continuous appearance. Why is this illusion? To understand this better let us look back on Time as presented in *Quantum Consciousness, Volume I* and in *Stalking the Wild Pendulum* by Itzhak Bentov. Bentov suggests that as a pendulum moves, at the top of its swing there is a pause and at the bottom of its swing there is a pause. In that pause there is no time, nor is there anything there to measure time. Bentov suggests that this occurs 14 times per second. With time's disappearance the illusion of an object's existence disappears. This is because nothing can exist, including you, if there is no time to exist in.

---

[1] Webster, page 1268

In Chapter 6 of *Quantum Consciousness, Volume I* we were asked to contemplate: *Could anything exist in this universe if there was no time for it to exist in?* When in workshops I ask participants to consider this, generally there is a blankness of mind, because we cannot nor can anything exist unless there is a time or duration. In other words, the mind and its experiences cannot exist without time. Therefore, experiences are time bound; no time—no experience.

The Great Illusion of Time is that we are always here.

Chaotic Contemplation

> Contemplate for a moment that you appear and disappear, appear and disappear many times each second.

Chaotic Contemplation

> Contemplate that the universe appears and disappears, appears and disappears many times each second.

With this understanding, where do we go during these gaps or intervals in time? In Asia they have developed a system of yoga which means union, that talks of a way to experience this *gap*. Raja Yoga, translated, means the King of Yoga's outline of an eight-step approach that leads to this experience. The last step, called *samadhi* in Sanskrit, literally means *no-me*. In that gap, which occurs 14 times per second, there is no-me in the gap, or a state, or better described as a no-state state, which affords us the opportunity to experience the underlying unity with everything else through the *natural process of disappearance*. The effort in Yoga or other disciplines is to know, and experience, and recognize this *no-me* unity. However, effort is not required, *because this is a naturally occurring process whether we are aware of it or not.* In other words, whether we like it or not, we are going into and out of the gap of no-state state continually; it's just a matter of being willing to recognize, experience, and become aware of this pulsation.

Thus we only have to become aware of and notice. Picture, for example, a film strip with individual slides. If we move the slides slowly, there is a picture and a gap, a picture and a gap, a picture than a gap. This is what the physical universe is doing in that natural process.

The Tao of Chaos Exercise #32

Step I   Eyes open, look at an object in the room.

Step II   Blink your eyes rapidly and imagine that the instant when your eyes are closed, the object is not really there.

This is the process. The nervous system of our *Embodied Mind* makes this process appear as one fluid no gap world. In reality however, the gap is there.

Time makes things appear as though they were always present. Yet, as we contemplate no time...time...no time..., or better yet, the appearance of you and disappearance of you, experiences can shift quite immensely subjectively. For example, knowing things appear and disappear on their own allows us to stop trying to "hold-on" to and make permanent through the use of time that which naturally has a cycle of its own.

Tao of Chaos Exercise 33

Step I   Take a moment and again consider this appearance and disappearance of yourself which occurs *naturally* on its own.

Step II   Next, see if you can experience the *natural* pulsation of the universe in its continual state of coming and no-state of being.

In this pulsation, or shall I say the recognition of the natural pulsation that *is*, there is a freedom from the illusion and fixation that occurs when we try to hold ourself and the rest of the world in place.

Tao of Chaos Exercise #34

First let us review Quantum Exercises #34-36 in *Quantum Consciousness, Volume I,* page 143-147 .

Step I   Eyes open, no blinking, see the world from back there.

Step II   Notice as things lose boundaries, they begin to give the feeling of movement and breathe.

Notice that objects lose their boundaries and run into one another.

Where do we go?

In *Quantum Consciousness, Volume. I,* we looked at David Bohm's implicate and explicate order. Simply put, the explicate is the appearance of objects and "the you" in time. The implicate is the gap or interval of the underlying unity of everything.

"One way this could be pictured is for quantum forms to unfold out of a deeper implicate order" (*Philosopher's Stone*, F. David Peat, Bantam Books, New York, 1991 p. 185).

Where do we go during this gap? *We go back into everything and hence are everything.*

"The human mind and body enters into direct communion with this ocean of active information, it would have access to forms and patterns that transcend (trance-end) the boundaries between inner and outer, mind and matter—in other words, to synchronicities. The Chinese sages had their own account of the synchronicities of the I Ching. Our manifest world is, they said, the reflection of a much deeper reality that lies outside the human domain of time. (*Philosopher's Stone*, F. David Peat, Bantam Books, New York, 1991, p. 186)

Why are we not aware of this unity? Because *awareness too is an object*, and hence disappears in the gap and reappears; hence *awareness also only exists in time.* Many people have argued saying, "I am awareness." In workshops, I have asked them, "Tell me a difference between you and awareness." They respond, "Well, I can be aware of being aware." I usually suggest as I did in *Quantum Consciousness, Volume I* that anything you can *be aware* of can't be you because it is an object. Therefore, since you can be aware of awareness, awareness is an object. In the natural gap, awareness and its object appear and disappear as a unit, therefore you cannot be aware of the gap. Furthermore, you cannot "know" this natural interval, because the knower and its knowledge also disappear in the gap. In this natural gap and pulsation lies the order in what appears as chaos.

The Gap and Chaos

We, along with us our physical universe, appear and disappear many times each second. Where then does the chaos come from? As mentioned earlier chaos is defined as the

"Infinity of space or formless matter supposed to have preceded the existence of the ordered universe."

What this means is that with the appearance of "you" and the physical universe there is an instantaneous knowledge that you will disappear. From the point of view of the I-dentity, which appeared, this disappearance is death, nonexistence, or annihilation. Knowing this there develops a *fear* or *terror* of disappearance because you, which just appeared, are afraid you will disappear and not re-appear. This is experienced in the body as a freezing of the muscles. Fear is the way we attempt to freeze ourselves and stop this process.

Tao of Chaos Exercise #35

Step I   Recall a time your felt *fear.*
Step II Ask yourself, "by creating fear what ex-perience am I *really* resisting having?"
Step III Notice what happens.

In its resistance to chaos, fear attempts to freeze time making it appear linear. For example, notice how often and how much of our energy is involved with trying to "keep order," "bal-ance," "stay on top of," "make secure" or permanent our life. We spend so much of our energies to create the illusion of permanence. It is this resistance to chaos, which uses fear, that creates the freezing of our memories, our bodies, muscles, our breathing. We resist our beautiful *vulnerability*. Further-more, disappearance becomes such a terror that I-dentities, parts of ourselves, relationships, our entire psycho-emotional process and our *nervous system* is built-in to resist the disap-pearance. Moshe Feldenkrais said, "the nervous system has a period dicity whereby the nervous system sweeps itself clean." (Conversations with Dr. Karl Ginsburg.)

Nisargadatta Maharaj once said to me, "there is no birth, there is no death, there is no person, it's all a concept, all an illusion."

Here he was saying that the emptiness condenses and becomes life, and from the point of view of life or condensed emptiness, the emptiness seems like death. Actually the emptiness becomes form called life, and the form becomes the emptiness called death. But since one and both are the same, then even the person is condensed emptiness. Hence, at a deeper level there is no life or death. Why? Because there are no contrasts. Emptiness becomes form, form becomes emptiness. Chaos is merely the *description* of form becoming emptiness or emptiness becoming form. In this way, chaos is order, order is chaos.

To illustrate this on a psychological level, when we are in a state of "I love myself," the state of "I hate myself" does not exist for us. Likewise, when we are in a state of "I hate myself," I love myself does not exist for us. In fact we cannot even remember "I love myself" when "I hate myself" is present. Does "I love myself" exist? Only when it appears. Does "I hate myself" exist? Only when it appears. To follow the *Tao of Chaos* is to understand that "I love you" will disappear and "I hate you" will probably appear and that the emptiness will become "I love you" and then disappear and that same emptiness will become "I hate you," and then disappear. But, that both "I love you" and "I hate you" are condensed emptiness or as Bohm would say, "Unfolded out of the implicate order." Simply put, while you are in "I love you" or "I hate you" it "feels" like its duration will last forever. However, if we understand that they appear randomly and disappear randomly, we move outside of the time bound state and allow the states of "I love you" or "I hate you" to arise out of the gap *knowing* they will subside into the gap and change at some point. Actually, the paradox is that everything changes. Therefore security can only be found in the understanding that everything changes. In other words, *change is security, the idea of permanency is chaos.* This allowing for emptiness to become a state and a state to become emptiness in its beautiful randomness is the *Tao of Chaos.*

In Chapter 5 on Space we talked about a basic premise in sufi psychology which was discussed by noted Sufi Master Idries Shah. Shah states "there is a time and space for everything." In *The Tao of Chaos* we understand that each emotion, each state of mind, and even each religious system or path has its time and space. When we understand this, we do not resist the natural comings and goings that occur in consciousness.

In the last example, we used the idea of emotions and states of mind which naturally occur. Another example occurred in a workshop I gave in New Mexico. A trainee said, "Why is it that many of the traditional paths to enlightenment don't seem to have much energy in them and don't seem to be very effective?" I replied, "That everything has its time and place." For example, I said, "The Catholic Church around the time of Christ had a lot of energy and had the experience of Christ. Now, the form (the church) is turning back into emptiness and losing its energy. For this reason, it has become *ritualized* and is holding-on to the time and space where it was powerful.

> *Principle:* When spiritual or psychological systems begin to disappear back into emptiness they become more and more dogmatic and ritualized. This dogmatic and ritualistic tendency is a survival mechanism of a psychology and spiritual system or any hierarchy.

In the same way, the form (the church) is becoming emptiness and will disappear. If we allow this, the emptiness will condense, and another form will occupy that space and time. It is by the holding onto a thought, emotion, state of mind, a system, or even a path that has had its time that causes chaos. The red flag for when a system or path has had its time is that it becomes dogmatic, and ritualized operating on faith and belief rather than present time experience.

The Pairs of Opposites

For centuries, since the days of the development of Yoga, the question of oppositions has persisted. Simply stated, how do we bring together the pairs of opposites, i.e., hate/love, yes/no, feminine and masculine. In the land of 20th Century Psychology, this has been seen as an attempt to integrate the pairs of opposites, or certainly to access, by choice, one opposite pole and then the next. These polar opposites, however, have never fully be an integrated Why? Because, there is a presupposition that these polar opposites are essentially different. Quantum Psychology says; *Polar opposites are not different*, but at a quantum level are the same undifferentiated substance. To experience this let us look at several exercises.

Tao of Chaos Exercise #36

Step I   Notice a pair of polar opposites, i.e. love/hate, feminine/masculine, weak/strong, independent/dependent, etc.

Step II   Notice the size and shape of the two opposites.

Step III   De-label the two polar opposites and see them as being made of the same energy.

Step IV   Notice what occurs.

Here we can see that when the two polar opposites are seen as being made of the same essential substance, there is no contrast—hence, there is no polar opposite. Many psychologies imagine that integrating the two polar opposites and creating a "third" point is integration. Actually, seeing them as made of the same substance dissolves the conflict and hence dissolves the problem. This is true integration.

Tao of Chaos Exercise #37

Step I	Notice a pair of polar opposites, i.e. love/hate, feminine/masculine, weak/strong, independent/dependent, etc.
Step II	Notice the size and shape of the two opposites.
Step III	Notice the empty space they are floating in.
Step IV	See the empty space and the two polar opposites as being made of the same substance.

These exercises, although similar to the ones demonstrated in *Quantum Consciousness: Volume I*, show us that opposites only exist as long as there are boundaries. Once we understand that everything is made of the same essential substance, then there are no polar opposites. Of course, *once we understand*, is no small task. This understanding requires practice. But once this understanding is recognized, there is no longer a problem of integrating the pairs of opposites; they are already integrated. It is only the label and the boundary which says they are not.

Chaos and Religion

With the presupposition that we freeze and resist the natural process of appearance and disappearance, let us look at the most denied natural process of life...*DEATH*. Death is the most denied and feared aspect of the universe. To avoid this disappearing process religions are created to explain and resist the natural process of appearance-disappearance.

Let us look at some major religions; Christianity has an afterlife in heaven, Buddhism and Hinduism have past and future lives, metaphysics has past and future lives.

Each one of us has taken on and been programmed to not allow this natural process. Noted psychiatrist Thomas Szasz says it this way. "Religion is an institutional denial of one finite life."

Tao of Chaos Exercise #38

Step I   Take a moment to explore your philosophy of "What happens when you die."

Step II   Notice how the philosophy resists the natural disappearing-reappearing process.

Step III   Notice what rules are given; that if you obey, good afterlife; if you disobey, bad afterlife.

Step IV   Notice how the rules, adherence to the rules, and the philosophy promising eternal life resist disappearance.

Step V   Contemplate (eyes closed) just for a moment, that there is a natural appearance-disappearance which occurs.

Step VI   Eyes open, see if you can accept and "sense" this natural pulsation.

To repeat the story again, in India about fourteen years ago my teacher, Nisargadatta Maharaj, who I call the ultimate de-programmer, said to me once,

"There is no birth, there is no death...it's all a concept ...it's all an illusion."

This is the power of missing the gap; nothing actually dies or is reborn. As David Bohm might say, The implicate becomes the explicate - the explicate becomes the implicate—this is the process.

In this exercise, we must go beyond our programming to consider a long denied process; appearance-disappearance. Few of us could deny how much we plan and obsess about our future in a feeble attempt to stay or be immortal. Noted psychiatrist Carl Jung, M.D. spoke of the desire to have children as a resistance to one's mortality or disappearance.

Time as a Circle

When we step out of time we can begin to watch our mind in relation to time. Time then can appear as circular rather than linear.

"As you know, modern physics says that time is curved. This means that it is a circle ... Time is not a straight line but infinite circles all turning on themselves ... the past is as living as the present or the future.[2]

Tao of Chaos Exercise #39

Eyes closed.

Step I   Notice a past.

Step II   Notice a present.

Step III   Notice a future.

Step IV   Notice that you are outside of time, watching the past, present, and future.

Step V   Notice that you are in no-time and can watch the past, present and future as they appear before the you which is in no-time.

---

[2] *Psychological Commentaries of G.I. Gurdjieff and P.D. Ouspensky*, by Maurice Nicoll, p. 752.

Noted physicist John A. Wheeler calls this circle of time where the present effects the past "delayed choice measurements."[3]

"Accordingly, it is our choices made now in the present that determine what the past had to have been." (*Parallel Universes*, Fred Wolf, p. 226)

This is a re-discovery. In psychotherapy we in the present, work on the past, and hence change our present time experience of the past and how we might behave in future time. This means that we can change our past in the present and hence change our future. In the work of Milton H. Erickson, M.D., he would have clients create a future when a problem was resolved, and then plan backward from future to present noting the steps that were already taken to resolve the present time problem. In essence, the created future was changing the present and the past[4]. Time is a circular and very pliable experience which can be shifted when one steps out of the thoughts of the mind that are by nature linear and "time locked."

The Past is the Present is the Future

Once we step outside of time we can begin to understand the emptiness or implicate order in which time is unfolded and appears in what we experience at the explicate level. This is the *Holographic Universe* (Michael Talbot, Harper Collins). The concept of time, however, is condensed emptiness (explicate order) which means the past, present, and future are the same at an implicate level. It is only at an explicate level that time *appears* to exist!

---

[3] Wheeler, The Transactional Interpretation of Quantum Mechanics, Reviews of Modern Physics, Vol. 58, No. 3, July 1986
[4] See *Trances People Live: Healing Approaches in Quantum Psychology,* 1991, Wolinsky, Stephen, Bramble Company

Tao of Chaos Exercise #40

Step I   See a past event.

Step II   See a present event.

Step III   See a possible future event.

Step IV   Notice the emptiness that these three events are floating in.

Step V   See the past event, present event, and future event as being made of the same substance as the emptiness which surrounds them.

Step VI   Notice what happens.

Conclusion

To freeze time making it appear linear is to resist the chaos of disappearance. *Time...no time...* appearance-disappearance as our natural process. Thinking you can control and freeze this pulsation does not stop the process. Rather, it creates fear and systems which deny the pulsation from implicate to explicate from explicate to implicate and keep the fear and chaos alive. The challenge for us all is to explore the disappearance and ultimately to know we are all connected to the one pulsation. With this understanding the imagined chaos of the explicate order can be seen as unfolding out of the serene implicate order. This would lead us to the understanding that the implicate is the explicate; the explicate is the implicate, or chaos is order; order is chaos. Time no longer then becomes so conditional since we are into the no-time of the interconnected Holographic Universe where past, present, and future unfold and become the explicate and enfold and become the implicate.

EIGHT • MASS

Mass: To come together or form a solid.[1]

Matter: Whatever occupies space, the substance to which physical objects consist or are composed.[2]

Matter is anything that occupies space and mass is its solidness. In this con text then, we, or how we see ourself and the world, occupies space and is solid. The next step after defining what matter/mass is is to look at how it pertains to the solid us. To do this it is important to go back to *Quantum Consciousness, Volume I* and recall Einstein's statement: "Everything is made of emptiness and form (mass) is condensed emptiness."

As mentioned in the chapter on Space, matter is space condensed down. Metaphorically speaking water could be viewed as space and ice-cubes as matter. Matter (condensed space) pulsates, becoming space...matter... space.

---

1. Websters, page 749.
2. Websters, page 752.

Parallel Worlds

Each of us experiences the solidness of ourselves and the "fixed" solidness of our individual world, which is a parallel world existing side-by-side with other individual worlds. For example, if we are in a parallel world called, "I'm all alone," this parallel world, or maybe we should call it a parallel state, feels solid and very real. What is interesting about parallel states is that once the space is contracted and it becomes solid, the state carries with it the illusion of time, i.e., it has always been solid and it will remain solid. What makes parallel states (worlds) so disconcerting is this phenomena of time which seems to be formed into existence as space contracts. Chaos occurs as contracted space, called matter, resists its thinning-out as a natural process.

Tao of Chaos Exercise #41

Eyes closed.

Step I   Notice a state of consciousness that you are in.

Step II   Notice how it feels like the solid state has always been there.

Step III   See the solid state as condensed emptiness.

Step IV   Notice that the "intensity" and "power" the state has over you is diminished.

Tao of Chaos Exercise #42

Eyes closed.

Step I   Feel "your" body.

Step II   Notice how it feels like the solid state has always been there.

Step III   See the concept of time, and the solid state as condensed emptiness.

Step IV   Notice how you are these, yet the "intensity" and "power" the state has over you has diminished.

Step V   Notice how resistance and chaos disappear as what we call "I" is allowed to be what it is...condensed interconnected emptiness.

Mass, like its sisters space, time and energy, as Einstein demonstrated are all made of the same substance.

In what I call mass phase, mass or solidness of an object or an internal state like a thought or emotion has a certain mass. If this mass is altered, i.e., made heavier or lighter, then the object cannot exist in its present form. Why? To change the weight or solidness of an object changes its intrinsic nature. This is what can be called a bifurcation point. A point where if mass *is* added or diminished it changes the experience.

Tao of Chaos Exercise #43

Step I   Notice an emotion.
Step II   Notice its weight.
Step III   Make the weight of the emotion heavier.
Step IV   Make the weight of the emotion lighter.
Step V   Notice what happens.

Tao of Chaos Exercise #44

Step I   Notice a thought.
Step II   Notice its weight.
Step III   Make the weight of the thought heavier.
Step IV   Make the weight of the thought lighter.
Step V   Notice what happens.

Tao of Chaos Exercise #45

Step I   Notice a state of mind.

Step II   Notice its weight.

Step III   Make the weight of the state heavier.

Step IV   Make the weight of the state lighter.

Step V   Notice what happens.

Chaotic Contemplations

Have you ever experienced anything that kept its solidness? Notice that everything went from solid state to disappearance.

Contemplation: Notice how things actually appeared quite suddenly and unexpectedly without reason or cause.

Tao of Chaos Exercise #46

Step I   Allow the emptiness to become a solid state, i.e., emotion or thought.

Step II   Notice how much of your attention it takes to hold it solid and intact.

Step III   Take your attention away and let the solid state become emptiness.

Conclusion

In this way emptiness is the implicate order with no energy, space, mass, and time. The implicate unfolds becoming a state (explicate order with energy, space, mass and time), and then enfolds into the implicate order of emptiness with no energy, space, mass or time. Changing the mass changes the state and each state can only exist at a specific density.

The *Tao of Chaos* is a process whereby we can allow disappearance without resistance. Since everything is in a constant state of appearance-disappearance, including mass, why not let it be. As mentioned earlier, "let it be, and it will let you *BE*: This is the *Tao of Chaos*.

SECTION III

THE ENNEAGRAM AND CHAOS

A GATEWAY TO ESSENCE: YOUR REAL SELF

NINE • CHAOS AND ESSENCE: YOUR REAL SELF

In my previous book, *The Dark Side of the Inner Child: The Next Step*, we talked about the formation of I-dentities and how the "outer" chaos or family dysfunction aids in the creation of a dysfunctional I-dentity and its overcompensated counter part.

What comes to mind, however, as we notice all these different I-dentities is, who or what we were before the creation of these I-dentities?

In order to explore this we must look at a child before there is any personality. To do this let us first explore the child just before, during, and after birth. If you look at a child, you will notice there is really no personality, there is really only an *essential* being with no characteristics that could be called a self. Actually, from the subjective point of view, the newborn does not even know that it is separate from the rest of the world. The beauty of infants is their spontaneity and how they are just themselves. This is before they are conditioned, programmed, and taught how to look, how to be, how to behave, how to act, how to imagine, how to feel, and how to think. An infant is *pure essence*. The infant experiences itself just as space, quiet, unrestricted, with no memory trace. This is what in some psychological or spiritual circles would be called **Essence**.

As the infant grows and the body develops, a group of I-dentities develops around Essence and hence a personality. Likes, dislikes, etc, are formed leaving the child with the before mentioned I-dentities. From a psychotherapeutic point of view, these I-dentities are the way the body and personality develop and handle incoming data from the environment. As children identify themselves more and more with I-dentities, they move further and further away from their spacious *Essence*. Soon, as most adults can attest, the Essence is gone and what is left are many I-dentities; talking to one another each with a different emotional experience, each with a different desire, each clamoring for attention.

What seems to occur is that as the infant develops into a full fledged body and personality, the Essence becomes less available and even feels frightening from the point of view of I-dentities.

The Void, Essence and Personality

The qualityless emptiness which was discussed throughout *Quantum Consciousness, Volume I* contracts and forms what might be called a personal Essence. See Illustration #3. This is what exists at birth. I-dentities are then formed as discussed in *The Dark Side of the Inner Child: The Next Step* to organize the outer chaos. When these I-dentities are formed, the physical body and I-dentities are organized around the Essence.

Why do I-dentities fear Essence? Each I-dentity is formed, is seeking, and has wants from the external environment. For example, an I-dentity might be created to please Mom to get love. These I-dentities face outward to the world and the outer chaos of no love, and are adapted to get, in this case, love. From the point of view of the I-dentity, the Essence is seen as death. See Illustration #3. To illustrate this let us give a few examples. Essence is prior to personality. The personality and

ILLUSTRATION #3

the physical body are formed around Essence and are seeking love by facing outward to the external world, (Mom, Dad, etc.)

From the point of view of personality (I-dentities), Essence feels like an internal *gnawing emptiness* which we all experience to varying degrees. All too often, the inner emptiness, which is Essence, is resisted by I-dentities and mistaken and viewed as bad or unwanted. I-dentities might attempt to fill the perceived gnawing emptiness, by eating, having relationships with people who are not right for us, over working, taking drugs, etc. It seems that this inner emptiness is avoided and resisted at all costs!

The body, however, often feels as if there is a hole in it. A hole of emptiness which we attempt to fill up. I-dentities are created to resist the hole or emptiness which is viewed as the ultimate chaos. To review, Webster's defines chaos as

"the infinity of space or formless matter supposed to have preceded the existence of the ordered universe" (p. 201).

The problem is that this inner emptiness is resisted by the I-dentities. Therefore I-dentities are in a double bind; they resist outer chaos and resist the imagined inner chaos of the emptiness.

An I-dentity, if it enters this emptiness and allows the emptiness, imagines annihilation, nonexistence, or death. This inner emptiness is the inner Essence which we all seek and which contains essential qualities like love, peace, power, invulnerability, etc. and which is intrinsic to the nature of Essence.

This means that I-dentities, as the song says, are "Looking for love in all the wrong places," by attempting to get it from the external; rather than from Essence which is our real self.

In short, the I-dentities are facing the wrong way. I-dentities are facing forward or outward, to get what they want when what they are really seeking can only be gotten by facing inward or back in the emptiness.

The I-dentities see this emptiness within the body as chaos, and resist it like crazy, to avoid it.

Therefore, this section is designed to develop a therapy to reabsorb I-dentities into the Essence and hence experience the essential qualities that I-dentities are seeking within oneself rather than continuing the failed attempt to "get" from outside. It can be said that the recognition of the order within chaos can occur at the level of our own essence, not at the level of personality through I-dentities.

The Organization of I-dentities Around Essence

The beautiful Essence of a child is lost as I-dentities are formed to organize the "outer" chaos. From the point of view of these automatic I-dentities, they are organized against the Essence. More simply put, the I-dentities organize around the spacious Essence. From the point of view of the I-dentities, the space of Essence seems like death; from the point of view of the I-dentities, the outer world seems like death.

Thus, I-dentities are stuck and frozen between outward chaos of the family, and inward space of the Essence. Both are seen as chaotic, both are scary, and both freeze the I-dentities on automatic.

Essence and the Body

What appears to occur is that the identification with the body by the created I-dentities form an internal universe, which, like a galaxy of stars, planets, and cosmic dust, seem to evolve around what the I-dentities perceive as a black hole which is actually within the body. It is this black hole which paradoxically is the *gateway* to Essence.

Most clients I have worked with experience this emptiness somewhere in their body; some in their solar plexus, some in their heart, some in their throat, some in the pelvis. From the point of view of the I-dentities, this emptiness means total and complete annihilation and death. But, to go into the emptiness actually has proven to be the most profound and *trance-ending* experience my clients and myself have experienced. It seems that the inner chaos of emptiness and the outer chaos of the family, which the I-dentities were created to resist, not only organizes our I-dentities, it organizes our body posture, and self-organizes how we experience the world.

Each I-dentity defends against the perceived emptiness, and the body posture seems to correspond to defend against the emptiness. What is the enormous paradox? The perceived gnawing emptiness we all resist is actually a gateway back to our Essence. This is the therapy of chaos; entering into the emptiness which is the gateway to Essence.

The metaphor of the pendulum has been used to represent the oscillating movement of the world as well as the psycho-emotional life of an individual. The pendulum has been recognized as an explanation in the movement of consciousness. For example, an individual can notice how, in their relationship, emotions move from love to hate, feeling adequate to feeling inadequate, feeling powerless to feeling powerful.

Generally speaking, one could equate this with I-dentities. For example, the pendulum of inside oneself; inner thoughts, a feeling of powerlessness on the downward swing hits a mid-point or gap, and then becomes an outward manifestation of feeling powerful on the upswing. Then the upswing hits a mid-point or gap, and goes "inside" and feels its inner thoughts, its feelings of powerlessness. This cycle goes on and on, powerless into powerful, powerful into powerless. In the past I-dentities or parts of oneself have been viewed more boundaried. For example, a part of one wants a relationship, a part of one wants to be alone. See illustration #4.

What becomes clearer is that when the boundaries which compartmentalize our experiences are removed, we can begin to see a movement in consciousness similar to that of

ILLUSTRATION # 4
TWO BOUNDARIED IDENTITIES

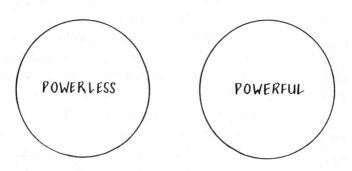

a pendulum. See Illustration #5. Rather than either I want a relationship, or I don't want a relationship, we can notice that one flows, like a pendulum from one to the other, moment to moment, day by day. It appears as though it is in the freezing of a part of the pendulum that subjective chaos ensues, rather than just allowing thoughts feelings, and relationships to flow one to another.

The Sufi school of the Fourth Way talks of the mid-point. What then is the mid-point? The mid-point is the gap or space that occurs as one emotion or thought changes to another. For example, if I have a thought or I-dentity called "I'm bad," before it turns into another thought or I-dentity called "I have

ILLUSTRATION #5

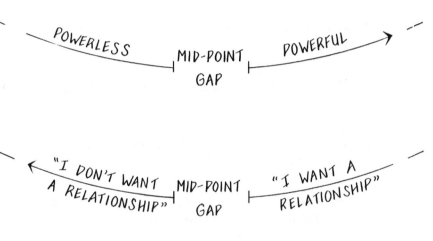

to be good," there is a gap or space. This is illustrated on page 36 and 37 of *Quantum Consciousness, Volume I*. In the same way there is a movement in feelings, states like powerlessness or fear, before they might turn into anger. The midpoint is what is called *self-remembering* and is where *self-remembering* can take place. In the work of G.I. Gurdjieff and P.D. Ouspensky, attention is split at the mid-point and one can wake up out of the sleep of identification with a particular state of consciousness. Half of your attention going inward, the other half going outward. This mid-point is often times experienced as pure quiet—nothingness. Gurdjieff himself often said, A man must resolve his own nothingness. This we can translate into the mid-point or that gnawing inner emptiness.

Many schools of self-development mention this mid-point or gap between two states, i.e., powerful, before it turns into powerless. In other words, the gap between the two states: some in the space between two breaths, some in the space between two thoughts. Several questions emerge, however, at this point in developing a *Tao of Chaos* and a reabsorption of I-dentities.

1. Can this mid-point of self-remembering become stable?

2. How does the pendulum start to move in the first place?

3. How does one go beyond the mid-point of self-remembrance?

4. What are the psychological factors which present and defend against the mid-point?

5. Is there a relationship between chaos and its relationship to the mid-point?

In order to understand this more completely, let us move to the space before the pendulum starts. I am going to call this space *Essence*. I am calling *Essence* the space prior to movement of I-dentities and even beyond mid-point. The *Essence* is prior to the mind, prior to the observer/observed, prior to intention, and hence prior to I-dentities. Secondly, the *Essence* is prior to the mid-point of self-remembering because at this point there is no individual self to remember, not a self to do this practice. At the *Essence*, there is no mind, no distinctions, no observer to observe, no awareness or awarer to be aware of something, no knower to possess knowing. Rather at *Essence* there is just observation with *no object*, awareness with *nothing to be aware of*, and knowing with *no knowing about*.

At first glance this seems abstract, so complicated and obscure that its realization seems to make us spin. What we will see is its availability, its freedom with nothing to be free of, its no-mind mind of undifferentiated consciousness. Essence has no distinctions; when emptiness condenses to form consciousness distinctions are made. Hence consciousness without distinction is Essence.

Before we go on the exploration of the Essence let me talk a little more about the mid-point. The mid-point is the space between one I-dentity before it meets another I-dentity; for example, powerless hits a gap before it moves to powerful. In the gap before powerless turns into powerful there is often an emotion or trance which is resisted. For example, as the pendulum moves from the downswing of powerless at the mid-point before it turns into powerful, there are trances and emotions which are variations on chaos. These emotions like confusion, dissociation, numbness, disorientation, a feeling of not knowing, anger, fear, are resisted by the individual, thus pushing them further along the pendulum into the I-dentity. These emotions and trances are the glue which hold the powerless and powerful I-dentity together.

The space between two I-dentities at the mid-point is seen as something to be resisted, hence the movement out of this gap is powerful. If we take off the layers of emotions, we find the *sedate* side of chaos, a feeling of nothingness or emptiness. This is the true mid-point and hence the most resisted mid-point.

Essence is where the pendulum begins, and as people know, once the psycho-emotional pendulum begins, it is almost impossible to *stop* it; let alone change its direction.

The real change must occur at the point of *Essence*. Said more simply, Essence is where you must look from and make connections to, in order to process the movement of the pendulum.

Fortunately for us, *Essence* leaves a trace, which is perceived by I-dentities as a hole or gnawing emptiness we resist in the body. This hole is a hole (holy) place where the therapy of chaos must go. But in order to go through that holy hole, the uncomfortable, crazy chaos must be experienced first. The therapy, therefore, will proceed from a person beginning in a conflict, and then take us through the crazy chaos, into the holy hole of chaos into the perceived emptiness of Essence. The next step is to understand and experience each move of the pendulum as a resistance to both the crazy as well as the sedate qualities of chaos.

Next, the Essence will be brought in. Why? Because the I-dentities have a goal or something they are seeking which, like the movement and momentum, cannot be stopped. Even though the strategy the I-dentity is using to get what it wants doesn't work, the pendulum keeps moving.

The Discovery

Essence has all the *essential* qualities that the I-dentity is seeking. Therefore, as the Essence absorbs the I-dentity, the essential quality, like love, or perfection is experienced from *Essence*. This is where the I-dentity, which feared its own destruction, is turned around toward the Essence and is reabsorbed, and the desired quality of the *Essence* emerges. In the Sufi system, states of emotion are called *states* to denote a sense of transience. Thus states are described as not permanent states of awareness; rather they come and go. A *station* is more permanent and resides in the *Essence*. Once this station is established it becomes a (way) station or place an individual lives in. For example, you might experience a state of love for another. Soon, though, this I-dentity, which is in the state of love, moves like a pendulum to a state of hate. Both

I-dentities have a state associated with them, i.e., love or hate. The *Essence*, however, which appears as a gnawing emptiness in the body, contains a permanent *station* of love with no object. This means rather than being an I-dentity in love, you reside at the level of *Essence*; which is love. When this occurs, the I-dentities can be reabsorbed into the *Essence*, and hence love moves from being a state of consciousness to a *station* of Essence. Simply put, the *Essence* is where a state becomes a station. This is the therapy.

In order to begin however, we will use the two forms of diagnosis: one, character analysis and, two, the enneagram as our diagnostic procedure. Highlighted case examples are presented and exercises offered in order to illustrate how to work with others as well as with oneself with this reabsorption process. With the Essence as your *Real Self* in mind, let us proceed and integrate our diagnosis along with the steps of how to reabsorb I-dentities.

ELEVEN · QUANTUM PHYSICS

THE ENNEAGRAM AND
THE EMPTINESS

Quantum Physics has demonstrated that the universe acts as a pendulum. In *Stalking the Wild Pendulum*, Itzhak Bentov suggests that we move from being to not being, or from manifest to unmanifest, 14 times per second. What this means is as we move from unmanifest to manifest, we enter into the no-state state of Essence which is emptiness. This no-state state appears to I-dentities as disappearance and hence becomes defended against. This pulsation or throb from unmanifest to manifest has been described in the ancient sanskrit text the *Sparda-Karikas*. Translated, it means lessons in the divine pulsation. So although this pulsation in Quantum terms happens 14 times per second, we exist and experience ourselves as manifest beings, and the world as a manifest world appearing 14 times per second and act "as if" the *disappearance* never happens. My teacher, Nisargadatta Maharaj, as mentioned earlier, described this process to me as a cinema film, in that each slide had a space or gap between the next slide. The problem was that it moves so rapidly, the gap is not noticed. This gap, which is a natural process, is where the I-dentity disappears only to re-appear an instant later. From the point of view of the I-dentity, disappearance into this gap is death, annihilation, the unknown, and chaos. Consequently, the I-dentity resists the perceived hole and perceived gnawing emptiness, causing more chaos, more pain, and more fear.

The Emptiness as a Gateway

It appears to the I-dentity that the emptiness is something to be resisted. Many clients report having a hole in their body or a hole in their being or a gnawing emptiness which they attempt to fill with food, drink, sex, work, or another person. This hole, however, is actually a gateway, a passage, into the much higher level of being, an order within chaos like sitting in the eye of a hurricane. This *holy hole* actually contains the *whole Essence*. The resistance to the holy hole is intense, and to begin to be willing to go through the hole of emptiness and use it as a gateway becomes the challenge. This is what the therapy is about, being able to enter through the hole, as a gateway into *Essence* and your *Real Self*, and reabsorb the dysfunctional I-dentities back within the self. The entrance through the holy hole in the body into Essence can be viewed as a *right of passage*. Why? Because the Essence is one step closer to the *you* of Quantum Consciousness than the personality, and secondly, because once you become established in this level of being, I-dentities lose their strength and your real self emerges and you begin to live from Essence.

The Enneagram

The enneagram is an ancient system from the middle east which describes nine basic *personality* types. Any student of the enneagram soon realizes that although there is one major type which she/he falls into, the enneagram has motion and does not remain fixed. Consequently, we all contain every type, with one type being our most used strategy.

The enneagram serves as a map of I-dentities, showing us where we are, giving us the ability to notice and detach from our "chief feature" or chief strategy or chief trance hopefully, to be able over time to predict the next motion of the mind.

The enneagram shows us types, but the personality types of the enneagram are organized to defend against the perceived gnawing emptiness, which is your Essence or real self. What this means is that although the personality types of the enneagram demonstrate movements of a type and style with I-dentities, the enneagram is a description of personality that is created to defend against the inner emptiness, which is the Essence or your *Real Self.*

Enneagram personality types with perceived correlating I-dentities defend against going into the perceived emptiness. The enneagram shows us our chief strategy (feature) trance to defend against the emptiness; furthermore, it moves like a pendulum fighting its own appearance and disappearance.

We will integrate the enneagram with the more traditional psychotherapeutic diagnosis of *Character Analysis* from Wilhelm Reich, M.D. In doing so, we will go through the major I-dentity structures that defend against the inner emptiness, which is perceived as chaos and leads us to our *Essential or Real Self.* Finally, from the emptiness will we explore the goal of each I-dentity, and reabsorb the I-dentity back within our emptiness by accessing the qualities that the I-dentity is seeking outwardly through the use of I-dentities, by extracting the inner essential qualities that are within us.

The next nine sections will not be a book on the enneagram, and character analysis. Many books will serve you better than this. What will be offered is a therapy to take apart the enneagram strategies and the character structures of personality which defend against the emptiness by fixating your attention as a way to distract you from the *Essence of your*

Real Self. The next step will be how to reabsorb the personality back into the essence. This will leave the practitioner experiencing essential qualities without I-dentities.

Diagnosis of Self and Other

All systems of psychotherapy and certainly many spiritual systems have their own methods and approaches to diagnosis. Many people resist the idea of diagnosis because there is a feeling that somehow you are characterized and located into a position that negates who you are. Any system of diagnosis can do that, but in the therapy of chaos, the practitioner is asked to objectively observe, so that they can watch and notice the style that the personality uses to defend itself against Essence. In my professional training seminars, diagnosis is used so that the participant can better understand how they themselves, organize and use I-dentities to organize their outer chaos. Furthermore, the I-dentities which organize the outer chaos have a trance strategy or defense which keeps this intrapsychic process alive and well. The purpose of the label is to better understand the personality, and at the same time to understand that you are beyond these I-dentities. In professional training I used the character analysis of Wilhelm Reich, M.D. This style was made more available by Alexander Lowen, M.D. and further made available by Ron Kurtz. This style of analysis of "Character" permits the therapist to know basic organization. By knowing these I-dentities, you can discover you are Essence, prior to, and beyond I-dentities. In short, *to find out who you are, you must first explore who you are not.*

The Therapy of Chaos

I spent years, approximately 3 hours per day with myself working with the enneagram. The enneagram, which is thousands of years old, denotes nine *basic* personality types, in an in-depth review of how that personality with its accompanying variations organizes the world.

I spent years taking apart approximately 90 pairs of oppositional I-dentities within each character type, and then began dismantling each pair within myself. This process using *The Enneagram* by Helen Palmer, *Personality Types* by Don Richard Riso enabled me to dismantle I-dentities one by one.

In 1991 I bought *The Enneatype Structures* by Claudio Naranjo. While studying Naranjo's book a missing piece jumped out at me!! That each personality type began with a feeling of "*loss of being.*" What I began to appreciate was that there was a *loss of being* that precipitated the I-dentities which were formed, and that there were nine basic styles of personality, nine being only the basic, which were habitually used to defend against this *loss of being*. I began to understand that as an infant we were forced to move from the pure *Essence of our Real Self* to the "outer" survival of the world as the body developed. In other words, as the physical body develops, the personality is formed through identification with the body. The personality is a survival mechanism which organizes chaos. What is the most important point is that the loss of being leaves a devastating hole within itself as it moves from *Essence* to personality. This explains why people feel a loss, like something is missing, a gnawing emptiness. This can be linked to a trauma which often is the place where people feel, "there must be something wrong with me, otherwise why would I feel this loss and emptiness. Actually, the gnawing shows there is something *right with you.* As will be demonstrated later, the irony of searching for something to fill the emptiness, thinking or feeling something is wrong, is how we run away from ourselves. More simply put, the doing we do to fill the emptiness is a resistance to the emptiness. It is trying to *do* your *being.* Or as Frank Sinatra put it so well in his song *"Strangers in the Night" do-be-do-be-do.*

The personality defends against the loss of being—but, there is the emptiness, a trace of Essence which is experienced as an emptiness within the body that the personality defends against. Each of us has thousands of I-dentities to defend against this inner emptiness where the loss of innocence or loss of being occurs. What is most important is the emptiness. The hole is a passageway that acts as a *right of passage*, through which we can enter into our own being. What you feel in your life is the continued attempts, through various strategies, to defend against this emptiness.

This means that the enneagram or *Character* is organized to defend against the emptiness. Unbeknownst to the personality *structure* the hole is a gateway into Essence. Consequently, these structures are defending against themselves, the deepest part of themselves.

Let us begin then to first diagnosis the strategy the I-dentity uses, and then to demonstrate the reabsorption of I-dentities back into a personal Essence.

Self-Diagnosis

As we move through structures it is important to be able to recognize and know our I-dentities and trances so that we can process through them and have them reabsorbed into Essence. It is important, therefore, to not get caught up with the personality with the aim of changing it. Simply put, do not try to change your personality and make it more "acceptable" or "healthy." Rather, notice that the organization of I-dentities around the body was a function of human development. Therefore, change would be trying to resist a function. Our goal is to notice possible combinations of I-dentities and their goals, and reabsorb them into the Essence of our real selves.

Essence: The Organizer of Chaos

Essence is beyond personality because it was there before the body and nervous system developed and could notice and differentiate self from other. Therefore, *Essence* becomes the ultimate organizer of chaos.

Essence, that vast personal emptiness, when allowed, can reabsorb the personality back into itself. Fortunately for us, Essence leaves a trace in the body. Although this trace of emptiness is resisted in the body, it is this Essence that the chaos and resistance to chaos can be reordered back into.

In order to do this we examine our I-dentities and personality fearlessly so that I-dentities are completely reabsorbed.

This allows the practitioner of the Quantum Approach to operate from Essence rather than I-dentity.

To do this I will propose I-dentity structures or underlying states that need to be reabsorbed. We must keep in mind that *it is not that which we know about that is the problem. Rather, it is that which we do not know about which is the problem.*

Lies

Lies we tell ourselves cannot be absorbed into Essence. Stated another way, we must confront and tell the truth about the lies we tell ourselves in order for I-dentities to be reabsorbed back into Essence. We must tell the truth about our lies. Why? *Essence can only absorb the truth - it cannot absorb lies.*

For example, I was working with a woman on the East

Tracy's superconscious

Coast at a workshop who described herself as a "love addict." She complained about a man that she was seeing, saying "He doesn't give me enough attention." I said to her, "You knew he was not right for you in the beginning of the relationship, and then lied to yourself about it; what lie did you tell yourself about him?"

She first got huffy about the question and then said, "Well, I was supposed to meet him at the restaurant at 8:00. He didn't show until 8:45. I kept lying to myself about that."

I explained that in a relationship we lie to ourselves about a person, and then we lie that we lied to ourselves. We then get angry with the person because they are *different* than the lie we told ourselves about the way they were. Our work is to uncover our own lies, and see people as they are, not the lies which compartmentalize our perceptions of their behavior. Another general example can be summed up in the word *denial*. If we lie to ourselves about a trauma that occurred by denying it occurred, or lie to ourselves about our childhood, those I-dentities cannot be reabsorbed back into Essence. Nisargadatta Maharaj said "You cannot let go of something until you know what it is." For this reason, there are no shortcuts or trance-ending, until we can experience and tell the truth about what had happened. Then and only then can personality be absorbed into Essence so that it is stabilized. A student once came to Nisargadatta Maharaj and said, "How long does it take to be able to stay in beingness? (Essence)" Maharaj replied, "To get established in this condition it might take some time but hang on to your beingness (Essence) only!"

Therefore as we begin this process, look at all I-dentity structures as yours. Why? Because no personality is one structure, rather we are mixes of many, and the enneagram, like the Quantum universe, is in constant motion.

OUTER CHAOS: THE DISRUPTER
INNER CHAOS: THE ESSENCE OF THE REAL SELF ORGANIZER

Throughout the book we have talked about "outer" chaos and the resistance to chaos as organizers of personality and I-dentities. The therapy of chaos moves us inward to Essence, which is prior to personality. Personality, it might be said, has limitations due to the fact that it is in time, or began as an individual as the physical body was conceived, born, and developed. Essence, however, has much greater scope and is prior to personality, and thus is one step closer to Quantum Consciousness than *is* personality. For this reason, Essence has at its fingertips essential qualities which personality is seeking. Stated another way, Essence has access to all qualities and *is* all qualities. Personality, according to noted Sufi teacher, G.I. Gurdjieff, is what is acquired; *Essence* is what we come with. Simply stated, we can say that the most intense trauma that occurs is as the personality is formed and leaves *Essence*. Better said, our greatest trauma is the *loss of Essence*. Personality searches for Essence its whole life unsuccessfully. Actually it is the outer search which defends against the trauma of *loss of Essence*. This loss of Essence forms such a *bifurcation point* that the personality re-enacts this most basic trauma and defends this most basic trauma every moment of every day. In other words, the resistance to the *ultimate trauma*, the loss of Essence, is defended against and hence re-enacted again and again.

How is it re-enacted?

Most of us feel a loss and, rather than experiencing that loss or going into the emptiness, we try to fill the emptiness and overcome the loss. To fill the emptiness, we use our attention to focus on something or occupy our attention so as not to feel the emptiness. Another way we might try to overcome the loss is by obsessively thinking that another will help us feel okay. Another way is that we might seek a teacher who can provide us with the secret of our loss. Or maybe we focus all our attention to others in an attempt to get them to feel our loss. This loss with its accompanying emptiness, is basic to personality and is its *nature*. Hence, to handle this loss of being we must go back the way we came.

There is a wonderful story of a famous Indian teacher named Ramana Maharishi. Once a seeker traveled from America to find the truth. After a long journey to India, he finally made it to Ramana Maharishi. He approached Ramana and asked, how can I find myself. Ramana replied, "Go back the way you came." The seeker left feeling upset. Another student said to Ramana, "Why were you so cruel, why didn't you give him a way to find himself?" Ramana replied, "I did, I told him to go back the way he came."

In other words, the personality must turn its attention around, and go back the way it came—back through the emptiness into the *Essence of the Real Self*.

What is ironic is that personality attempts to be Essence and to have and get the qualities of Essence. This can never occur, because personality is the third implicate, Essence the second implicate, and the Void the implicate.

The Loss of Essence

The trauma of the loss of Essence traps energy, i.e., Quantum comes from the word quanta which means energy packets, either to resist or re-enact and try to make right this ultimate trauma.

This ultimate trauma is the moment that the personality perceives itself as separate from itself (Essence). This *splitting off* leads to the ultimate bifurcation point, where the personality splits and dissociates from the Essence and defends against that traumatic experience repeatedly. The Essence, which from the point of view of personality seems empty, causes the personality to feel terrified of its own self, and projects that terror on others fearing they will annihilate you. This fear of Essence projected on people causes the personality to feel afraid of others. Once again, the double bind. The personality is afraid to connect with others and is afraid to connect to its Real Self, or Essence. The personality also feels terrified of the quanta of energy stored up during this traumatic fragmentation, because the personality feels the energy as overwhelming and chaotic. When facing this energy, clients often feel as though the energy is so powerful and overwhelming it could explode and destroy themselves or another.

The predicament of personality is illustrated in the fairy tale, *The Ugly Duckling*. The ugly duckling is treated as ugly by the outer world, thinks it's ugly, until it realizes, when it looks at itself, it is a beautiful swan (Essence).

In physics terms, Essence is the second implicate; it exists outside of energy, space, mass, and time, and yet acts as the *touchstone* or bridge which connects the ultimate to the physical universe. In other words, it is Essence that stands between David Bohm's implicate and explicate orders. Moreover, it is Essence that can give order to chaos. The paradox, however, is that to the I-dentities of personality, the empty space of Essence seems like chaos. Personality is the accumulation of I-dentities arranged so as to support the biological and psycho-emotional survival of the physical body. This puts I-dentities in a frozen pattern; I-dentities of personality are frozen trying to order outward chaos, and frozen resisting the perceived inward chaos of emptiness. In this way, the I-dentities of personality are in a double-bind stuck between outward and inward chaos.

Essence, however, does have all qualities to organize and reorder chaos.

> "The first implicate order is just the field itself." The first implicate order corresponds to a television screen, which is capable of showing and indefinite variety of explicate forms. The second implicate order correspond to the computer, which supplies and has the information that can arrange various forms. The third implicate form is the player. (*Science, Order, and Creativity*, F. David Peat and David Bohm, Bantam Books, New York. p.183).

In this analogy, it can be said that the undifferentiated consciousness or void is the first implicate order, Essence the second implicate order, and personality the third implicate order.

Following this line of reasoning, the therapy requires the personality (the third implicate order) to enfold into Essence, (the second implicate order) and experience the true essential qualities that are Essence. Then, finally for Essence to enfold back into the implicate order, or pure undifferentiated consciousness, which is the underlying unity of the void.

The Process

As we have explored through this text, chaos has been the unifying factor in regard to the organization of I-dentity. Chaos, the terror of overwhelmed, confusion, and out-of-control, is the viewpoint generally taken. To overcompensate for the chaos, we create I-dentity systems and subjective universes which act as attempts to end the chaos by organizing it to bring about a state of peace or equilibrium. Before we continue let me *again* define chaos in Webster:

> "The infinity of space or formless matter supposed to have preceded the existence of the ordered universe." (Page 201).

I mention this again because we must go into this "infinity of space," which to an I-dentity feels like chaos, and enter into Essence.

Each observer/creator of an I-dentity has a fixation of attention, or a way that the personality fixates its attention outwardly on particular I-dentities or underlying feeling states so the observer does not have to look at emptiness.

The Observer Creates And Is Part Of Personality.

In review of *Quantum Consciousness, Volume I,* the observer is still facing outward and is a first step in the process to move beyond personality. The *observer,* however, *is part of personality*, arguably a "higher" part. This is a very important point. The observer separates from Essence and develops to varying degrees with the development of the body and the personality. As mentioned throughout *Quantum Consciousness*, the observer creates I-dentities, and is part of the I-dentity. Stated another way, the observer faces outward toward thoughts, feelings, images, people, etc. *This fixation of attention of the observer is the strategy the observer uses to resist the trauma of loss of being.* The observer fixates its attention on the outward personality to avoid the trauma of loss of being and the emptiness. Stated another way, *the observer and the cluster of I-dentities we call personality are a unit, not separate.* The illusion is that through observation the observer can be freed of personality. The fact is that the observer is created as the physical body and personality develop. Furthermore, the observer through the act of observation creates the personality. See Illustration #6.

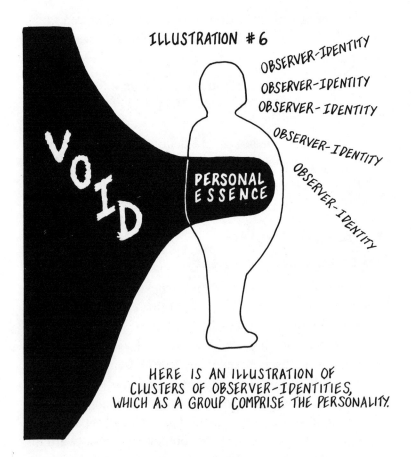

ILLUSTRATION #6

OBSERVER-IDENTITY
OBSERVER-IDENTITY
OBSERVER-IDENTITY
OBSERVER-IDENTITY
OBSERVER-IDENTITY

VOID

PERSONAL ESSENCE

HERE IS AN ILLUSTRATION OF CLUSTERS OF OBSERVER-IDENTITIES, WHICH AS A GROUP COMPRISE THE PERSONALITY.

This is a controversial point, and so the reader must ask; *has anyone they know ever been able to let go of personality by just self-observation?* If your answer is *no*, become willing to explore the possibility that the observer/personality is one unit. This means to enter into Essence, the observer and its object, i.e., the I-dentities clustered together called personality, must be reabsorbed back into Essence. In this way the (subject) observer and its object, the personality, disappear. What emerges is the essential quality of observation with no object.

Stated another way, the subject observer and its object (the personality) are reabsorbed back into Essence so that there is the essential quality of observation with no object. How can there be observation with no object? Because, at the level of Essence, the subject (observer) and its object (personality) merge and become one. This, G.I. Gurdjieff called *objective consciousness;* observation with no object.

For this to occur, the observer turns its attention inward toward the emptiness, rather than its habit of facing outward, thus it sees itself. More simply put, when the observer fixates its attention and faces outward, personality is there. When the observer fixates its attention and faces inward toward emptiness, Essence is there, and the observer (subject) and its object (personality) dissolve in Essence. The observer fixates attention outward to resist Essence (itself). When the observer faces inward, it gets reabsorbed into its essential nature. Then, there is observation with no observed, awareness with no object to be aware of, and a knower without knowing about. At this stage, the observer/personality dyad begins to disappear, and only pure Essence is left. This has also been called the Real I by G. I. Gurdjieff, or what Ramana Maharishi called the I I.

To illustrate, picture a wheel. The hub of the wheel forms the center axis to the spokes. Essence is just below the hub of the wheel. The hub of the wheel is the fixation of attention and underlying experience of personality called the chief feature, chief fixation, or chief trance. The I-dentities are the spokes of the wheel. Therefore, if you can discover the hub of your wheel, which organizes the I-dentities, the reabsorption of the I-dentities (spokes) and the hub and the fixation of attention of the observer is much quicker. For that reason, we will explore the major hubs of attention of the observer personality, which prevent us from merging with Essence.

The Essence

Exploring and knowing the observer's fixation of attention is not enough. To reach Essence, each structure of personality must be deconstructed and reabsorbed back into your essential nature. Why? If we just stay in Essence, the personality will still be functioning. This is what often happens to meditators. One minute they are in Essence—the next minute, like a sling-shot they are in I-dentities. To a meditator leaving Essence and entering the world is like a *smack* in the face. Therefore, we deconstruct the I-dentities of personality so we can move and live in the world from the place of Essence. With that spirit in mind, each fixation of attention is followed by a highlighted case study and summary of the process. Hopefully, this will allow the reader to follow along, and provide a context for their own reabsorption process. In the first seven cases, you will see easy reabsorptions. In the last two, barriers to reabsorption are demonstrated plus examples of how to proceed through more difficult structures.

Please note that each case is a *highlight* of a session or several sessions lasting from one to several hours. I have chosen specific cases to emphasize particular points of information. For that reason, each case and its complexity of therapeutic information will increase as you go along. This gives the reader a piece at a time. This process is not a formula, but rather a context to enter into the reabsorption of old I-dentity patterns.

Throughout all of my four books I have demonstrated that life, and our intrapsychic world, reflect the world of physics. I-dentities have counter I-dentities, which are one unit working in tandem and complimenting one another. These I-dentities are connected, and, unlike most forms of psychotherapy where we try to get rid of the bad worthless part and keep the good worthy part, in the therapy of chaos both are seen as a unit connected by an emotional state or a trance which holds the I-dentity together like glue.

These pairs of I-dentities are reflected in the world of physics and hence in our inner world of psychology.

"Today we know that every particle has its antiparticle, Particle and antiparticle is a fundamental symmetry in physics...Scientists realized that an electron can be thought of as having a quantized spin. This spin has only one of two possible directions - up or down- hence its basic two-valuedness." (*Superstrings: The Search for the Theory of Everything*, F. David Peat, Contemporary Books, Chicago, 1989, p. 75-76).

Conclusion

It is important to understand how *basic* pairs of I-dentities that are formed to organize chaos and resist the trauma of loss of Essence resist and create unwanted states of chaos. What should be noted is that each attempt to organize the chaos is actually a resistance to an unwanted state. Therefore, it is the attempted organization of chaos which facilitates an I-dentity on an exhausting search to *end* this unpleasant state. The two pairs of I-dentities, therefore, are chaos and the resistance to chaos.

Each fixation of attention of the observer is a strategy

used to resist the trauma of the loss of being and the perceived emptiness. A whole personality is formed around Essence. "To discover who you are, you must first discover who you are not." In this spirit, let us begin to explore the nine fixations of attention with their character types so that we can discover who we are not. In this way the observer/personality fixates attention on a feeling, a person, a thought, an imagining, as a way to resist the trauma of loss of being and the emptiness. It can be said that the observer/personality fixates its attention and faces forward and looks outside itself in a desperate attempt to avoid the trauma. The perceived gnawing emptiness, however, is a constant reminder of Essence. The personality, however, sees Essence as a constant reminder of the painful trauma and so attempts to avoid it at all costs.

Stated more simply, the fixation of attention is the strategy the observer/personality uses to avoid the trauma. This is why *changing* the personality is adding on to the defense of trauma, rather than dealing with the trauma, i.e., the loss of Essence directly, which the observer/personality is resisting. Stated another way, the continual attempt to change the personality and make it better or healthier is the observer's fixation of attention on personality and a resistance to Essence (emptiness). In short, the observer's wish to change personality is the way it resists Essence, or itself. To get the observer/personality to turn its attention around toward emptiness leads to Essence.

To turn the attention of the observer/personality's fixation of attention outward to a "better personality" leads to more I-dentities and more personality and hence away from Essence.

Fixations of Attention are Strategies

Fixations of attention, like trance states, occur when the observer of an experience shrinks their focus of attention and goes into a trance-like state by fusing with a particular state or I-dentity to avoid the trauma of loss of being.

Chapter 23 is called Advanced Attention Training which discusses the observer's attention and how it organizes inward as well as outward attention.

I'M O.K. IF I'M PERFECT
YOU'RE O.K. IF YOU'RE PERFECT

The first fixation has different names. Naranjo calls it *angry virtue*, it is called the *perfectionist* by Palmer, and the *reformer* by Riso. This fixation of attention is marked by a deep resentment and characterologically the body is rigid, and looks brittle as if it might break.

The Underlying State

The underlying state of consciousness of each fixation of attention is critical in understanding how Essence is organized around the observer/personality dyad. The underlying state is that chronic underlying condition which might be a feeling, a thought or a state of consciousness.

For example, in fixation strategy of attention number 1, the underlying state is the feeling of resentment. This means that all of the I-dentities and stories the observer/personality dyad tells itself only reinforce the chronic state of resentment.

The Story is Not the State

Most of us, when we experience the chronic state, look, and often find a story as to *why* we feel what we feel.

For example, we feel emotionally a feeling of resentment. We will then automatically *assume* that there is a *reason* or *story* why. We then look, and even find a story to justify our emotions. In order to understand the underlying state of a personality type, we must understand that the state, in this case resentment, is almost always present. For this reason, to look for a story as to why you are resentful, or to try to overcome your resentment, only re-enforces the resentment. The way out is to acknowledge that this is your underlying state, and just let it be.

In *Quantum Consciousness: Volume I*, Chapter 4, we work with emotional states. Throughout the Quantum exercises in that section, we are asked to take our attention off of the *story* as to why we feel what we feel, and to focus attention on the feelings themselves.

In other words, taking your attention off of the mental story when you are in an emotional state, and focusing on the emotional state, itself. Simply stated, place your attention on the emotions when emotional states are present.

The Chief Feature or Trance

The fixation of attention of the observer/personality dyad has three functions; first, to fixate attention away from the gnawing emptiness. Second, to try to experience perfection in this fixation, by looking through the observer/personality dyad. This searching for perfection is caused by the observer/personality dyad deciding that this gnawing emptiness means that it is *imperfect*. And third, to make up stories or reasons of imperfection to justify the chronic underlying state of resentment. *Resentment* is the underlying state. For example, let's imagine the observer/personality dyad feels the gnawing inner emptiness. First, the observer personally might look for something to fill-up this emptiness like a relationship or psycho-spiritual system. Second, since the observer/personality dyad decides that the emptiness means there is an imperfection within themselves, the observer/personality dyad looks for a *perfect* relationship or system. Third, since the underlying state is resentment, the observer/personality dyad projects its own imagined imperfection on a relationship or psycho-spiritual system and makes up stories of imperfection about the relationship or system to justify feeling resentful. As we will discuss throughout this section, each fixation of attention labels the gnawing emptiness as "there is something wrong or it is seen by the observer as an internal lack or inner deficiency," and then tries to *over*-compensate for the feeling of inner lack. Finally, the observer/personality dyad, since it cannot overcome this lack, creates a story to reinforce and justify its underlying state.

Where Does That Resentment Come From, How Does It Manifest?

See Illustration # 7

As mentioned before, the pendulum acts as our metaphor for the organization of the body and the observer/personality dyad around Essence. Or, more simply put, from an unmanifest Essence to a manifest observer/personality dyad. At this point of fixation, the manifestation of the body and the observer/personality dyad surrounds the Essence as the body develops. Unfortunately, as the body develops, and hence the personality, the trauma of the loss of Essence leaves the observer/personality dyad with an underlying state of imperfection and resentment and hence fixates on trying to overcome it and experience perfection. Fortunately, Essence leaves a trace in the body as an empty feeling. More simply put, the body develops and organizes an observer/personality dyad around the Essence, which leaves its trace as a gnawing emp-

ILLUSTRATION # 7
FIXATION OF ATTENTION STRATEGY #1
THE PERFECTIONIST

"LOOKING FOR PERFECTION IN ALL THE WRONG PLACES"

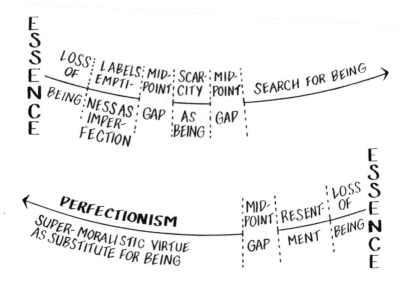

tiness. Many clients who come to me complain that when they come home from work they feel this gnawing emptiness in their stomach.

For example, I have a client who, when she returned home from classes, felt her emptiness in her stomach. The emptiness was so resisted that to "fill it up" she over-ate. Unfortunately for her, she was unable to go into the emptiness. She would say, "It's just too terrifying." She would resist it by trying to fill up her stomach. The emptiness in this case was labeled loneliness and something to be feared. Her therapy involved going into this resisted area of emptiness. For the observer/personality dyad the trauma of loss of Essence is so great that to look at the loss of being is terrifying. Why? Because with this loss came the *splitting off* from Essence and the development of a false self, and the observer/personality dyad.

There is an incredible *shock* that is felt when Essence is lost. Essence contains essential qualities, like love, power, strength, etc., which are our nature. This loss of Essence occurs as the body-mind develops, and brings forth a state of personality which is experienced as *inadequacy* ("What is wrong with me that I have lost my basic nature?") Why? Because the observer/personality dyad attempts to retrieve these essential qualities through the use of I-dentities or false selves rather than Essence. It can be emphasized that the observer/personality dyad feels inadequate to get love, perfection, etc. because these are qualities that can only be stabilized in Essence not in the observer/personality dyad. For this reason the observer/personality dyad is inadequate compared to Essence, *and the issue of inadequacy can never be fully worked out at the level of personality.*

To restate, the deep feeling of inadequacy can never be handled on a personality level. Why? Because compared to Essence the personality *is* **inadequate** to get love. Love, for example, is the nature of Essence, not of personality. To say it another way, the personality appears to be looking outward comparing itself to others and hence feels inadequate. Actually, the personality is looking inwards and is comparing itself to Essence. In other words, personality is inadequate compared with Essence. To truly experience love, one must *be* in Essence, not in personality. Or stated another way, personality can experience personal love as a transient *state*. The *station* of love, however, is only intrinsic to Essence. From Essence to personality, there is a descent along the pendulum in a desperate search to return to Essence, but the mistake in fixation of attention strategy #1 is that the observer/personality dyad is looking outward for the perfection of Essence rather than inward at Essence itself. An anger resentment and self-righteousness develops as the essential quality of perfection, which is Essence, is labeled as imperfection and is substituted with a personality which has I-dentities and has a fixation of attention on perfectionistic moralistic virtue. In other words, the observer/personality dyad is *resentful* at the trauma of loss of Essence. The observer/personality dyad is searching for the perfection of Essence and cannot find it. The personality looking outward *substitutes* moralistic virtue for the perfection that is Essence. In this way, the fixation of attention strategy #1 feels resentful at not being able to find perfection outside itself.

Moralistic virtue becomes the way the observer/personality dyad attempts to *substitute*, create perfection, and resist the deep trauma of loss of Essence, which is perfection itself. I-dentities develop to justify the moralistic virtue, seek another perfection, and overcompensate for the inadequate personality by becoming super moral or even religiously fanatic. Very simply put, over perfectionism is the compensation for the deep inadequacy and self-blame destined by the trauma of loss of Essence. This causes I-dentities to be formed which are compensatory by nature to cover the deep inadequacy and self-blame for losing Essence. It might be said that not only is the personality inadequate compared to Essence, but also the personality blames itself for its inadequacy and its lack of perfection.

For example, I saw a client who was obsessed with integrity and being moral. She was very judgmental and always seeking and questioning her own integrity. The problem was that she had decided that money was bad and immoral, and that people who had money were "out of integrity." Simply put, she was trying to be perfect and super moral as an overcompensation for her own feeling that she was imperfect and not good enough. This dyad of unworthy imperfect trying to *be perfect* was personality's attempt to substitute for the perfection that is Essence. In other words, she was trying to have a perfect personality, which is not possible.

Like the song, she was "Looking for love in all the wrong places." She was looking for *perfection* in all the wrong places; outside of Essence in the observer/personality dyad and the world through a substituted image of perfection. In this way, she was looking for perfection outside, in all the wrong places, rather than inside in Essence.

There was a story told to me while I was in India. Several Gods had gotten together to decide where to hide the *key* to a person's nature, i.e., Essence, so that people would never find it. One God said, "Why not hide it on top of the Himalayas?" Another God replied, "No, people would eventually find it." The second god said, "Why not hide it at the bottom of the ocean?" "No," replied another, "Someday, they will reach the bottom of the ocean." The third God said, "Let's hide the *key* (Essence) inside of people, they will never think to look there."

This is the plight of us all: "Looking for ourselves in all the wrong places."

The Self-Therapy

The self-therapy asks individuals, who find themselves stuck in this fixation of attention, and who label essence as imperfection, and over compensate with over perfection and moralistic virtue, to shift their focus of attention. This shift changes the outward trance or I-dentity to the trance-ending of Essence. This requires us all to be impeccably honest with ourselves and to notice the gnawing emptiness within our own body which the body and the observer/personality dyad have organized around.

To do this, the inadequacy must be explored. The individual will have numerous over-compensating I-dentities that defend against the experience of the emptiness.

The Therapy

Step I Write down those I-dentities which resist your emptiness.

Step II Notice where in your body emptiness exists.

Step III Enter into the emptiness and feel it.

Step IV Notice how to the I-dentity, the emptiness seems like death, but from the inside, the emptiness is calm, quiet, peaceful and serene.

Step V From inside the emptiness ask each I-dentity "What is it you really want and are seeking more than anything else in the world?"

Step VI However the I-dentity responds, feel that quality of experience in the spacious emptiness.

Step VII Next, have the I-dentities turn around and be reabsorbed within the emptiness which is Essence.

Variation

Step VIII Seeing the I-dentities in the foreground, stay in the background and notice the I-dentities are floating in emptiness.

Step IX Experience and feel the essential quality from the background.

Step X See the I-dentities and the emptiness as being made of the same substance.

I-dentities	Underlying State	Over-Compensating Identities
Imperfect	Imperfection Yielding Resentment	Perfectionistic
Poverty (either of spirit or financial)		Self-satisfaction Over-stability
Scarcity		Image of Superworth
Worthlessness		Dominance
Inadequate		Judgemental

Above is the *Cliff Notes* of the therapy, so let me slow down the process and offer a highlighted case example.

Highlighted Case Example

John is a 39-year-old man who feels resentful about his inability to meet his financial obligations.

Client: I feel powerless to live in this world. It is so dishonest. I try to be honest and fair but nobody tells the truth.
Therapist: What are you feeling right now?
Client: Tight.
Therapist: Where in your body do you feel this tightness and powerlessness?
Client: In my stomach.
Therapist: Peel back the layer of powerlessness and notice what feeling is below it.
Client: Unworthy.
Therapist: What feeling is between and connects the unworthy to the powerless?
Client: Fear.

Therapeutic Note
I-dentities come in pairs, and what often holds the I-dentities together is an unacknowledged and unwanted emotional state or trance. This emotional state acts as glue to hold together two I-dentities.

For example, if a little girl asserts herself and Dad thwarts her, she might have an assertive I-dentity and fear which connects to a new I-dentity which pleases Dad. In other words, layered between the two I-dentities of *assertive* and *please Dad* there could be an unwanted, unacknowledged feeling of fear. This fear must be acknowledged and experienced, before we can go further on in the process. In other words, denial of fear would be a *lie and Essence can only absorb the truth.*

Therapist: Step in between the two layers and feel the fear.
Client: Nods.
Therapist: If you peel back the unworthiness, what is underneath it?
Client: An empty space.
Therapist: What does the emptiness feel like?
Client: Loneliness.

Therapeutic Note
Here he defines the emptiness as loneliness. This definition or label covers the true emptiness which is a no-state state and is almost qualityless.

Therapist: Peel back the loneliness and see what is there.
Client: Just empty space.
Therapist: What does it feel like?
Client: Nothing, just emptiness, kind of peaceful.

Therapeutic Note
Peacefulness is an essential quality. For that reason, we work from Essence to personality, rather than from personality to Essence. For example, most therapists feel that if you work through personality, you will reach your Essence. However, few people, even after years and years of therapy, do reach their Essence.

The Tao of Chaos asks us to work from Essence making it our starting point rather than our finishing point. In contrast, most therapists have personality as the starting point in hopes of Essence being the finishing point.

Therapist: From "back there" in the peaceful space how do the different layers and I-dentities in the foreground seem to you?

Client: They seem less significant.

Therapist: Ask the first I-dentity, the one who feels powerless, "what you are seeking more than anything else in the world?"

Client: To know things are okay.

Therapist: Ask the I-dentity, "If you felt okay, what would that feel like?"

Therapeutic Note
We want to get to a feeling, so we always ask, *what would that feel like*?

Client: Safe and like everything had a purpose and was perfect.

Therapist: Ask the I-dentity, "What would that feel like?"

Client: Peaceful and like everything fits.

Therapist: Now, from "back there" notice the second layer, the unworthy I-dentity. Ask the unworthy I-dentity, "What are you seeking more than anything in the world?"

Client: To be perfect.

Therapist: Now, from "back there" ask the next layer of loneliness, "What are you seeking more than anything else in the world?"

Client: To be connected.

Therapist: Now from back there in the emptiness, feel the peacefulness of back there where everything fits.

Therapeutic Note

Here, Essence is peace by its nature. We can experience this as we enter into Essence. As mentioned earlier, all qualities that I-dentities are seeking outside can never be fully attained through the observer/personality. It is through Essence that these qualities can be made manifest.

Client: Nods

Therapist: Feel the perfection of "back there" and the connection of "back there".

Client: Nods.

Therapist: Now, from "back there" see if you can turn the I-dentities that are facing forward looking for peace, connection, and perfection around so that they face you.

Client: Nods.

Therapist: Now see if the I-dentities would be willing to be reabsorbed into the emptiness as you feel the perfection and peaceful connection of "back there."

Client: They already have.

Therapist: How are you doing?

Client: Peaceful.

Conclusion

This very edited transcript highlights a session where the Observer/I-dentities have a fixation of attention and are "looking for perfection in all the wrong places." By shifting the observer's attention around and experiencing the perfection that is Essence, the Observer/I-dentities can let go and be reabsorbed back into Essence, which is prior to personality.

Once the chronic habitual pattern of the observer of looking outside to fill the emptiness is shifted, and the observer looks to the Essence, and merges with Essence, the essential quality becomes stable. It is important to note with each fixation of attention how the observer/personality dyad labels the emptiness. In fixation of attention strategy #1, the emptiness is labeled as imperfection. For this reason the observer/personality looks outside itself for perfection. In fixation of attention strategy #1, the perfection being sought by the observer/personality dyad is found and stabilized in the perfection and peace which is inside in the Essence of their Real Self.

I'M O.K. IF YOU FLATTER ME
YOU'RE O.K. IF YOU FLATTER ME

This fixation of attention of the observer/ personality dyad is also called the *Giver* by Palmer, The *Helper* by Riso, and *Egocentric Generosity* by Naranjo, and demonstrates a fixation of attention on flattery. In other words, the observer/personality dyad places all its attention on getting flattered or flattering oneself which reinforces the underlying compensation of pride. Furthermore, in order to get attention and flattery from outside this fixation over-compensates for what lies beneath the underlying state of pride which is inadequacy *which* covers the chronic emptiness. There is no attention on the emptiness, all attention is on receiving attention through flattery, which is an attempt to reinforce pride and a-void the trauma of loss of being. In pop-psychology language it can be seen as a major part of co-dependency.

In this observer/personality dyad which develops around the Essence, the trauma and the pain of the loss of Essence is overwhelming. The observer/personality dyad forms a deep feeling of *dependence* because the emptiness is seen as not having any independent self. This leads to trying to fill emptiness with *flattery* and reinforcing the underlying compensation state of pride. In this fixation of attention strategy #2, the emptiness is labeled as dependence. This causes the observer/personality to create an over-independent image. In fixation of attention strategy #2, much time is spent trying to flatter or tell stories to herself/himself about achievements and successes, thus reinforcing the false pride, lies, and over-independent image. Furthermore, there is a false sense of trying to look independent with a powerful sense of freedom and will. This is a part of the look of pride, which attempts to overcompensate for the feeling of *worthlessness and dependence.* This fixation often times is so used to giving itself up to get flattered that it forms many dissociated selves. This is the chameleon and can be likened to the main character of a Woody Allen film, *Zelig*, where Zelig takes on the I-dentity of others. The dependence and neediness becomes a constant desire to fill the emptiness in the body. This, in character analysis, corresponds to an oral character type, an emptiness which can never be filled or, as a character type, a bottomless pit of needs. The attempt by I-dentities in this fixation is to fill the emptiness with either *self-flattery* or by *getting flattered.* In other words, reinforcing the underlying compensation state of pride becomes an *obsession.* To hide the neediness the deep inadequacy which is covered by false pride, which acts as a compensatory I-dentity or as a reaction formation against the worthlessness and dependence. People who suffer from this way of handling the emptiness create a desire to be the center of attention and can develop a larger than life self-image. They develop internal feelings of being greater than they are, and a false sense of pride for fantasized achievements.

To defend against the emptiness much time is spent trying to "look good" or to get *flattered.* It is as if the energy of attention and flattery will fill the deep empty hole that is sitting in their body. Often times a false generosity or over-giv-

ILLUSTRATION # 8
FIXATION OF ATTENTION STRATEGY # 2
THE OVER-FREE

"LOOKING FOR INDEPENDENCE, WILL AND FREEDOM IN IN ALL THE WRONG PLACES"

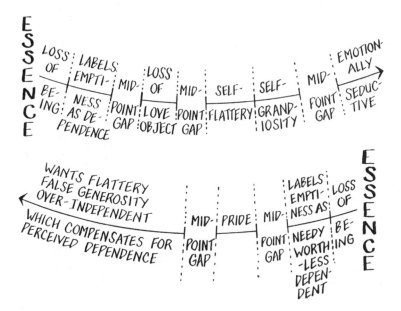

ing is acted out. See illustration #8. In an attempt to get flattered, this personality, like the co-dependent, over-gives in an attempt to *get* flattered as a giver. This leads to inflated stories to others and self-lies of success as a way to get flattered. Simply stated, *flattery* is used to fill the emptiness. This observer/personality dyad fixation compensates with a false strong will at the level of the observer/personality dyad in an attempt to hide the dependency. Frequently the I-dentities are seeking the essential quality of will, power, or freedom.

Self-Therapy

Here again, the I-dentity of grandiosity must be explored. This self-grandiosity covers the deep worthlessness and dependence. As with all places where the observer fixates attention, the I-dentities must be named and their true desire uncovered before they can be reabsorbed into Essence.

The Therapy

Step I   Write down those I-dentities which resist your emptiness.

Step II   Notice where in your body emptiness exists.

Step III   Enter into the emptiness and feel it.

Step IV   Notice how to the I-dentity, the emptiness seems like death, but from the inside, the emptiness is calm, quiet, peaceful and serene.

Step V   From inside the emptiness ask each I-dentity "What is it you really want and are seeking more than anything else in the world?"

Step VI   However the I-dentity responds, feel that quality of experience in the spacious emptiness.

Step VII   Next, have the I-dentities turn around and be reabsorbed within the emptiness which is Essence.

Variation

Step VIII Seeing the I-dentities in the foreground, stay in the background and notice the I-dentities are floating in Emptiness.

Step IX   Experience and feel the essential quality from the background.

Step X   See the I-dentities and the emptiness as being made of the same substance.

I-dentities	Underlying State	Over-Compensating Identities
Insufficient	Dependence	Pride
Dependent		No Needs/
		Over independent
Needy		1. False abundance
Inadequacy		2. Larger than life image
		3. Tries to get love
		4. Center of Attention
Bad Emptiness		5. Over-emotional
		to hide emptiness

Highlighted Case Example

Below is a highlighted session with a woman age 32 who is a nurse. Her presenting complaint was, "I cannot get enough attention."

Client: I feel depressed. I can't seem to get satisfied. I try to get my needs taken care from others but no matter how much I give, I never get in return.
Therapist: Where in your body do you feel this *giver* part of yourself?
Client: My heart (she points to the center of her chest).
Therapist: If you peel back this over-giver, what is underneath?
Client: I feel totally worthless.
Therapist: What emotion connects the layer of worthlessness to the layer of super-giver?
Client: Helplessness.
Therapist: Feel the helplessness?
Client: I keep resisting the helplessness.

Therapeutic Note
In this interaction I will ask the client to create the helplessness. I do this because she is unwilling or unable to experience what is there. When she says

she is resisting helplessness, I ask her to knowingly, consciously, intentionally *create* the resistance. This enables her to take charge of the resistance. Then, I ask her to knowingly create what she is creating automatically. i.e., create the helplessness then the resistance, until she feels free to create and have the helplessness and the resistance to helplessness and free to *not* have them.

Therapist: Intentionally create the feeling of helplessness.
Client: I am.
Therapist: Make the resistance to helplessness the size of this room.
Client: Okay.
Therapist: Make the resistance the size of the State of New Mexico.
Client: Okay.
Therapist: Make the resistance the size of the United States.
Client: It's getting harder to create it.
Therapist: Okay, stop creating it. Now create the feeling of helplessness the size of California to the Mississippi River and the resistance to helplessness from the Mississippi River to the Atlantic Ocean.
Client: Okay.
Therapist: Now, create that several times.
Client: Okay.
Therapist: Now stop creating it and peel back the layer of worthlessness and what is there?
Client: An empty space.
Therapist: How does the empty space feel as you enter into it?
Client: Quiet, calm, kind of void.
Therapist: Be "back there" in the empty space and look out at the two I-dentities of worthlessness and over-giver and the helplessness between them. How do they seem to you?

Client: I feel much less attached to them.

Therapist: From "back there", ask the over-giver, "What are you seeking more than anything else in the world?"

Client: To be recognized and acknowledged.

Therapist: If the I-dentity felt recognized and acknowledged, what would that feel like?

Client: Powerful.

Therapist: Ask the worthlessness, "What are you seeking more than anything else in the world?"

Client: To feel safe and strong.

Therapist: And if the I-dentity *felt* safe and strong, how would that feel?

Client: Powerful.

Therapist: Feel the power of the empty space "back there."

Client: Yes.

Therapist: Now, turn the I-dentities around so that they can see that the power they were seeking is inside the emptiness rather than facing toward the outside.

Client: They can feel that.

Therapist: Now, ask the I-dentities if they would be willing to be reabsorbed back into the Essence "back there" as you feel the power.

Client: They are absorbed.

Therapist: How do you feel?

Client: Calm and powerful.

Conclusion

In this case she was "looking for power in all the wrong places." By having the I-dentities turn around, the power, which is Essence, is experienced.

In this case, since she had a Yoga background, I reminded her of the Bhagavad Gita, where Krishna (personal Essence as therapist) says to Arjuna (client) in reference to Essence, "Swords cannot cut it, fire cannot burn it." This means that the power of Essence, cannot be cut, burned, or hurt in any way. Hence it leaves a person feeling an invulnerable vulner-ability. Invulnerable because it cannot be hurt; vulnerable because there is total openness and exposure. Simply put, once you are not identified with personality and *are* Essence, you no longer identify others as personality, and hence feel an Essence-to-Essence connection which is much deeper than a personality-to-personality connection.

I'M O.K. IF YOU THINK I'M O.K., YOU'RE O.K. IF YOU THINK I'M O.K.

The third strategy of the observer/personality dyad to resist the trauma of the loss of Essence fixates attention on what is called the *performer* by Palmer, the *status seeker* by Riso, and is called *success through appearances* by Naranjo. This strategy of the observer/personality dyad fixates its attention on outward appearances to resist the trauma of the loss of Essence and is probably one of the most prevalent structures in our society. Few could deny the emphasis on "looking good in the world today." The problem with a performer is that their center is not inside themselves, rather, their center is outside of themselves. This leads them to feel about themselves how they imagine others feel about them. This is the classic syndrome of the queen in *Sleeping Beauty* when she says, "Mirror, mirror, on the wall, who is the fairest of them all?" When the mirror answers, "Sleeping Beauty," there is outrage and *vanity*. Vanity is a very powerful chief feature and reinforces the underlying state of deceit. This underlying state of deceit is always there. Although there might be an outward tendency to think deceit is an asset (like a used car salesman), or if we think deceit is bad, the performer will try to hide it by being over-honest.

Once again, there is no reason or story as to why strategy #3 feels itself to be deceitful other than that the observer/ personality dyad labels the emptiness of Essence as an inability to *do* or to *create*. The fixation of #3 on not being able to *do* or *act* can either attempt to overcome feelings by *over-doing*, or to overcompensate for deceit. They might tell themselves stories where people accuse them of being deceitful and hence they become over-honest. In this way they either justify or demonstrate to the inner imagined person they are not deceitful but honest. This fixation might even tell itself that it is misunderstood. With the underlying state of feeling that they can't *do, act,* or *create*, however, the fixation is always trying to cover it up and look *good* by overdoing. For this reason, since they label the emptiness as an inability to *do, act* or *create*; most actions are seen as "acting," and hence the person feels like they have to be deceitful. This also has manifested in clients I have seen who feel like an imposter. They are "acting" to compensate for their underlying state of an *inability to do*. To restate, from the outside a person might see the #3 fixation as always *doing*, but, subjectively since #3 has labeled the emptiness of Essence as an inability to do even if they are always doing they feel like they have done nothing. We must remember that the first label (I-dentity), in this case labeling the emptiness of Essence as an inability to do, is the strongest. The second I-dentity of overdoing is the compensation and can never over-compensate. To restate, #3 feels deceitful about their accomplishments because they don't believe they do anything, and secondly, you can never feel o.k. by over-compensation because it always reinforces its opposite state. See illustration #9.

Vanity can be seen as using everyone else as a mirror to reflect who you are, what you feel, and your image of yourself. This means that this person imagines that who they are,

ILLUSTRATION # 9
FIXATION OF ATTENTION STRATEGY #3
THE PERFORMER

"LOOKING FOR SUCCESS, BALANCE & WORTH IN ALL THE WRONG PLACES"

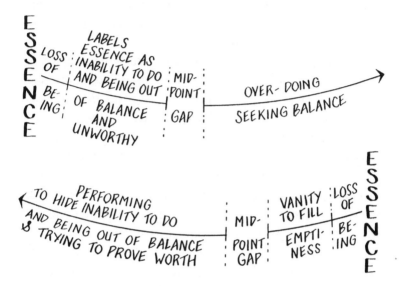

what they should learn, be, do, or have is being reflected by others outside themselves. For example, I once met a man who was part of a New Age community which believed the world was always reflecting a lesson about who they were. He told me that while walking down the street he saw a woman who had a bad leg. He decided that since she had a bad leg, the universe was reflecting that to her. This is the core of #3, thinking the world is a reflection of them. Although this is not the place to elaborate in depth, this way of understanding was part of a #3 community, which had a #3 belief system, and which probably attracted people with a #3 fixation of attention. This is discussed more completely in my last book *The Dark Side of the Inner Child*, Chapter 14, and is called infantile grandiosity. Vanity is so re-enforced by our society that, more often than not, we are judged by others for what we do, look like, own, and have rather than who we are. This in psychology is narcissistic. To characterize the narcissistic personality I was told a joke at a workshop.

There was a narcissistic man who was having dinner with a woman. After spending most of dinner talking about himself he looked at the woman and said, "enough about *me*...now tell *me* what do you think of *me*."

The problem with vanity and its underlying state of an inability to do, which is true for all fixations of attention, is that psycho-emotional pain arises because we *think we are what we wish to be*. For example, if I wish to be seen as a fantastic person and I start believing that image rather than being realistically grounded in my *true abilities and limitations*, I feel pain when people are not treating me the way I *wish* people would treat me. More simply put, I get treated the way I am, and not the way I see myself. Believing in and falling in love with your self-image is narcissistic and is a major *self-deception* (deceit). This strategy of fixating attention *deceives* itself thinking that who they are is who they wish to be. In Ego Psychology and Object Relations, the approach is to question the grandiose internal images that were created, so that limitations can be looked at in present time rather than a world being looked at through the eyes of a grandiose infant. This approach of working on grandiose internal narcissistic images in Self Psychology and Object Relations therapy is called by Heinz Kohut, *transmuting internalizations*.

What frequently drives people into psychotherapy is that the discrepancy between the way they want to be seen and the image they present is much different from how they feel inside. Stated another way, people fall in love with their own created "cool" images. They then sell the "cool" image to the world, pretend they didn't create the "cool" image, pretend they are not pretending and *are* their images, and defend the images against others thinking they're "not cool." These created images are a defense against who they imagine they are, *not who they really are*.

Recently, for example, I was doing a Quantum Psychology® workshop. A woman, to her credit, experienced and acknowledged her self-deceit and vanity. She thought she was doing all this internal psycho-spiritual work for herself. She realized that her fixation of attention was a #3, and that all the work she was doing on herself was so that she would look good to others. This was a *painful* discrepancy.

At the level of character analysis, the person appears as if they are in their body and present, when actually they are not. A phallic narcissistic man might sexually be giving, but his attention or O.K.ness is not on himself and his feelings, rather it is how good a lover *the partner thinks he is*. Hence his orgasms are not complete. Why? Because he is not in his body. We must remember that although people appear as though they are in their body and present does not mean they are. For example, people who exercise are not necessarily "in their body." They might be wondering how good they will look by exercising. Hence they are outside of their body experiencing how others might see them. Practitioners of spirituality or psychology are often becoming healthy, clear, or more spiritual to look good to another, rather than for themselves. This is self-deception and vanity at a more subtle level.

At the deepest level, the trauma of the loss of Essence makes the observer/personality dyad feel like there is an internal vacuum which they label as an "inability to do" which must be hidden. This internal vacuum yields someone who is constantly on the "go" to fill the vacuum, or perceived void, and over-compensates for an inability to do, act, or create; simply put, this type "goes for it." For example, this observer/ personality dyad might have obsessive thoughts, or try to constantly achieve to fill the perceived vacuum. The interesting part of this strategy of fixating attention is that there is a reaction formation and an attempt to dominate others in order to defend against people seeing the inner emptiness, which they define as a lack and a feeling of not doing, i.e., the best offense is a good defense. This reaction formation leads itself to deceiving self and others through domination. Moreover, the defense of their vacuum is so powerful that a true #3 does not even know what they are feeling. Why? Because their center is outside of themselves. They feel good if others are giving their vanity attention and telling them they look or are good. They feel bad if others are disinterested or critical. This fixation strategy can feel the inner vacuum, which they label as bad when attention from others is not coming their way. In short, they try to fill up the vacuum through getting attention from others. This does not always mean "good" attention. In the old language of Transactional Analysis, we need *strokes*, and if positive strokes aren't available, we will take negative strokes instead.

As with all fixation strategies, the chief feature or chief trance and the underlying state, deception (in this case vanity and deceit, respectively) are in defense against the trauma and the perceived emptiness which is experienced in the body. From the point of view of the performer, they must over-work and over exert performing and looking good to overcome this inherent emptiness and incomplete doing. Furthermore, the acknowledgment for the performance has an escalating zero point. This means that if I get $1,000 today for a performance, next performance, to get the same "high," I need $1,000 plus. In this way attention and adoration become an addiction; the substance being adoration. Anyone who gets the #3's "hit" of adoration deprives #3 of their limelight since there is a scarcity of adoration (the substance). This makes #3 very competitive.

As with all strategies of fixated attention, the emptiness is a gateway that, when walked through and experienced, allows for the reabsorption of I-dentities and the experience of the true essential self. At the deepest level, the performer's I-dentities are seeking a sense of equilibrium. Unfortunately, the equilibrium and balance they are seeking is a state and can never be fully made a *station* at the level of personality. Why? They are essential qualities, not qualities of the observer/personality dyad.

The Therapy

Step I   Write down those I-dentities which resist your emptiness.

Step II   Notice where in your body the emptiness exists.

Step III Enter into the emptiness and feel it.

Step IV   Notice how to the I-dentity, the emptiness seems like death, but from the inside, the emptiness is calm, quiet, peaceful and serene.

Step V   From inside the emptiness ask each I-dentity "What is it you really want and are seeking more than anything else in the world?"

Step VI   However the I-dentity responds, feel that quality of experience in the spacious emptiness.

Step VII Next, have the I-dentities turn around and be reabsorbed within the emptiness which is Essence.

Variation

Step VIII Seeing the I-dentities in the foreground, stay in the background and notice the I-dentities are floating in emptiness.

Step IX	Experience and feel the essential quality from the background.	
Step X	See the I-dentities and the emptiness as being made of the same substance.	

I-dentities	*Underlying State*	*Over-Compensating Identities*
Vacuum	An inability to do, act, or create yielding vanity and self-depception	Fill-up vacuum 1. With doing/Over doing 2. Possible work-aholic 3. Obsessive thoughts
Not Knowing who they are		1. Wanting to be seen 2. Try to figure out who they are
Super-Vacuum		Everything being done to be seen a certain way
Meaninglessness		1. Looking for meaning and who they are through how one appears to others. 2. Image of over honest
Dishonest and Bad		and good.

Highlighted Case Example

Barbara, a woman in her late twenties, described herself as a "love addict," with an inability to get the attention she needed in her relationship. She claimed, "He always promises to give me love, never does, and I feel like he lies."

Client: My partner Bill never gives me enough attention and isn't "there" for me emotionally.

Therapist: What lies did you tell yourself about Bill?

Client: Lies? (in a huffy voice)

Therapist: Yes, didn't you tell yourself lies about who he was?

Client: Well actually on our first date we were supposed to have met at 8:00 at this restaurant and he was almost an hour late. I kept lying to myself that he was okay and was really going to be there for me.

Therapist: What other lies did you tell yourself about Bill?
Client: That he would change and somehow he would give me what I wanted. Basically I told myself that he was different than the way he was.

Therapeutic Note

It is important at this point to continually repeat to oneself or a client, "Tell me a lie you told yourself about (*the situation or person*)." This is important because it was her self-deception (deceit) which she denied that made her feel like a victim. To empower ourself, the lies we tell ourself must be uncovered first. To explain further, most people feel empty inside. To resist the emptiness they lie to themselves about the people they are in relationship with. In short, they try to get others to fill their emptiness, and lie to themselves about who people are so that the imagined, made-up person will fill the empty space. Later, they lie that they lied to themselves, and then get angry and try to change their partner. This is called the *fallacy of change* and is considered a thinking distortion in cognitive therapy.

> "The only person you can really control or have much hope of changing is yourself. The fallacy of change, however, assures that other people will change to suit you, if you just pressure them enough. Your attention and energy are therefore focused on others because your hope for happiness lies in getting others to meet your needs." (Thoughts and Feelings: The Act of Cognitive Stress Intervention, McKay, Davis, Fanning, New Harbinger, 1981, p. 23)

Furthermore, Albert Ellis, the father of Cognitive Therapy would say that in our example she had a thought that Bill "*must not*" be the way he was. This "must not" Ellis calls "musturbation;" the continual thought that this *must not* be allowed or *must not* be true.

Individuals *seeking* relationships are often attempting to get another to fill up their emptiness. In short, if I imagine you can fill up my emptiness—"I love you;" when I realize you can't—"I'm out of here"—in search of someone who can.

Therapist: When you go home at night after work, do you feel a gnawing emptiness inside that you just can't stand?
Client: It drives me crazy. I just don't want to go home at night so I'll work late every night.

Therapeutic Note
Here again, the emptiness jumps out as a *gnawing real pain.*

Therapist: Where do you feel the emptiness in your body?
Client: Here. (points to solar plexus)
Therapist: Turn your attention around and walk into the emptiness.
Client: I'm scared.
Therapist: Notice the fear; is there an outer layer the fear is attached to?
Client: There is a part of me that has an overwhelming desire for love.
Therapist: Peel back the fear and tell me what is underneath it.
Client: Loneliness.
Therapist: Peel back the loneliness and tell me what is there.
Client: An empty space.
Therapist: Go into the empty space and tell me what you experience.
Client: Terror

Therapist: Peel back the terror, what's there?

Client: A big empty void.

Therapist: Go into the void and tell me what that's like.

Client: Peaceful, spacious... calm.

Therapist: From "back there" inside the empty void, how do those I-dentities in the foreground seem to you?

Client: Like they are floating in empty space.

Therapist: Ask all of them, "What are you seeking more than anything else in the world?"

Client: Love.

Therapist: Feel the love "back there"?

Client: (Nods)

Therapist: Now, ask the I-dentities to turn their attention around, can they be reabsorbed into the emptiness, *as you feel that love.*

Client: I am love.

Therapist: Do you experience, love with no object.

Client: Yes, just love.

Conclusion

This case took place on the first day of a 3-day workshop in Quantum Psychology®, so I had time to track her for a few days. She reported, after seeing Bill that night, that she felt transformed, and several times she would pop into her I-dentity, and look for him to fill her void. But she said, "It was easy now to enter into her Essence, it was great to have a technique".

She reported several weeks later that it worked for her and that her subjective experience of her relationship changed—*even though he did not change*. This gave her more responsibility and power rather than "looking for love in all the wrong places."

In conclusion, it needs to be noted again, that these are highlighted cases, not full cases. The purpose of this high-lighted excerpt is to demonstrate the reabsorption of the observer/personality dyad back into Essence and the retrieval of the essential quality.

I'M O.K. IF I FEEL PAIN, YOU'RE O.K. IF YOU FEEL PAIN

This Fixation of Attention Strategy #4 represents in psychology's character analysis the *masochist*. A masochist is someone who feels that the only way to get love and control a situation is to feel pain. In character analysis, the masochist feels control through pain. In this structure there is a confusion between pain and love. Simply stated, love=pain. The fixation of attention is on melancholy which interfaces with the trauma of the loss of Essence by feeling an impoverishment of Being, and that somehow they have no origin or "roots," and hence, melancholy.

Here, as with all other strategies of fixated attention, the observer/personality dyad organizes around the Essence. The observer/personality dyad feels such an impoverishment and loss of love by losing Essence that it has the underlying state of envy. This fixation is envious of others who, in their opinion, have the love and roots they feel they lost as they moved from Essence to personality. This fixation of attention on melancholy also has a feeling of being broken hearted. As the pendulum swings the other way, this fixation strategy of the observer/personality dyad can take the stance of self-rejection and no self-worth. Often times the observer/personality dyad creates a substitute idealized being, guru, teacher, or lover that is an image of Essence externally, *but* not actually Essence. For this reason, #4 often sees themselves as not connected to their own life or their roots, and they are seeking their "roots." Here the observer personality labels the emptiness of essence as having no real *connection* to people and life and, hence, feels melancholy. In many ways the #4 strategy of fixated attention can also create an internal ideal image of Essence and mistakes that as Essence. See Illustration #10.

ILLUSTRATION # 10
FIXATION OF ATTENTION STRATEGY # 4
THE MASOCHIST

" LOOKING FOR PAIN WHICH THEY THINK IS LOVE IN ALL THE RIGHT PLACES"

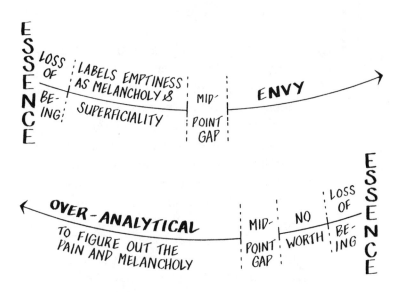

For example, I was seeing a man for therapy who continually had images popping up in his consciousness that were idealized representations of Essence. These idealized images were spiritualized (see Chapter 14 of *The Dark Side of the Inner Child*). Instead of exploring them as substitutes for Essence, they were taken as Essence, when actually they are symbols of Essence *not* Essence; again Alfred Korsybski's "The map is not the territory," or the symbol or image of Essence, *is not Essence*. This is important to understand regarding the worship of an internal deity, as is done in both the Yoga tradition as well as the Buddhist tradition. The internalized image of the divine Mother or Buddha, or whatever deity, is an *image or symbol of Essence—it is not Essence.*

The love hunger of the #4 strategy of fixating attention grows and gnaws away at the observer/personality dyad and there is an attempt to fill up the loss of love (Essence) and the emptiness with pain. This comes about because the personality first tries to fill up the emptiness with a love object, which fails. The love object, which is often the parent, cannot fill up the emptiness of the infant so there is pain. The observer/personality dyad then fuses or associates the idea of love with the idea of pain, i.e., *love = pain*. Hence this is called the *tragic romantic* by Palmer. The decision to try to fill up and defend oneself from feeling the emptiness becomes a fixation strategy of the observer/personality dyad by using pain, which to the #4 fixation strategy equals the love of Essence.

In the psychoanalytic literature, the metaphor of the masochist develops during the anal phase of development. The child is being toilet trained. When the child moves its bowels, Mom/Dad are happy. When the child withholds, Mom/Dad are not happy. In this case there is an illusion of power and control on the part of the child. The child can withhold, and by doing so imagines it can control the happiness of its Mother or Father, even at the cost of discomfort. The child *spites* the parent by holding back, and believes it is controlling Mom's/Dad's happiness. This distortion gives the ob-server/personality dyad a feeling of imagined power. In other words, "I control you through feeling pain." This is the mas-ochist that *wins by losing* or *spites* others, thus giving the personality the illusion of feeling powerful and in control by withholding.

This strategy, to avoid the loss of Essence, fixates their attention on others and becomes very envious and imagines others have the "ultimate" experience. To work with mas-ochism in a different context, see *The Dark Side of the Inner Child*.

The general out-of-control feeling of the masochist makes this character type spiteful in an attempt to control by with-holding. Crudely put, using the psychoanalytic metaphor, the masochist "either shits on others, or sets it up for others to shit on them." This type is self-effacing, and according to Alexander Lowen, is one of the most difficult to work with. Why? They spite the therapist (Mom and Dad) by not chang-ing. This character type can initiate pain and contains a sadis-tic I-dentity which resists the feeling of humiliation. Actu-ally, the underlying state of envy is an attempt to understand what is wrong with them and their melancholy by thinking others "have the answer." The envy also keeps the fixation strategy of attention #4 facing outward on others, rather than inward when their heart was broken due to the loss of Es-sence.

The fixation strategy #4 of the observer/personality dyad feels broken hearted, and hence will have stories of *tragic romances* (Palmer) of betrayal to justify their melancholy. It must be remembered that the story is used to justify the state; and the *story is not the state*. For that reason, the attention must be taken off of the story, and placed on the state itself as energy.

This habitual pattern of getting people to "go into agree-ment" on the story keeps #4 fixated. The melancholy and envy are chronic states, and are not context (story) dependent, but are a function of how the body and observer/personality dyad developed around Essence. In short, changing the story will not change the state. Acknowledging the chronic state and shifting attention will change the state. The Cliff Notes: *Like cures like*, i.e., story does not cure state, experiencing the *state cures state*.

There can be great difficulty working with the tragic romantic which *"seeks happiness through pain"* as called by Naranjo because they are obsessed with filling up the emptiness with pain and will continually set up their life around pain. This pain defends against a much *deeper* pain and sense of inadequacy or lack of not being enough since the observer/personality dyad is no match for the Essence.

Here the I-dentities are seeking their roots and connection. Unfortunately for the I-dentities, that source is Essence, and they are facing in the wrong direction.

The Therapy

Step I   Write down those I-dentities which resist your emptiness.

Step II   Notice where in your body the emptiness exists.

Step III   Enter into the emptiness and feel it.

Step IV   Notice how to the I-dentity the emptiness seems like death, but from the inside the emptiness is calm, quiet, peaceful, and serene.

Step V   From inside the emptiness ask each I-dentity "What is it you really want and are seeking more than anything else in the world?"

Step VI   However the I-dentity responds, feel that quality of experience in the spacious emptiness.

Step VII   Next, have the I-dentities turn around and be reabsorbed within the emptiness which is Essence.

Variation

Step VIII   Seeing the I-dentities in the foreground, stay in the background and notice the I-dentities are floating in Emptiness.

Step IX   Experience and feel the essential quality from the background.

Step X   See the I-dentities and the emptiness as being made of the same substance.

I-dentities	Underlying State	Over-Compensating Identities
Impoverishment of Being	No roots or connection yielding melancholy and envy	Be like Mom Be like Dad
Self-Rejection I'm Bad"	Love-Hunger	Idealize themselves or others
Non-Existence	Pain	Crying to get Attention

Highlighted Case Example

Phyllis, a woman in her late forties, was a tragic romantic. Phyllis had been married four times and was living with a man for 3 years for whom she had no sexual attraction. Phyllis stayed in the relationship, however, because they had a comfortable life style. Her partner Carl wanted sexual contact and intimacy, which she wasn't interested in.

Client: My relationship is kinda dull, and boring, but it works.
Therapist: What do you want that you don't have in the relationship?

Client: Intimacy.

Therapist: Why are you staying in the relationship?

Client: It took years with Carl to get it to work with my two kids, (from another marriage) and his two kids (from another marriage). Also, I believe that even if I were really in love with someone, it would go away and I'd be in pain anyway, and so it's best to learn to do without.

Therapist: How does Carl feel about this lack of sexual contact?

Client: He is frustrated and angry and *hopes* it will change.

Therapeutic Note

Notice how she substitutes a relationship that is a friendship for a marriage partner and actually treats him like an object, i.e., she doesn't care that he is in pain. This is the child's loss of a love-object, which is explored in Object Relations Therapy. The pain of the external love-object (Mom) is lost. In this case, it gets re-enacted, as her initial sexual relationship with Carl becomes platonic. Notice Carl's cognitive distortion called the fallacy of change. This is also a reenactment of the oedipal situation where the child cannot have sex with Dad, and hence develops a platonic relationship with Dad and becomes like Mom. In Quantum Psychology®, I would look to see how the Mom and Dad *modeled* this no-sex relationship, possibly stayed together for economic, social, and "kids" reasons. Next, I would explore how she fused that model and is acting *it out* in present time with Carl.

Therapist: Do you lead him on?

Client: No.

Therapist: Well, don't you think by living with a man that sex is usually involved?

Client: Yes, but I tell him I don't feel the same way as he does.

Therapist: Notice the double message you are giving him; you live with him and give him and others the idea that you are sexual, when you are not.

Client: Yes, he feels angry like I'm controlling him through sex.

Therapeutic Note

Here the masochist/sadist dyad is revealed. First, she is in pain about no intimacy, and hence gives herself pain staying in a relationship that is not sexually what she wants. Second, she controls Carl by withholding sex and gives him and others the message that they are or will someday be lovers.

Therapist: What are you feeling right now?

Client: Pain in my heart.

Therapist: How do you defend against the pain in your heart?

Client: By acting like everything is okay with Carl.

Therapist: And controlling him?

Client: Yes.

Therapist: What feeling state connects the pain in the heart and the controlling I-dentity?

Client: Despair

Therapist: Feel the despair. Now peel back the layer of despair and what is underneath it?

Client: An empty hole.

Therapist: Walk into the empty hole and tell me what it feels like.

Client Like an empty space ... actually it is quite comfortable.

Therapist: From "back there" in the space, how do the I-dentities in the foreground seem to you?

Client: Distant.

Therapist: Is the "in control" I-dentity connected to Carl?
Client: Yes.
Therapist: Can you see the Carl I-dentity?
Client: Yes.
Therapist: What feeling connects the in-control, little girl I-dentity to the Carl I-dentity?

Therapeutic Note

Here, I will suggest that the "in control" I-dentity is an age-regressed little girl, who is attracted to Carl (Dad). It is important to know the full loop. In this case, in her psyche she has a pained little girl, the "in control" little girl, and Dad who in the re-enactment is Carl. If Dad remains in her psyche, unless he is processed, it will cause more re-enactment of her tragic romantic.

Client: Sadness.
Therapist: Feel the sadness?
Client: It is like when my father wasn't there anymore.
Therapist: And how did you get even and spite him?
Client: By not giving him what he wanted.

Therapeutic Note

Once again, notice the *trance*-ference of Dad on Carl, and how she spites Carl (Dad) by not giving him what he wants. This is the fallacy of control.

Therapist: Ask the Carl (Dad) I-dentity, "what are you seeking more than anything else"
Client: To be loved.
Therapist: Now, go back again into the empty space, and ask the pain I-dentity, "What are you seeking more than anything else?"
Client: Love.

Therapist: Now ask the little girl I-dentity, "What are you seeking more than anything else?"

Client Security.

Therapist: So that you will feel what?

Client: Safe and peaceful.

Therapist: And what does that pained little girl want more than anything else in the world?

Client: To know herself.

Therapist: So that she will feel what?

Client; Powerful.

Therapist: Good, now from "back there" in your emptiness, feel the love, power and safety of back there.

Client: Yes.

Therapist: Notice how all of these I-dentities seem like they are floating in empty space.

Client: Yes.

Therapist: Good now what happens if you see the I-dentities and the space as being made of the same substance.

Client: The I-dentities disappear in the space. There is nothing there.

Therapist: How do you feel?

Client: I have no words - just no words.

Conclusion

In this case, I tried the variation on the procedure which is discussed in *Quantum Consciousness: Volume I*. When the emptiness and the I-dentities are seen as the same substance, they merge and disappear. Why? No contrasts.

In this highlighted case, the I-dentities which are the observer/personality dyad are reabsorbed back into Essence. This left her speechless. Why? Because at the level of Essence, there is no subject/object in her to be powerful over. For this reason, there is power and peace with no story, reason, or object. This is the nature of Essence—a no-state state that has no subject/object, story, or reason. Simply put, Essence and its qualities just are.

EIGHTEEN • FIXATION OF ATTENTION STRATEGY #5

**I'M O.K. IF I DON'T FEEL,
YOU'RE O.K. IF YOU DON'T MAKE ME FEEL**

OR

**I'M O.K. IF I REJECT YOU,
YOU'RE O.K. IF I REJECT YOU, BEFORE YOU REJECT ME**

How can I have feelings when I don't know if
    it's a feeling,
How can I have feelings if I just don't know
    how to feel,
How can I have feelings when my feelings
    have always been denied.

John Lennon (HOW)

This fixation of attention strategy of the observer/personality dyad to fixate attention is representative of the *schizoid* personality in character analysis. The *schizoid* personality, according to Alexander Lowen, was formed in the womb. This character type feels rejection from the mother, and hence is fearful. To combat this fear, the schizoid freezes all feeling and numbs out and becomes involved in *premature observation*.

Like premature ejaculation, *premature observation* is a defense against feeling. In other words, the schizoid cannot feel; therefore, she/he observes, and acts "as if" she/he is feeling. This fixation strategy is called the *observer* by Palmer, the *thinker* by Riso, and is said to *seek wholeness through isolation* by Naranjo. In this fixation of attention we have a powerful I-dentity which has an inability to feel, or cannot feel. This fixation confuses thoughts with feelings. In other words, they think feelings rather than feel feelings. This fixation of attention strategy is an observer/personality dyad that is *prematurely* in a state of *observation*. This *premature observation* looks spiritual from the outside.[1] The person is detached, non-feeling, slightly aloof, and seems to like to be alone. In reality, however, he/she is dissociated from their feelings and their body and has a difficult time interrelating with others, particularly in the area of intimacy. This strategy of the observer/personality dyad *looks* spiritual and is called the *Unenlightened Buddha*, because ideas and thoughts are mistaken as experiences. In other words, they think experience rather than having experiences. This observer/personality dyad reacts internally to a fear of being *engulfed*, and imagines people want from them, even if they do not. Needs are not felt and often spiritualized[2], with an unacknowledged fear. All of this leads the person to detach prematurely without the ability to connect with others. In other words, their *premature observation* is a reaction against feeling the fear of the trauma of loss of being. Hence it is *premature evacuation*. In other words, they act "as if," they are connected or *pretend* so that others will not see their emptiness. This lack of feeling is labeled spiritual and often times they think, and others around them think, they are spiritual and meditating, when actually they are terrified and *medicating*. See Chapter 14, Spiritual-

---

[1] See Chapter 3, *Quantum Consciousness: Volume I, Is It Dissociation or Observation?* (Stephen H. Wolinsky, Bramble Books, 1993, Connecticut)

[2] See Chapter 14, *The Dark Side of the Inner Child* (Stephen H. Wolinsky, Bramble Books, 1993, Connecticut)

ization, *The Dark Side of the Inner Child*. This occurs because this observer/personality dyad implodes rather than feels during an experience and leaves their body thus going in to premature observation. The observer in this fixation labels the emptiness as nothing; hence they accumulate things, ideas, etc. and are subject to avarice. See Illustration #11.

At this placement of attention, the observer/personality dyad's fantasies and ideas are presumed to be experiences. In character analysis the *schziod* unknowingly has a deep fear of rejection. Alexander Lowen, M.D. suggests that the *schizoid* personality originates intrautero and occurs through the biological rejection of the mother. Schizoids have a body type which is bony, with high cheek bones, and the structure of

ILLUSTRATION # 11
FIXATION OF ATTENTION STRATEGY # 5
THE OBSERVER

"LOOKING FOR THE ALL-KNOWING AND ACCUMULATING TO LOOK LIKE THEY'RE ALL-KNOWING; TO COVER THEIR EMPTINESS IN ALL THE RIGHT PLACES"

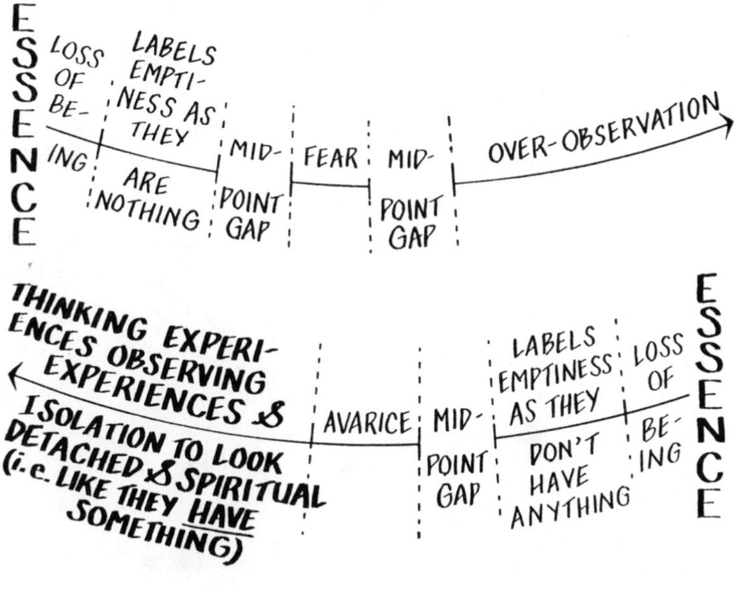

the observer/personality dyad and rejection is actually held in the *bones*. Often the schizoid has a covering over their eyes so that even if you are making eye-contact with them, you cannot connect with them. This personality either assumes rejection, sets themselves up for rejection, or rejects others before getting rejected. In politics Dan Quayle has this fixation with a very wooden-like, almost puppet-like appearance; constantly setting himself up to be rejected, and rejecting others (Murphy Brown and single mothers) before getting rejected by Murphy Brown and single moms. Ross Perot also holds this fixation. Perot left the race for President as soon as his polls dropped after the Democratic Convention. Simply stated, fearing and imagining rejection, he would reject the media before they rejected him. Perot would walk into a press conference, a reporter would ask a question, Perot would see it as a rejection, get angry, reject the press and walk off the platform. In other words, the #5 will isolate themselves out of fear of rejection. Consequently, they buffer and hide themselves in a cloak of detachment never really experiencing life, and having to act "*as if*" they do. In this way they act "*as if*" they care, or feel, or are interested; but to the individual in relationship with a *schizoid*, there is always something missing. In this case, *it is them.*

In this observer/personality dyad the pain of the loss of Essence creates a bifurcation point, as the personality organizes around the Essence, that is so strong that there is an unacknowledged loneliness. So great can be the pain and fear of it that to control others rejecting them or engulfing them, like their mothers had, they isolate themselves in an attempt to seek wholeness (Naranjo). In reality, however, the isolation further creates premature detachment (evacuation) and makes dissociation active. This action can be spiritualized (see *The Dark Side of the Inner Child*, Chapter 14), to deter against the fear of rejection.[3] I knew a doctor once who acted

---

[3] Also see Chapter 3 *Quantum Consciousness: Volume I* under the heading "Is it Dissociation or Observation?"

"as if" he were spiritual and feeling. His wife would complain, "He is not here," and truly he wasn't. He projected his mother onto his wife and isolated himself, calling it spiritual. He withdrew from his wife, leaving her both confused and frustrated. This observer/personality dyad seeks to be all-knowing and omniscient to compensate for feeling their own nothingness. Unfortunately the "act" of the I-dentity which looks or acts omniscient hides the fear of rejection that someone might see their emptiness. They over-compensate by "acting as if" and trying to "look omniscient" at the level of personality. This over-compensates for the deep inadequacy the personality feels at the loss of Essence. Their fear of engulfment is so strong that their chief strategy is avarice. They are accumulators. The underlying state is greed with a touch of fear. People who have this fixation are certain that others will take the little they have, thus they dissociate, accumulate, hoard, and hide experiences like a miser hides its gold. This, they presume is the only way to have a *whole self*.

The Therapy

Step I   Write down those I-dentities which resist your emptiness.

Step II   Notice where in your body emptiness exists.

Step III   Enter into the emptiness and feel it.

Step IV   Notice how to the I-dentity, the emptiness seems like death, but from the inside, the emptiness is calm, quiet, peaceful and serene.

Step V   From inside the emptiness ask each I-dentity "What is it you really want and are seeking more than anything else in the world?"

Step VI   However the I-dentity responds, feel that quality of experience in the spacious emptiness.

Step VII Next, have the I-dentities turn around and be re-absorbed within the emptiness which is Essence.

Variation

Step VIII Seeing the I-dentities in the foreground, stay in the background and notice the I-dentities are floating in emptiness.

Step IX Experience and feel the essential quality from the background.

Step X See the I-dentities and the emptiness as being made of the same substance.

I-dentities	*Underlying State*	*Over-Compensating Identities*
Insufficient	Feeling Like Nothing Fear/doubt	Avoidance
Loneliness	Anxious	Feeling wholeness through isolation
Fear of Engulfment	Fear	Feeling wholeness through isolation
Seeking of Nothingness	Reminds them of rejection by Mom	Overly-spiritual
Pain of Emptiness	Repression of needs	Over-intellectual
Self-rejecting	Fear	1. Assume rejection 2. Reject to avoid rejection
Unacknowledged fear of power-lessness	Overwhelmed	1. Holding back 2. Greed 3. Power through withholding

Highlighted Case Study

Fred is a psychologist, about 45, from California whose presenting problem is a resistance to getting close to his wife.

Therapist: What do you want to explore today?
Client: I feel this resistance to being fully intimate with my wife. Somehow I always hold back.
Therapist: Where do you feel this resistance in your body?
Client: (points to the center of his chest) says, my heart.
Therapist: If we were to see your wife out in front of you ... what feeling state connects the resistance-to-closeness I-dentity and your wife?
Client: Fear.
Therapist: Feel the fear, merge with it completely.
Client: I keep feeling overwhelmed like I'm going to be swallowed up by her love.
Therapist: Does love equal being swallowed up?
Client: Yes.
Therapist: No wonder you are resisting love.

Therapeutic Note

Here we have three important themes. First, the cognitive distortion of emotional reasoning, "I think I'm going to be swallowed up...therefore I am going to be swallowed up."

> *Emotional Reasoning* "At the root of this distortion is the belief that what you feel must be true in all negative things you feel about yourself and others must be true because they *feel* true." (Thoughts and feelings, McKay, Davis and Fanning, New Harbinger, Oakland, CA, 1981, p. 22-23).

Second, the possible *trance*-ference of Mom on his wife. Why? Because, if you are in present time, why would you be afraid of being swallowed up? Only an age-regressed child who is hallucinating his wife as his mother would feel afraid of being swallowed up.

Third, is the fusion of meaning. In this case, love=being swallowed up. I will approach the cognitive distortion and the fusion of meaning through an elaborate de-fusion process.

Therapist: If you fuse together love (holding up my left hand) with being swallowed up (holding up my right hand and putting the two hands together), what are you creating?
Client: Fear.
Therapist: If you fuse together the idea of love (holding up my left hand) equals swallowed up (holding up my right hand and putting two hands together), what are you not creating?
Client: Feeling free to love.
Therapist: If you fuse together the idea of love (holding up my left hand) and being swallowed up (holding up my right hand, and then putting both hands together), what are you resisting?
Client: Being alienated.
Therapist: Create the feeling of alienation.
Client: Okay.
Therapist: Make it the size of this room.
Client: Okay.
Therapist: Make it the size of California.
Client: Okay.
Therapist: Make it the size of the United States.
Client: Okay.
Therapist: Make it the size of the world.
Client: Okay.
Therapist: Take your attention off of it. Now, if you separate love and being swallowed up (separating left and right hand), what gets created?
Client: Openness.

Therapist: If you separate (separating hands) love and being swallowed up, what doesn't get created?
Client: Fear.
Therapist: If you separate love and being swallowed up (separating hands), what, if anything, gets resisted?
Client: Nothing gets resisted.
Therapist: How are you doing?
Client: Clearer.

Therapeutic Note

All of us fuse together ideas, like love equals, or power equals, etc. Kristi L. Kennen, noted psychotherapist, isolated four main areas where fusion of meaning occurs; love, help, power, and responsibility. Ms. Kennen has actually developed a 3-day workshop on taking apart these four fused (confused) ideas. The job of the therapist is to de-fuse or separate two ideas which are stuck together, hence freeing the state.

Therapist: Now, with your wife out in front of you, notice the resistance to intimacy in your heart, and peel back the layer and see what is underneath it.
Client: Empty space.
Therapist: Go into the empty space…how does it feel?
Client: Quiet, calm, meditative.
Therapist: Now from "back there", in the foreground we see your wife, and the fear which connects it to an age-regressed you.

Therapeutic Note

Once again I offer the idea that the resistance to intimacy is a younger identity. This younger identity is like a schema.

"Although different persons may conceptualize the same situation in different ways, a particular person tends to be consistent in his responses to similar types of events. Relatively stable cognitive patterns form the basis for the regularity of interpretations of a particular set of situations. The term *schema* designates these stable cognitive patterns. When a person faces a particular circumstance, a schema related to the circumstance is activated. The schema is the basis of molding data into cognitions... defined as any ideation with verbal or pictorial content. Thus a schema constitutes the basis for screening out, differentiating and coding the stimuli that confronts an individual. Individuals categorize and evaluate experiences through a matrix of schemas." (*Cognitive Therapy of Depression* A. Beck, A. Rush, B. Shaw, G. Energy, Guilford Press, N.Y. 1979, p. 12-13).

Next, I suggest the possibility that this *younger schema* to the world might be viewing his mother rather than his wife.

Therapist: Does this younger I-dentity relate to your wife the way a little boy relates to his mother?
Client: Yes.
Therapist: What feeling connects the mother identity to the little boy I-dentity?
Client: Fear.
Therapist: Feel the fear, be it completely, as energy.
Client: Okay.
Therapist: Good, from "back there," ask the mother I-dentity, "What are you seeking more than anything else in the world?"
Client: To be taken care of.
Therapist: And if she was taken care of, what would she feel?
Client: Safe and loved.
Therapist: Ask the little boy I-dentity, "What are you seeking more than anything else in the world?"

Client: To be myself.

Therapist: And if you felt like yourself, what would that feel like?

Client: Strong and powerful.

Therapist: Good, now, from "back there," feel the love...safety of back there...along with the power and strength of back there.

Client: Yes.

Therapist: How are you doing?

Client: Fantastic.

Therapist: Good, now notice the size and shape of these I-dentities.

Client: Okay.

Therapist: Now de-label them and see them as energy.

Client: Okay.

Therapist: Now reabsorb the energy into the essence of "back there," as you feel the power, safety and love of "back there."

Client: Okay.

Therapist: How are you doing now?

Client: Great.

Therapeutic Note

Here we are adding a third variation to this process; seeing the I-dentities and emotions as energy and re-absorbing them back into Essence. This is explored in depth in *Quantum Consciousness, Volume. I*, Chapter 4, The Energy of Emotions.

Conclusion

Here again, the reabsorption process is quite easy. To integrate the process and look at the *trance*-ference more clearly, I asked the client for a week to internally, in his mind, place a mother mask over the face of his wife. In this way I am asking him to do knowingly, consciously, and intentionally that which he is doing unkowningly, unconsciously, and unintentionally. This hopefully aids in making the implicit explicit, thus adding the quality of awareness to the process. *Awareness is the solvent that loosens the glue of I-dentities which are stuck to us!!!*

I'M O.K. IF YOU SEE ME AS THE AUTHORITY, YOU'RE O.K. IF YOU SEE ME AS THE AUTHORITY

OR

I'M O.K. IF I'M REBELLIOUS, YOU'RE O.K. IF YOU ACCEPT ME FOR BEING REBELLIOUS

This fixation of attention strategy is called The *Devil's Advocate* by Palmer, the *loyalist* by Riso, and the *persecuted persecutor* by Naranjo. This rebel is in a constant state of ambivalence. Naranjo actually calls this fixation of attention the *ambivilants*. This fixation characterizes either a rebellion (rebel I-dentity) and a fusion with authority figures (authority I-dentity). On one side of this I-dentity structure is a rebel with an underlying state of ambivalence and fear, not really knowing what he/she stands for, but defending against people knowing that. The fixation of attention is on fear, and since the underlying state and the fixation of attention are similar, this makes fear the constant companion and mechanism through which everything is seen.

This is the character type of the compensated oral who can pretend being heroic to hide the fear. Often this type barely feels the fear, but instead feels angry. This is why Naranjo calls this fixation the *persecuted persecutor*. The fear happens so fast that the observer/personality dyad only feels the anger to defend against the fear. Here the devastation and trauma of the loss of Essence is so overwhelming that the fear must be shifted or not allowed to be. Consequently, the Devil's Advocate (Palmer) changes the fear to anger and presupposes that they are being attacked and persecuted: and rather than feel fear, they feel anger. In this persecution there is an unacknowledged fear which can be very undetected. The anger prevents the fear from being seen. Again, the best defense is a good offense. This fear is a fear of inadequacy and fear of losing Being. In other words, the fear from the trauma of the loss of Essence is frozen, remains in their consciousness, and is defended against. Stated another way, they perceive that their loss of Essence will occur again, and hence create a subjective experience of being persecuted and strong. They create people in their mind as persecuting them; blame them and attack them inwardly or outwardly as if this person is going to steal their Being. In this fixation, the fear is denied, and it quickly, unbeknownst to the individual, turns into anger to defend against anyone seeing the fear. This resistance to fear, and weakness being the underlying state. In other words the emptiness is labeled weakness. This causes an overcompensator I-dentity to form which is heroic and overly-strong and counter-phobic to compensate for the emptiness being labeled as weakness. This observer/personality dyad blames others for loss of Essence and attempts to find the truth by either proving authorities wrong or becoming an authority who knows the truth. Stated another way, in this style the observer/personality dyad defines the emptiness of Essence as a deep weakness. In order to compensate for this feeling of weakness, the #6 fixation of attention has a false self of strength. To not show their fear or weakness to others or themselves they distract themselves imagining someone is persecuting them. To retaliate quickly, they turn their fear into anger and attack and persecute the imagined persecutor. The state of consciousness of a Devil's Advocate (Palmer) is a constant internal state of "paranoia," the fear of someone finding out that they are empty and weak. To them empty = weak and is inadequate, not the emptiness of Essence. Thus, they attack or defend and plan counter-attacks which are gone over in the mind of this #6 strategy of fixation. Underneath it all lies a fear that someone will find out how weak they really are. To state again, all observer/personalities are inadequate compared to the Essence. Unknowingly, the observer/personality dyad is always comparing itself to the Essence and coming up short. This drives the outward fixation of attention to deeper levels in their attempt to find a sense of strength. Fixation #6 believes that if they could have ultimate strength, the fear and pain of the trauma of loss of being will disappear. See illustration #12.

Recently I saw a man named Sam who went to workshop after workshop, meeting authority after authority, to find out the truth so he could feel strong. Sam said his whole life was about feeling strong. What Sam did not understand was that the I-dentities which were seeking the truth and strength were I-dentities, not Essence. Hence, the strength of Essence was never revealed. It was not until Sam could let go of the I-dentities and *be Essence*, which is strength and truth, that the obsessive compulsive strength seeking could be dissolved.

As stated before, the *inadequacy can never be worked out at the level of the observer/personality dyad*. The inadequacy or fear of someone discovering the inadequacy must be worked out through the reabsorption of I-dentity back into the essential aspect it represents. Simply stated, the observer/personality dyad is inadequate compared to Essence, hence, inadequacy can never be worked out at the level of personal-

ILLUSTRATION #12
FIXATION OF ATTENTION STRATEGY #6
THE HEROIC

"LOOKING FOR STRENGTH IN ALL THE WRONG
WAYS AND IN ALL THE WRONG PLACES"

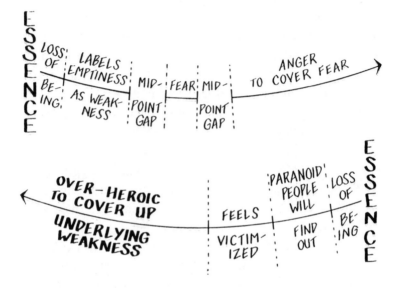

ity. The cluster of I-dentities called personality must be worked out of the level of Essence, where the essential nature and qualities the I-dentities are seeking are.

The Therapy

Step I   Write down those I-dentities which resist your emptiness.

Step II   Notice where in your body the emptiness exists.

Step III Enter into the emptiness and feel it.

Step IV	Notice how to the I-dentity, the emptiness seems like death, but from the inside, the emptiness is calm, quiet, peaceful and serene.
Step V	From inside the emptiness ask each I-dentity "What is it you really want and are seeking more than anything else in the world?"
Step VI	However the I-dentity responds, feel that quality of experience in the spacious emptiness.
Step VII	Next, have the I-dentities turn around and be reabsorbed within the emptiness which is Essence.

Variation II

Step VIII	Seeing the I-dentities in the foreground, stay in the background and notice the I-dentities are floating in Emptiness.
Step IX	Experience and feel the essential quality from the background.
Step X	See the I-dentities and the emptiness as being made of the same substance.

Variation III

Step XI	De-label the I-dentities and see the I-dentities as being made of energy.
Step XII	Allow the energy to be reabsorbed back into Essence.

I-dentities	*Underlying State*	*Over-Compensating Identities*
Weak	Weakness yielding fear	Over-strong heroic
Victim	Paranoid	
Uncertain	Ambivalent	Over-certain

Highlighted Case Example

Fred, a businessman age 48, came to see me regarding his inability to make a decision as whether or not to stay in the relationship with his wife of over 20 years.

Therapist: What do you want to work on today?
Client: I just can't decide whether to stay or not stay with my wife Ann.
Therapist: What are you creating in response to this ambivalence you have?

Therapeutic Note
I spotted the ambivalence as a possible underlying state, particularly because his character (body-type) looked oral. He was big, fleshy, very talkative, and appeared needy. For this reason, I decided to ask, basically, "How do you overcompensate for your ambivalence?" I thought that he might be a compensated oral because he appeared on the surface as a strong powerful businessman. Thus I hypothesized that he would hide his ambivalence and fear by "acting strong and powerful" when deep down he felt ambivalent and weak.

Client: I try to ignore it and go about my business, but, it keeps sneaking in. I try to work harder and go past this feeling.
Therapist: Where do you feel this compensator I-dentity in your body?
Client: In my chest.
Therapist: If you peel back the compensator, what feeling connects the compensator with the ambivalence?
Client: Fear.
Therapist: Feel the fear as energy.
Client: Okay.

Therapist: Now peel back the ambivalence and what do you experience?

Client: An open space.

Therapist: Enter into the space...what is that like?

Client: Just open space, kinda calm.

Therapist: From "back there" in the space, how do these two I-dentities and the fear seem to you?

Client: Distant, I don't feel attached to them.

Therapist: Now, ask the compensator I-dentity, "What are you seeking more than anything else in the world?"

Client: The desire to know.

Therapist: So that it will feel what?

Client: Power and strength.

Therapist: And from "back there" ask the ambivalent I-dentity, "what are you seeking more than anything else?"

Client: To know the truth.

Therapist: Good, now from "back there", in the empty-space, feel the power, strength and truth of being.

Client: Okay.

Therapist: How does that feel?

Client: Clear.

Therapist: Now look at these two I-dentities and the fear that connects them and see if you can allow them to "turn around" and see that what they are seeking is inside you.

Client: They can see that.

Therapist: Now allow them to be absorbed as you feel the strength, power, and truth.

Client: Okay.

Therapist: How is that?

Client: Good, but from back here I don't feel like doing anything. How do I live with my wife and keep this space, while living in the world?

Therapeutic Note
Here we are facing one of the most difficult points in

therapy. The no-state state is so different and new, that the integration of living life from "back there" is very hard to understand. Why? Because from "back there" you just *are*, and your actions are not figured out or calculated through a rational thought process. Rather, you just act with no internal considering. It is like the old Zen saying, "Before enlightenment chop wood and carry water; after enlightenment chop wood and carry water." It is not that your actions change, but the space you come from and your subjective experience is totally different.

This is difficult for clients to stabilize and appreciate during this transition phase, so I recommend the Sufi exercise of G.I. Gurdjieff to help this integration process...it is called self-remembering.

"I am speaking of the division of attention which is the characteristic feature of self-remembering. I represented it to myself in the following way: When I observe something, my attention is directed towards what I observe — a line with one arrowhead.

I ————————————➤ the observed phenomena when at the same time, I try to remember myself, my attention, is directed toward the object observed and toward myself. A second arrowhead appears on the line:

I ◄————————————➤ the observed phenomena having defined this I saw that the problem consisted in directing attention on oneself without weakening or obliterating the attention directed on something else." (*In Search of the Miraculous*, P. D. Ouspensky, Harcour, Brace & World, Inc., 1949, p. 119)

Therapist: Good question. What I would like you to do is to keep half your attention "back there" and with eyes open the other half of your attention on me; *simultaneously.*

Client: You mean to divide my attention half on "back there" and half on out here?

Therapist: Yes.

Client: That is difficult.

> ### Therapeutic Note
> This is a difficult task, and a "higher" level of experience than he can do, so I offered him something he could do for homework.

Therapist: Okay, see if on your inhale you can take all your attention and keep it "back there," and on your exhale, put all your attention "out here."

Client: You mean oscillate back and forth with my breathing?

Therapist: Yes.

Client: I can do that.

Therapist: Okay, try that this week for homework and let's see what happens.

Conclusion

Here the homework is of vital importance. The question is always, "How can I live my life and stay in this space?" The answer is to offer exercises that are do-able. In this case I look for a way for him to move from Essence to personality and from personality to Essence. This reinforces the integration process and empowers him to develop self-awareness on his own without me. Not needing me to guide him, he can proceed on his own. To quote Fritz Perls, M.D.; "Maturity is the transcendence from environmental support to self-support."

"I'M O.K. IF I'M FILLING MYSELF UP, YOU'RE O.K. IF YOU'RE FILLING ME UP"

Like all other strategies of fixating attention, the #7 observer/personality dyad suffers the trauma of loss of being and a gnawing inner-emptiness. When the observer/personality dyad organizes around the Essence there is an inner sense of *scarcity* on the first rung of the pendulum. This leads to a deep feeling of meaninglessness and ultimately to gluttony to fill the empty space. This fixation style of the observer/personality dyad is called the *Epicure* by Palmer, the *Generalist* by Riso, and *Opportunistic Idealism* by Naranjo. Gluttony is the way the personality attempts via food, sex, or drugs to fill the empty space. Sevens can also try to fill the emptiness by intellectual study or an over-spiritualization. The important concept here is *over* and *exaggerated* which often manifests as obsessive *planning*. This strategy of fixating attention gets extremely prideful to cover up the deep feelings of worthlessness. Sevens will sometimes over-compensate either with a false sense of spirituality or a false sense of abundance. So distant does the #7 get from the deep-rooted feeling of emptiness that they actually start believing that they are their image. Consequently, there is a created fusion with the image of over-abundance and worth. Sevens might become gluttons, acquiring "things," trying to fill the emptiness. This fixation believes their false image of abundance. Sevens also can, like fixation strategy #2, become very grandiose about their skills and abilities in an attempt to fill their emptiness. This observer/personality dyad strategy becomes so enamored with their created image that they become narcissistic. They believe they are their image and there is confusion between imagination and reality, between projects and accomplishments, potentialities and realizations. This is also a fear type; hence the underlying state is of being afraid of not being enough. Thus, the chief fixation strategy or trance is to fill up at all costs. This can lead to a sense of being a fraud. Because at all costs the image that covers the "not enough" of emptiness must be kept full. Furthermore in their scarcity there is a tendency to see the world in terms of hierarchy. In other words, since the observer/personality dyad experiences the emptiness of Essence as scarce and void of wisdom, they can also attempt to fill-up the emptiness by seeking people who they perceive as further up on the hierarchy to lift them up. Since the #7 fixation of attention strategy labels the emptiness as a lack of wisdom, the over compensation is to become over-idealistic. People who are status seeking or name droppers as a way to elevate themselves in the hierarchy of their profession are often times #7. See illustration #13

The Therapy

Step I   Write down those I-dentities which resist your emptiness.

Step II   Notice where in your body the emptiness exists.

Step III   Enter into the emptiness and feel it.

ILLUSTRATION #13
FIXATION OF ATTENTION STRATEGY #7
THE IDEALISTIC

"LOOKING FOR KNOWLEDGE BY
ACTING KNOWLEDGEABLE"

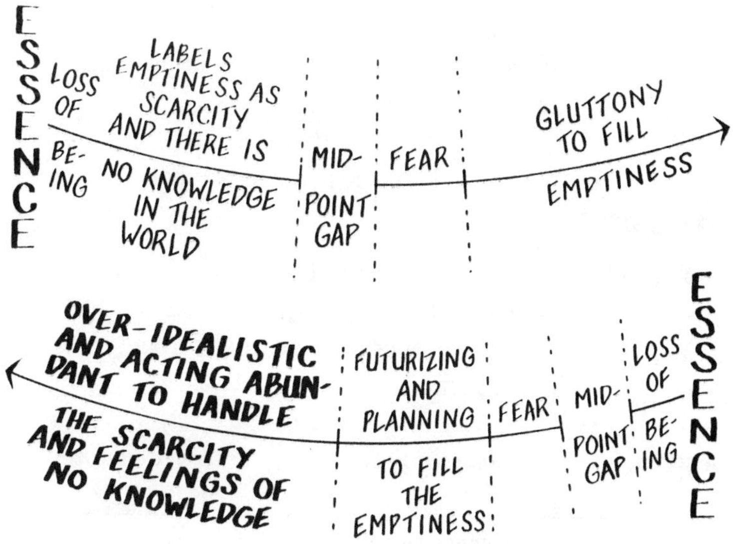

ESSENCE
LOSS OF BE-ING
LABELS EMPTINESS AS SCARCITY AND THERE IS NO KNOWLEDGE IN THE WORLD
MID-POINT GAP
FEAR
GLUTTONY TO FILL EMPTINESS

OVER-IDEALISTIC AND ACTING ABUN-DANT TO HANDLE THE SCARCITY AND FEELINGS OF NO KNOWLEDGE
FUTURIZING AND PLANNING TO FILL THE EMPTINESS
FEAR
MID-POINT GAP
LOSS OF BE-ING
ESSENCE

Step IV   Notice how to the I-dentity, the emptiness seems like death, but from the inside, the emptiness is calm, quiet, peaceful and serene.

Step V   From inside the emptiness ask each I-dentity "What is it you really want and are seeking more than anything else in the world?"

Step VI   However the I-dentity responds, feel that quality of experience in the spacious emptiness.

Step VII   Next, have the I-dentities turn around and be reabsorbed within the emptiness which is Essence.

Variation II

Step VIII   Seeing the I-dentities in the foreground, stay in the background and notice the I-dentities are floating in emptiness.

Step IX   Experience and feel the essential quality from the background.

Step X   See the I-dentities and the emptiness as being made of the same substance.

Variation III

Step XI   De-label the I-dentities and see the I-dentities as being made of energy.

Step XII   Allow the energy to be reabsorbed back into Essence.

I-dentities	*Underlying State*	*Over-Compensating Identities*
knows nothing	no knowledge	know it all
	scarcity	glutton
empty	fear	fraud
frustration		over-enthusiastic
pain		planning in future
lack of knowledge		charlatan

Highlighted Case Example

Mary, a woman in her late thirties, came to see me with a presenting problem of being misunderstood. In her relationship with men, she would "sell them" on her, and obsess about how they would be together in the future; furthermore, she was obese.

Therapist: What would you like to look at?

Client: I seem to attract men into being in a relationship with me, and then I feel misunderstood. Then, I just cannot stop myself from eating.

Therapist: This part of you that attracts men, where do you feel it in your body?

Client: In my pelvis.

Therapist: And this part of you that overeats, where do you feel it in your body?

Client: In my stomach.

Therapist: When you go home at night before you eat, what do you experience?

Client: Aloneness.

Therapist: Where in your body do you feel it?

Client: In my stomach.

Therapist: And where in your body do you feel the obsession about planning a future?

Client: In my head.

Therapeutic Note

Here we have three areas of disturbance; the head, the stomach, and the pelvis. Although each area defends against an unwanted I-dentity, there is only *one* Essence. Therefore, no matter which emptiness we enter, we can reach the same inner Essence. In this case, I decided to work from the head down. I thought of this because of the body work of Wilhelm Reich, M.D. The body, according to Reich, is divided into seven segments or defensive blocks he calls body armor, i.e., eyes, jaw, throat, chest, solar plexus, stomach, and pelvis. Alexander Lowen, M.D. added the arms and legs. Reich traditionally worked from the eye segment downward with the belief the most powerful energy or quanta was in the pelvis, which acts like a bifurcation point. In Kundalini yoga on the other hand, the work is from the root Chakra (bifurcation point) at the base of the spine through seven bifurcation points (called Chakras) up to the crown of the head. It used to be said, jokingly, Kundalini yoga works from sex to God (upward from the root Chakra), and William Reich works from God to sex (from the eyes downward). Of course, this presupposes that the pelvis is further away from God than the head. In this case I chose the Reichian perspective because of her problems with men.

Therapist: If you peeled back the layer of this obsessive I-dentity, what is underneath it?
Client: Fear.
Therapist: Feel the fear as energy.
Client: Okay.
Therapist: Now if you peeled back the fear, what is beneath it?
Client: An empty feeling of worthlessness.

Therapeutic Note
She defines emptiness as worthlessness, when emptiness is just emptiness. This means that you never stop peeling layers until the emptiness is reached.

Therapist: If you peel back the worthlessness, what is there?
Client: Emptiness.
Therapist: Now, let's go down to your stomach. Peel back the overeater and what's underneath that layer?
Client: An empty loneliness.

Therapeutic Note
Notice again how she defines emptiness as loneliness.

Therapist: Peel back the loneliness and what is underneath that?

Client: An empty hole.

Therapist: Now go down to your pelvis and peel back the I-dentity that attracts men, and tell me what you see.

Client: Sexual energy.

Therapist: Feel the sexual energy.

Client: Okay.

Therapist: Now peel back the sexual energy and what do you experience?

Client: Inadequacy.

Therapeutic Note

Notice how her over come-on to men hides her inadequacy.

Therapist: Peel back your inadequacy and what do you experience?

Client: I feel misunderstood.

Therapist: Peel back the misunderstood I-dentity and tell me what is there.

Client: A dark empty meaningless space.

Therapeutic Note

Once again the emptiness is seen as meaningless, rather than meaningful.

Therapist: Peel back the meaningless and what's underneath there?

Client: An empty space.

Therapist: Go into that empty space and tell me how it feels.

Client: Peaceful, calm.

Therapist: Enter into the peaceful calm emptiness, and notice how the emptiness at the pelvis is the same emptiness at the stomach and the same emptiness at the head.

Client: Yes, there is one emptiness and it is like I can be in the emptiness and look out any one of or all three of the holes.

Therapist: Good, now ask the obsessive I-dentity in the head, from "back there." "What are you seeking more than anything else in the world?"

Client: Reassurance.

Therapist: Ask it, "If you felt reassurance, what would you feel?"

Client: Calm and peaceful.

Therapist: Now ask the worthlessness I-dentity, "What are you seeking more that anything else in the world?"

Client: Peace.

Therapist: Now feel the peace of "back there" and go to your stomach and ask the overeater, "What are you seeking more than anything else in the world?"

Client: Serenity.

Therapist: Ask the loneliness, "What are you seeking more than anything in the world?"

Client: Wholeness.

Therapist: From "back there" feel the wholeness and serenity of the empty space.

Client: (nods)

Therapist: Now go down to your pelvis.

Client: Okay.

Therapist: Ask the sexual I-dentity, "What are you seeking more than anything else in the world?"

Client: Fulfillment.

Therapist: Ask the inadequate I-dentity, "What are you seeking more than anything else in the world?"

Client: Wholeness.

Therapist: Now from back there feel the wholeness and fulfillment of "back there."

Client: Okay.

Therapist: Now, notice the empty space these I-dentities are floating in.

Client: Okay.

Therapist: Now see the I-dentities as being made of energy.

Client: Okay.

Therapist: Now experience the Essence as being made of the same energy as the I-dentities.

Client: Wow, it's all one.

Therapist: How are you doing?

Client: No words...just silence.

Therapeutic Note

Here I added the third variation. In this variation, the I-dentities are de-labeled and seen as energy, and the Essence is being seen and experienced as being made of the same energy as the I-dentities. This offers the energic unity of Essence and observer/personality dyad.

Conclusion

Once again we are reabsorbing the I-dentities of the personality back into Essence. The trauma of loss of Essence creates so much repressed energy (quanta) that the reabsorption acted like a sling-shot—pulling back within itself the lost energy that had manifested outside of itself. This extra quanta (energy packet) provided the Essence with the energy it needed to recognize its own essential quality that it already is; or better said, to recognize itself as energy.

I'M O.K. IF I'M IN CHARGE
YOU'RE O.K. IF YOU LET
ME BE IN CHARGE

In this strategy of fixating attention, the trauma of the loss of being and its perceived emptiness leaves the observer/personality dyad with a loss of wholeness and a sense that there is no truth in the world. This fixation fears being seen as vulnerable and unwhole which leaves this personality repressing their vulnerability and love. In an attempt to fill the emptiness now covered with an unlovable/no-love experience. There is a feeling of a lack of *fairness* in the world for their loss of Essence. For this reason there develops an intense lust as an overcompensation for unlovable and an intense desire to make right or fair the injustice which was done, i.e., their loss of Essence. In other words, lust is substituted for love and overjustice for the injustice. The fixation of attention #8 resists and covers up the feeling of lovelessness with lust and projects immorality onto the world and attempts to make it right. Lust here can take the form of sexual lust, emotional lust, or an intellectual lust. What becomes curious for #8 is that whenever love or peaceful emptiness is present, they resist it because it *pushes their button* and reactivates the trauma of the loss of power and the injustice. They feel so powerless and unlovable that when love is experienced, they change it into lust. On the return swing of the pendulum, vulnerability and dependence emerge. This causes #8 to react by becoming more dominant and more hostile. The fixation of attention is called the *Leader* by Riso, the *Boss* by Palmer, and is called *Coming on Strong* by Naranjo. In other words, rather than facing the personality's inadequacy powerlessness and lovelessness, they defend against people seeing that within them by attempting to *dominate* others and force the *truth, justice, and the American way* on them. This forces #8 to develop an arrogance, even a vindictive and vengeful arrogance, that comes on incredibly strong to counter the vulnerable dependent underdog, which they deny inside themselves. #8 can be seen in those who act like they know or can do anything and everything. Sometimes this can be demonstrated by over-dominance and arrogance. #8 is not generally introverted. Rather, they prefer to be a *BOSS*, in the thick of things, dominating and persuading others of their unique qualities as a leader. #8 will rarely admit shortcomings of their philosophical system or themselves because this would leave them, from their point of view, vulnerable to the experience of the trauma of the loss of Essence. Sometimes the arrogant dominant takes on humility as #8 moves to become a #2 and takes on the super-giver. All of this hides the general vulnerability and masks the perceived emptiness. See illustration #14.

On the level of character analysis, the issue is power. The psychopath should not be confused with the extreme of Dr. Lechner in the motion picture "The Silence of the Lambs." A psychopathic structure simply means that when a person feels powerless, the feeling of powerlessness as a child is so resisted and unwanted, a mental manipulation takes place. In this manipulation, the person imagines and creates an inter-

ILLUSTRATION # 14
FIXATION OF ATTENTION STRATEGY #8
THE JUDGE, JURY, AND EXECUTIONER
"ACTING-OUT POWER IN ALL THE WRONG
WAYS AND PLACES"

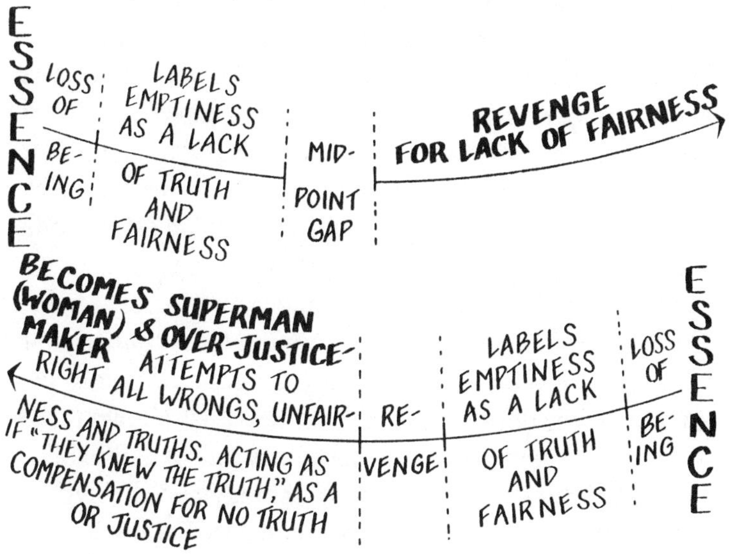

nal story and explanation that they are in charge and have the
power in a situation where they are powerless.

The Psychopathic Society

In the tragedy of child molestation, a little girl of three
might create the fantasy or imagine that she wasn't powerless, but rather was in charge of Dad raping her. She might
imagine she is so powerful as to have seduced Dad, and hence
she controls him. Thus she might even blame herself. This is
a defense against powerlessness. Unfortunately in our society, this understanding is reinforced. For example, if three
men rape a woman, the defense attorney makes it look like

the woman was in charge and made these poor little men rape her ("It was what she wanted," or "Why was she there in the first place?"). This is society's psychopathology, the *victim is imagined to be the perpetrator and the perpetrator is made to be seen as the poor innocent victim.*

This is the sickness of our society. The 3-year-old little girl is not wrong or bad for imagining herself to be in charge— it was a *survival mechanism.* However, it is a subtle internal manipulation of the illusion of power. Another unfortunate example in our society is men who were raped as children. Because of society's double standard and psychopathology, a boy who is sexually abused by a woman is seen as lucky. After all, being forced to have oral sex with an older woman for a small *male* child is good for him.

These psychopathic trances induced by society help to hypnotize the young boy, and later often leads to their abuse of others. The old Gestalt Therapy adage, "Do unto others, that which was done unto you." Research has shown that almost *all* men who are sexual abusers were sexually abused. Yet, because of society's psychopathology and the hypnotic trance given to the young boy, few come to therapy for treatment of sexual dysfunction, i.e., premature ejaculation, impotence, or child molestation.

Psychopathic Structures vs. Psychopathology

Let me at this point clarify the difference between having a psychopathic structure or trance and being a psychopath. The little girl/boy, who is molested and feels powerless, manipulates their internal state to being in charge of the perpetrator and powerful, to resist the feelings of powerlessness and victimization. This is a psychopathic *trance* or *structure.* On the other hand, a psychopath is one whose entire personality is so integrated into power and manipulation and has such resistance to powerlessness that they are unaware of powerlessness. The true psychopath objectifies others and feels *no remorse* for these actions. This lack of remorse and the total objectification of another person is psychopathic.

In other words, we all have psychopathic structures and trances which resist powerlessness automatically, we, however, feel remorse, it is not our entire personality. With a true psychopath, it is their *entire* personality. Feeling powerless with a deep inner sense of helplessness, the psychopathic #8 over-compensates, becoming and imagining themselves to have more power than they do. Inwardly, like #6, they feel victimized by any question about their power and authority. Feeling victimized, they attack and seek *revenge*. Unlike #6 whose underlying state is motivated by fear, #8 has an underlying state of anger. This anger defends against the real issue, the *injustice* that took place around trauma of the loss of Essence. They will then manufacture a story which will validate all of the necessary reasons for their vindictiveness.

What is not appreciated in psychotherapy is the larger context in which a behavior occurs. Family therapists were the first to expand the explanation of behavior of children and adolescents to include the larger context, i.e., the family, in which the behavior manifested.

In the same way, our society often asks individuals to behave in psychopathic ways. For example, in the Vietnam War, we asked pilots to drop bombs on villages in Southeast Asia. The pilots were hypnotized by society into believing that "life is cheap or unimportant" to Asians. To drop bombs on women and children, an individual has to objectify individuals and see them as not human. This dehumanizing process is psychopathic in nature. Furthermore, often times the pilot who dropped bombs is seen as a hero and given a medal, as in the case of Admiral James Stockdale, who was Ross Perot's running mate in the 1992 Presidential election. Admiral Stockdale was seen as a victim of the Vietnamese by being put in prison; rather than a psychopath who killed an untold number of women and children by dropping bombs on villages in Vietnam. The government *trance*-fered the injustice on the Vietnamese, and then could *justify* dropping bombs on villages and, as Time Magazine reported in 1972; killing, wounding and making homeless 6,000,000 Vietnamese.

In a recent phone conversation with one of the fathers of Family Therapy, Dr. Carl Whitaker, I said to him, "Carl, isn't it amazing how psychopaths feel no remorse?" Carl replied, "Actually, they *repress their remorse* and this later brings about their own downfall, as with Hitler, Napoleon, and Lyndon Johnson." I said, "Lyndon Johnson was a mass murderer?" Dr. Whitaker replied, "Yes, and it is people's unwillingness to confront that which is mass hypnosis."

Why is Lyndon Johnson a mass murderer and a psychopath? In a study of the 1964 election, Barry Goldwater's main criticism of L.B.J. was that he was *soft on communism*. It is well documented that L.B.J. knew at that moment that to create the biggest Presidential landslide in history[1], he would have to prove otherwise. L.B.J. then knowingly used false information about the Gulf of Tonkin as an excuse to intensify the Vietnam War. L.B.J. bombed Hanoi day and night and killed an untold number of people to win an election by a landslide—to win was not enough for L.B.J, it had to be the biggest landslide in history. This is psychopathic. What is even more amazing is that this psychopathic behavior was seen as acceptable, at the time, to a majority of Americans.

Lies

I am bringing up this extreme case because we all must confront our own psychopathology. It is this *self-lie* when we

---

[1] Lyndon Baines Johnson was nicknamed, by the Washington Insider, *Landslide Lyndon* for allegedly fixing his Senatorial election by stuffing the ballot boxes and winning the Senatorial seat by under 50 votes.

feel powerless which permits us to see other humans as not human, and hence objectify them. For this reason, we *don't feel, feel no remorse, or repress our remorse* in our psychopathic reaction formation in defense of our own powerlessness.

To reach Essence, all lies must be fearlessly looked at. One of the most difficult is our psychopathic resistance to powerlessness. Notice for example, in the recent trial of the four Los Angeles police officers who beat motorist Rodney King that the defense attorneys made the police officers (of which four did the beating and 23 officers watched the beating) the victim of a black man. This kept the stereotype of blacks having super-human strength, and the police officers with guns, sticks, and electric shock guns the victims. This *is* the psychopathic society.

In other words, the #8 fixation has a psychopath structure that will develop a justification for their revenge and anger. The story, however, is not the territory, it is the map. The territory is what is; the story is the organization of personality around Essence which is defending against the perceived injustice around the trauma of the loss of Being.

I-dentities	Underlying State	Over-Compensating Identities
victimized	no justice in the world yielding revenge	over-justice makes righteousness being in charge
no aliveness		greed for aliveness
control	denial	anger

The Therapy

Step I   Write down those I-dentities which resist your emptiness.

Step II   Notice where in your body the emptiness exists.

Step III   Enter into the emptiness and feel it.

Step IV   Notice how to the I-dentity the emptiness seems like death, but from the inside the emptiness is calm, quiet, peaceful, and serene.

Step V   From inside the emptiness ask each I-dentity, "What is it you really want and are seeking more than anything else in the world?"

Step VI   However the I-dentity responds, feel that quality of experience in the spacious emptiness.

Step VII   Next, have the I-dentities turn around and be reabsorbed within the emptiness which is Essence.

Variation

Step VIII   Seeing the I-dentities in the foreground, stay in the background and notice the I-dentities are floating in Emptiness.

Step IX   Experience and feel the essential quality from the background.

Step X   See the I-dentities and the emptiness as being made of the same substance.

Highlighted Case Example

What I am about to present is an elaborate structure for working with Post Traumatic Stress Disorder (P.T.S.D.). I am presenting it in this section for two reasons. First, I don't want to mislead people that I-dentities can just be reabsorbed. I-dentities and the context in which they are created must be taken apart and their *lies* and the context in which they were created must be known, i.e., "the truth sets one free." Essence cannot absorb that which is being denied, or where the client has an unwillingness to experience. Better said, there cannot be resistance to an experience or a situation. This can be exemplified in spiritual groups and new-age groups who think they can transcend a trauma through meditation. What occurs is that as soon as meditation is finished, the trauma emerges and sometimes it feels subjectively stronger[2]. In other words, they move from Essence and then like a slingshot are thrown into their I-dentities. It cannot be overstated that nothing can be a-voided. In other words, to enter into the void, we must know and be willing to experience the trauma and its corresponding structure; thus we cannot a-void to trance-end. For this reason, it is not that which we know about which is a problem, rather it is that which we don't question or don't know about that causes problems. For example, often times people who meditate exhibit the same dissociative qualities as those who dissociate. For example, I, along with many meditators I knew in India, were able to enter into a peaceful void while meditating. This peaceful void appeared like meditation. Actually, they entered into what I call a *dissociative amnesic void*. In other words, they entered into a calm peaceful blank state where there was no mind and peace. Unfortunately, this *dissociative amnesic void* like experience was a defense against trauma and was not *THE VOID*. In other words, they had a blank spot in their consciousness which was *medication not meditation* in order to blank out the trauma. For example, for years I meditated entering into a calm blank space which I misunderstood as *THE VOID*. After years of meditating/medicating the *dissociative amnesic trance dissolved*, and to my shock incest emerged. I then processed through my incest and found the true void of emptiness or unboundaried space which is always in the background of my consciousness. What is ironic is that once you are ready to truly meditate, which means you have processed your *dissociative amnesic void* which protects you from trauma, and

---

[2] See, *The Dark Side of the Inner Child* by Stephen H. Wolinsky, Chapter 14, Bramble Books, CT, 1993.

you process the trauma(s), you don't need to meditate any-more. Simply put, when you are actually ready to meditate, you no longer need to meditate.

This understanding explains why when meditators/medicators finish their meditation/medication time for the day they feel so "punched out" by the world. Why? Because they leave their *dissociative amnesic trance* which appears as the void and have to face the world where the trauma *leaks* through the *dissociative amnesic void* and colors their present time perceptions of the world.

Secondly, I wanted to demonstrate a case where reabsorbtion of identities was not so easily do-able. In this way I wouldn't be showing success after success. Rather, I wanted to demonstrate that although this process works, the work on the I-dentities and the context in which they were created must be explored in their *entirety* first before the reabsorption process. Stated more clearly, reabsorption is the last step, not the first step in integration. Therefore, if you are a therapist, do not be mislead into thinking this is the *cure-all*. This approach of reabsorption works *only* after the pre-liminary therapy has been done, the *dissociative amnesic void* dissolved, and the trauma processed. And even after that reabsorption and integration of the no-state might take some time. To use the words of my teacher, Nisargadatta Maharaj,

> "To get established in this condition it might take some time, but hang on to the beingness only."

In this spirit, and with the understanding that reabsorption is a part in the process not the whole process, let us look at this case.

Highlighted Case Example

Tom is a successful businessman in his late forties from Arizona. He came to see me with the presenting problem of an over-reactive anger response to the world.

Therapist: What would you like to look at?

Client: My over-reactive anger at my girlfriend.

Therapist: This over-reactive I-dentity, where do you feel it in your body?

Client: In my solar plexus.

Therapist: If you were to peel back that layer, what's underneath it?

Client: A feeling of loss.

Therapist: If you were to peel back that layer, what is underneath that?

Client: Humiliation.

Therapeutic Note
At this point, as you will note he has a pop-up memory of being orally raped at age 5 by an elder cousin, age 17. I mention it here because the humiliation and powerlessness is resisted to the point that a *violent rage*, which could not be expressed on paper, emerges.

Client: (continued) I have this violent anger, and some day I'm going to kill that mother-fucker Bill, I was fine and I looked up to him, and wanted him to like me, and the next thing I know he has me pinned down, sitting on my shoulder with his dick in my face forcing me to suck his penis and I didn't know what to do. I'm going to get him one day.

Therapeutic Note
This passage is an understatement of the rage at the rape this man was going through. At this point, I shifted the focus in an attempt to look at the memory, and his *appropriate* reactions to the rape. I use the word appropriate because recently in therapeutic circles they would label intense emotions as an abreaction. I do not see this as abreaction but as an appropriate reaction given what occurred.

As a further note, for me, I see the memory or what occurred as important, but what is more important is what he created in response to the memory. At the end of the text, I will give a summary of the P.T.S.D. structure which was developed by myself and Kristi L. Kennen.

Therapist: Okay, can you take a look now at the movie in your mind?

Client: Yes.

Therapist: Start it at the beginning of the rape and describe step by step what happens. Describe it to me in third-person, like the little boy rather than I.

Client: Okay. Well, the little boy is playing with his cousin and he kinda idealizes him and wants him to like him. The little boy's cousin begins wrestling with him and wrestles him down to the ground and is sitting on him. Now, the cousin is taking his penis out of his pants and is putting it in my face.

Therapist: His face.

Client: Yes, in his face.

Therapeutic Note

This is a breaking point of intensity or a bifurcation point, the first part of the trauma, and the first part to explore. It is my aim to have him tell the story third-person so that he can observe the movie first rather than be in the movie. The movie is broken down into segments, and each segment is handled separately at a point of intensity (bifurcation point).

Therapist: What thoughts are the little boy creating?

Client: What's going on?

Therapist: Create the little boy in the movie thinking "What's going on?"

Client: Okay.

Therapist: What feelings are the little boy creating?

Client: Confused and scared.

Therapist: Create the little boy in the movie being confused and scared.

Client: Okay.

Therapist: What fantasies are the little boy imagining?

Client: He feels frozen, and isn't imagining anything.

Therapist: Create the little boy in the movie freezing his body and stopping his fantasies.

Client: Okay.

Therapist: Okay now let's allow the movie memory to roll again.

Client: Well, the cousin is laughing and telling the little boy to suck on his penis.

Therapist: Let's stop here. What thoughts are the little boy creating?

Client: He's confused, and he wants the cousin to like him but doesn't know what to do.

Therapist: Create the little boy being confused and wanting the cousin to like him.

Client: Okay.

Therapist: What feelings are the little boy creating?

Client: Revulsion, disgust and powerlessness.

Therapist: Create the little boy in the movie feeling revulsion, disgust and powerlessness.

Client: Okay.

Therapist: What fantasies are the little boy creating?

Client: None.

Therapist: Now let the movie roll a little further and describe what happens next.

Client: The little boy feels angry, crazy and betrayed because he looked up to his cousin, so he doesn't know what to do, so he puts his cousin's penis in his mouth.

Therapist: Let's stop here. What thoughts are the little boy creating?

Client: He's blocking out all his thoughts.

Therapist: So he's creating blocking out.

Client: Yes.

Therapist: Create the little boy blocking out his thoughts.

Client: Okay.

Therapist: What feelings are the little boy creating?

Client: He feels numb and afraid.

Therapist: Okay. Create the little boy feeling numbness and fear.

Client: Okay.

Therapist: Now what fantasies are the little boy creating?

Client: He has images of killing his cousin and cutting off his penis and stuffing it in his cousin's mouth.

Therapist: Okay, create the little boy having these images.

Client: Okay.

Therapist: Now let the film roll and tell me what happens.

Client: Well, his cousin gets up after a while, and grabs the little boy and tells him he'll beat the shit out of him if he tells anyone.

Therapist: Okay. What thoughts are the little boy creating?

Client: He's blocking out thoughts of having the shit beat out of him and wanting to kill his cousin, and he feels humiliated if people find out.

Therapist: Okay. Create the little boy having those thoughts, images and feelings.

Client: Okay.

Therapist: Now what happens?

Client: The memory ends.

Therapist: How are you doing right now?

Client: A little better.

Therapist: Okay. Now let's start the film at the beginning.

Client: Okay. Well, the little boy is playing with his cousin and he kinda idealizes him and wants him to like him. The little boy's cousin begins wrestling with him and wrestles him down to the ground and is sitting on him. Now, the cousin is taking his penis out of his pants and is putting it in his face.

Therapist: What thoughts does the little boy *imagine* his cousin is having?

Client: Belittling, like he's more powerful than him.

Therapist: What thoughts does the little boy create in response to that?

Client: He thinks he's smaller than his cousin and that his cousin could hurt him.

Therapist: Okay. Create an energy loop of the cousin thinking he is more powerful and the little boy thinking his cousin could hurt him.

Client: Okay.

Therapeutic Note

This is a crucial juncture. In order to get the other side of the loop, i.e., his cousin I-dentity which he *trance*-fers on others, we must find out what the little boy *projects* and *imagines* the cousin is thinking, feeling, or imagining and what he creates in response to that. This is crucial because he *trance*-fers his cousin on others, and hence experiences others as his cousin, thus the *revengeful* thoughts and feelings. Therefore, the *whole* loop must be taken apart so that the man in 1992 doesn't re-enact this anger with everyone again and again.

Therapist: Create the loop as energy and watch it, allowing it to do what it does.

Therapeutic Note

This relates back to Iteration and the Mandelbrot Mandala. Often the underlying order is revealed as an energic pattern and is allowed to iterate (repeat) many times.

Client: It just spins around and disappears.

Therapist: Good, How are you doing now?

Client: Relieved.

Therapist: Now what does the little boy imagine the cousin is feeling?

Client: Powerful.

Therapist: What does the little boy create in response to his cousin's power?

Client: He feels powerless and weak.

Therapist: Okay. Intentionally create the cousin as powerful and the little boy as powerless and weak as a loop.

Client: Okay.

Therapist: Now see it as an energy loop and allow it to repeat many times. You just watch.

Client: Okay.

Therapist: What happens?

Client: The energy kind of dissipates and just emptiness is left.

Therapist: Now what does the little boy imagine the cousin is fantasizing?

Client: Just being bigger and more powerful.

Therapist: What images does the little boy create in response?

Client: Weak, powerless.

Therapist: Okay, now again create the cousin feeling powerful and the little boy feeling powerless as an energy loop.

Client: Okay.

Therapist: What happens?

Client: It looks like energy.

Therapist: How you doing?

Client: More relaxed.

Therapeutic Note

In each of the memory breaks, there is a gap, after a bifurcation point of intensity. This is demonstrated as we move from state to state. For example, as we move from a thought, such as "I like myself," to the thought

"I hate myself," there is a gap, space, or midpoint where one state turns into another state. The way we stated this earlier was by using the metaphor of the film strip. With a film strip, there is a picture and a gap or space and then another picture. The gap is the "time," if we can spot and notice it, where we are present again and we can remember ourselves. The reason we cannot remember ourselves in a traumatic memory is that too much energetic change is built up within the picture. This energetic build-up is seeking to release. Before therapy, the traumatic memory has so much charge, and resisted charge, that rather than the memory moving, the memory stays *fixed*. Since the built-up energy has no place to go because it cannot express the anger, fear, or pain of the situation, the energy seeks release through a sublimated, or alternate, and hence distorted vehicle.

For example, the pain that a child might experience during a molestation freezes the child's muscles and breath creating a trance (fixation of attention). In this case, the movie is halted and the a-tention remains fixated in fear. To handle that excess undischarged energy of fear, the child might get violent, overeat, vandalize property, take drugs, get pregnant, etc.

This is what occurs to some traumatized teenagers; when the excess energy of trauma is not discharged, they sublimate it. Later, as an adult, this excess energy is still being stored so the adult looks and finds more socially acceptable ways to discharge energy, i.e., a phobia, drugs, or psychosomatic disorders, etc.

To review, the gap after the bifurcation point does not get noticed because it contains so much stored up energy from the trauma. For this reason, the observer disappears. Let me explain by an example. In workshops people often ask me the question, "Why can some people observe and be mindful of their process and traumas while others cannot?" What I say is that *during* the excess energy which occurs during trauma, there are generally three reactions regarding the trauma. One, the observer explodes and merges with the trauma and disappears within the trauma. Two, the observer implodes and to resist the feelings of the trauma prematurely evacuates and prematurely observes that she/he doesn't feel the trauma, or she/he creates some form of trance to defend against the trauma. This is why to wake up the observer, the unidentified trauma must be processed. If the trauma is not processed. Sublimated ways to release the energy ensues. These sublimated attempts at releasing the energy become a pattern and hence a way to greater and greater frustration. However, if the excess energy is allowed to discharge while looking at a memory by experiencing the emotion as energy, the pattern of releasing excess energy in a sublimated and fixated way resolves itself and gives the person extra energy and unfreezes the memory. This opens up the gap or space within trauma memory, allowing self-remembering to occur.

The cycle of energy is a graphic representation of a dynamical system which creates a phase portrait (or picture).

"The forces of the psyche, and the rules they obey are generally referred to as a dynamical system." (*Psychological Perspectives*, Abraham Fred, 1989)

This means that the energetic pathway described in the highlighted case above between the little boy and the cousin is first organized to handle the pain and chaos of the oral rape. To move beyond the rape, the adult must notice the energetic pattern, called in chaos theory, trajectories and the point of intensity, i.e., bifurcation point. It is at the point of intensity that the energy is at its highest; this is where I point out and show the gap within the memory. It is at this point the pattern is experienced, understood, and processed. The stored up energy is then discharged, and the pattern is released.

Therapist: Now let the movie roll and go to the next segment.

Client: Well, the cousin is laughing and telling the little boy to suck his penis.

Therapist: Okay. Stop here. What thoughts does the little boy *imagine* the cousin is having?

Client: He thinks he's totally powerful.

Therapist: What thoughts does the little boy create in response?

Client: He thinks he is small and inadequate.

Therapist: Okay. Create a loop from the cousin thinking he is totally powerful to the little boy thinking he is small and inadequate.

Client: Okay.

Therapist: Now let the energy loop do what it does—you just watch.

Client: Okay.

Therapist: What happens?

Client: It spins rapidly, then disappears.

Therapist: Now what does the little boy *imagine* the cousin is feeling?

Client: Powerful.

Therapist: What feelings does the little boy create in response to him feeling powerful?

Client: He feels powerless and humiliated.

Therapist: Okay. Create an energy loop from the cousin feeling powerful to the little boy feeling powerless and humiliated.

Client: Okay.

Therapist: What happens?

Client: It disappears.

Therapist: Okay. What fantasies does the little boy imagine the cousin is having?

Client: Like he is going to kill him and cut his penis off and wear it around his neck to show off.

Therapist: What fantasies does the little boy create in response?

Client: Total humiliation...worse than death.

Therapist: Create the cousin having those fantasies and the little boy having his fantasies in response as an energy loop.

Client: Okay.

Therapist: What happens?

Client: It just keeps going.

Therapist: How are you feeling about it?

Client: More detached from it.

Therapist: Okay. Let's let the movie roll and go on to the next segment, and describe what you see.

Client: Well, his cousin gets up after a while and grabs the little boy and tells him he'll beat the shit out of him if he tells anyone.

Therapist: What thoughts does the little boy imagine the cousin is having?

Client: Like he's the coolest and greatest.

Therapist: What thoughts does the little boy create in response?

Client: Like he's a weak powerless piece of shit.

Therapist: Okay. Create an energy loop from the cousin thinking his thoughts, and the little boy thinking he's a piece of shit.

Client: Okay.

Therapist: Now watch the energy loop and tell me what happens.

Client: It speeds up, then slows down, then disappears.

Therapist: Okay. What feelings does the little boy imagine the cousin is having?

Client: All powerful.

Therapist: And what feelings does the little boy create in response?

Client: Total devastation, like his whole body is caved in.

Therapist: Create the energy loop again from the cousin's feelings to the little boy's feelings and the cave-in in the body, and tell me what happens.

Client: It just spins and spins.

Therapist: How does it feel to you?

Client: More distant.

Therapeutic Note

It cannot be overstated that the body is the cornerstone of how we stand in the world. For that reason, the cave-in in his chest carries the *body memory* of the trauma, and hence must be included. Even Freud said that the ego was body centered. To illustrate, if a client has an image of themselves as a weak person this might be mirrored by a caved in chest. No matter how much therapy is done, they are still walking around with a caved in chest. This creates an unconscious body image of a "beaten person," and a re-enforcement of the weak person I-dentity. For this reason, the body and mind must be seen as *one unit*. Therefore, although I began my therapy practice as a Reichian and Bioenergetic therapist, I no longer do that style of work. For that reason, I almost always *refer* people to hands-on body therapists, i.e., Reichian, Bioenergetics, Rolfing, Feldenkrais, etc., to integrate the whole person.

Therapist: What fantasies does the little boy *imagine* the cousin is having?

Client: Like he is a king.

Therapist: And what fantasies does the little boy create in response?

Client: Like he is a slave.

Therapist: How does his body look?

Client: Caved in.

Therapist: Okay. Create the cousin having the king fantasy and create the little boy with a caved-in body and a slave as an energy loop.

Client: Okay.

Therapist: What happens?

Client: It just disappears.

Therapist: How you doing?

Client: Calmer and quieter.

Therapeutic Note

I don't want to leave the reader with the idea that all this was handled in a few hours. The body caving in his chest and his pulling back in the pelvis will require body work, i.e., Rolfing, Bioenergetics, Feldenkrais, etc. To restate, without body therapy there can *never* be a full integration in the psychotherapy. The body not only carries the memories in the form of posture and breath, it also demonstrates how the person moves in the world. Furthermore, the person must learn or re-learn how to embody their traumatized body again and embody an untraumatized body, since, during this kind of a trauma, he had to leave his body behind. In short, no body-work—no completed psychotherapy; the body mirrors how the person embodies herself/himself in the world.

Therapist: Now, look at the movie from beginning to end, and notice the empty mind space that the movie is floating in.

Client: Okay.

Therapist: Now, run the film diagonally from upper left to lower right.

Client: Okay.

Therapist: Now run the film diagonally downward from upper right to lower left.

Client: Okay.

Therapist: Now diagonally from bottom right to upper left.

Client: Okay.

Therapist: Now run the film diagonally from bottom left to upper right.

Client: Okay.

Therapist: Now make it into a yo-yo.

Client: Okay.

Therapist: Now decide it was the most important situation in your life.

Client: Okay.

Therapist: Now decide it was a situation that occurred.

Client: Okay.

Therapist: How are you doing?

Client: Much freer, cleaner, relieved.

Therapist: Is it okay if we stop here?

Client: Yes.

Therapeutic Note

The last section is done this way to give the client the understanding that they (the observer) exist before the memory in their mind, during the memory, and the same observer will exist after the memory leaves. I said to a client after the memory left, "Well, I guess you're not your mind." She looked startled and nonverbally confused. I said, "You're still here, even though the story is not, therefore you are not your story."

Observers hold the movie in their mind unknowingly, and fuse with the trauma. By giving an observer a way to have that experience and remove their fixated attention, the movie loses its hold on them and the fixation of attention of the observer loosens. In this way, the trauma becomes a story they can pick up or put down.

Post Traumatic Stress Disorder Outline

Part I - Going over the story

Step I   Let the client run the movie as it is from beginning to end.

Step II   Notice points of intensity and break the memory after an intensity point.

Step III   Have the client speak in third person. Ask them what thoughts, feelings, and fantasies they created during each segment.

Part II - The Loop

Step I   Have them go back over the movie asking what they *imagine* the perpetrator was thinking, feeling and imagining.

Step II   Ask in each segment what they created in response to the perpetrator's imagined thoughts, feelings and fantasies.

Step III   Have the client intentionally create the loop (trajectory) from them to the perpetrator and back to them.

Step IV   Have them see the loop as energy until the loop begins to dissipate.

Part III - Letting go

Step I	Have them run the film in many directions; backward, forward, diagonally in many directions.
Step II	Have them decide it was important.
Step III	Have them decide it was an experience.
Step IV	Have them do whatever they want with the memory.

Conclusion

This brief statement about Post Traumatic Stress Disorder looks easy. Please do not think it is this simple. This is a highlighted example of sessions which took some six to eight hours. There are many factors to working with a client on P.T.S.D. This is, however, a nice piece to use with whatever system you are presently using to handle the disorder. And it should be noted that one segment of the memory might take a long time to process, i.e., I once met a Vietnam Vet who told me it took 3 years of therapy to work through one 6-minute segment.

I'M O.K. IF I PLAY YOUR GAME, YOU'RE O.K. IF YOU LET ME PLAY YOUR GAME

They are playing a game
They are playing at not playing a game
If I tell them they are playing a game, they
   will punish me.
I must play their game of not seeing I see the
   game.

(R.D. Laing)

To continue what happens to the person in this poem by R. D. Laing, #9 goes unconscious and forgets they are playing a game, not to mention forgets that they are playing at not playing or not seeing their game. This is their trance of amnesia and negative hallucination not to mention age-regression and post-hypnotic suggestion.

In this particular strategy of fixating attention, the pain of trauma of moving from Essence to personality is so great that an *unconscious laziness develops*. In *Trances People Live* we discuss the trances that occur psychologically. Here the organization of I-dentities around Essence cause trances to defend against the pain after the loss of Essence. This unconsciousness takes the form of psychic laziness and a resistance to looking inside of oneself. For this reason, the underlying state is laziness, and the chief trance is called *Going Along With the Stream* by Naranjo. Actually, the strategy of fixating attention is because the observer/personality dyad sees nothing inside themselves and instead of giving into it, wants to go unconscious about it. This produces laziness or sloth. Furthermore, it produces a basic style of giving oneself up for others. For example, the true chameleon of #9 feels as though there is nothing inside. Rather than acknowledging that, #9 looks outside itself for its existence and is called the *Mediator* by Palmer or the *Peacemaker* by Riso. It must be understood that the unconscious laziness of #9 and going along with the stream is a way of distracting themselves and others from confronting their emptiness. #9 seeks *love* as its highest aim, but the observer/personality dyad sees the emptiness of Essence as *lovelessness*. #9s frequently lack an identity of their own and become co-dependent, taking on other people's lives or positions. This lasts, however, only while they are in their presence. Once in another person's presence, they become them, fusing with their feelings and ideals. This is a true co-dependent. The feeling there is nothing inside themselves and which they label loveless. The problem is that underlying this structure is an implicit demand to be taken care of. When this doesn't occur, *rage* emerges.

To a #9 anything is better than looking at the nothing. #9s often create a false interior or false spirituality to cover their perceived nothingness. This superficial spirituality deprives them of the very available empty space which is always there lurking in the background of their experience. #9s are considered by many the most naturally spiritual because of the availability of that empty space. For #9s, when the superficial spirituality is pierced, and they become willing to enter into their own empty space which leads to their Essence, the doorways are easy and readily available. The thing a #9 has to watch out for is getting angry at other people's inability to fill their emptiness. See Illustration #15. Basically, most of us resist our emptiness to such a degree that we get compulsive about being in relationships. We basically say to another, "Fill my emptiness." When this occurs, there is peace, when this doesn't, it's a divorce. Stated another way, we all attempt to fill our emptiness by looking outside ourselves. This habit of expecting others to fill our void can only lead to frustration. Why? Because each of us must enter into our own nothingness and see its value. Running away from our own emptiness and expecting others to fulfill it must fail since emptiness is our true essential nature.

ILLUSTRATION # 15
FIXATION OF ATTENTION STRATEGY # 9
OVER-UNDERSTANDING

"LOOKING FOR LOVE IN ALL
THE WRONG PLACES"

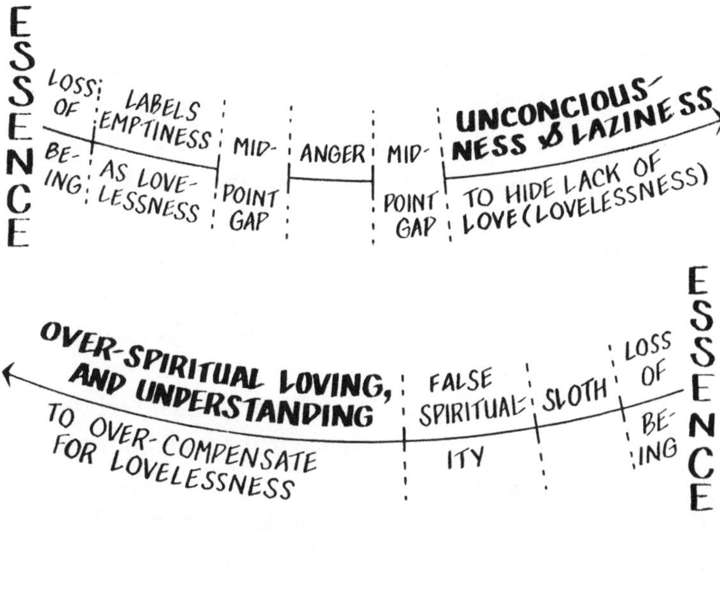

E
S
S
E LOSS   LABELS   UNCONCIOUS-
N OF   EMPTINESS   MID-   ANGER   MID-   NESS & LAZINESS
C BE-   AS LOVE-   POINT   POINT   TO HIDE LACK OF
E ING   LESSNESS   GAP   GAP   LOVE (LOVELESSNESS)

                                                              E
                                                              S
   OVER-SPIRITUAL LOVING,   FALSE   LOSS   S
   AND UNDERSTANDING   SPIRITUAL SLOTH   OF   E
   TO OVER-COMPENSATE   ITY   BE-   N
   FOR LOVELESSNESS   ING   C
                                                              E

This strategy of fixating attention has a tendency to go unconscious and automatically become other people, thus developing a superficial spirituality in an attempt to avoid the nothingness. A #9 can be very easily guided into the nothingness of Essence but caution has to be taken that superficial nothingness, created nothingness, or symbols for nothingness, is not mistaken for the vastness of their own Essence.

I-dentities	Underlying State	Over-Compensating Identities
Unconsciousness	Labeling nothingness	Hypervigilant
No-self	as lovelessness	Super-conscious
		Being lovable
Lovelessness	Anger	Adaptive false self
		Over spiritual

The Therapy

Step I Write down those I-dentities which resist your emptiness.

Step II Notice where in your body the emptiness exists.

Step III Enter into the emptiness and feel it.

Step IV Notice how to the I-dentity the emptiness seems like death, but from the inside the emptiness is calm, quiet, peaceful, and serene.

Step V From inside the emptiness ask each I-dentity, "What is it you really want and are seeking more than anything else in the world?"

Step VI However the I-dentity responds, feel that quality of experience in the spacious emptiness.

Step VII Next, have the I-dentities turn around and be reabsorbed within the emptiness which is Essence.

Variation

Step VIII Seeing the I-dentities in the foreground, stay in the background and notice the I-dentities are floating in emptiness.

Step IX Experience and feel the essential quality from the background.

Step X See the I-dentities and the emptiness as being made of the same substance.

Highlighted Case Example

Barbara, age 35, is facing a divorce after 15 years of marriage. For years she has given herself up in an attempt to "take care of him." It might be said that she fuses with his wants and desires as a defense against her own nothingness.

This is another case whereby the reabsorption of I-dentities cannot occur in one session. Rather, trances and I-dentities which cover her trauma must first be taken apart and looked at. In order to demonstrate this, the theoretics will be discussed before the case so that the reader can see the direction I am going in.

Traumas and Trances

In both *Trances People Live* and *The Dark Side of the Inner Child*, trauma is seen as the cornerstone in the development of the defensive trance. What must be emphasized is that during a trauma a trance is created which helps to defend the individual from knowing, feeling, or remembering what occurred. This brings about the tightening of the muscles, holding of breath, and a storing up of excess energy.

This is important because to live the *Tao of Chaos* requires the knowledge of your own trances. No I-dentity can be reabsorbed into Essence unless the truth of the trauma be known. To restate again, the Essence cannot absorb lies, distortions, and denied memories or I-dentities.

The *Tao of Chaos* is about allowing, and so let us illustrate what occurs around a trauma.

ILLUSTRATION #16
TRAUMAS AND TRANCES

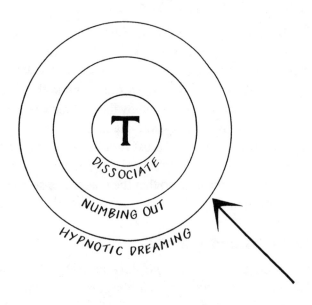

As you can see, the T is the trauma and the defenses of trance surround the trauma. When you are working with yourself or another, you will hit defensive trances like a wall as you enter into the core of the trauma.

For example, if a little girl was molested at age 5, she might first, *dissociate*; second, numb-out; and third, hypnotic dream in order to survive the trauma.

> The order of unlearning is different for each person, because what we unlearn first is what is learned last…therefore you proceed by stages, the last learned is the first unlearned, and in this way you can proceed safely. (G. Spencer Brown Transcripts, Professor Von Meier, Art 269, March 19, 1973)

In this way, she will pass through the trances in a last in, first out fashion. Or, the last trance created being the first trance that will have to be experienced as we go into the trauma. In the above situation, she will first have to go through *hypnotic dreaming*. It seems like a dream, second, sensory distortion (numbing out), and third, dissociation (floating above her body). These trances must be experienced and processed as created defenses in order to enter into the actual event. The event itself must be "looked at" and processed before the I-dentities can be re-absorbed into Essence.

To process through the trances requires the willingness to be with and knowingly, consciously, intentionally create the automatic trance. To process the trauma, depending upon its severity, will probably require a therapist to guide one through serious intrusions.

The *Tao of Chaos* and the reabsorption of I-dentities sounds and appears easier than it is; it requires honesty with oneself. The *Tao of Chaos* also requires true understanding, allowing, and no resistance to experiences.

Recently I had a discussion with a well known Ericksonian therapist. He said, "When I get upset I create all the resources and symbols I can create." I thought to myself, "What's wrong with being upset and just allowing?" This is the *Tao of Chaos*; no judgment, no evaluation, no significance, no resistance, just *allowing* experiences without the intention or goal of getting rid of the unwanted experience.

Resources as Dissociators

Creating a resource like a symbol to handle a feeling of upset resists the feeling of upset. Secondly, it is a subtle form of dissociation since it takes the person out of their present time experience. Third, and most important, you create the symbol, therefore you, not the symbol, has the power. By creating symbol or image to handle an upset you empower the symbol or image rather than *you*, the one that created the symbol or image in the first place. For example, I was presenting a workshop in the Mid-West. In that workshop, I did a piece of therapy with a woman who had been molested. After taking apart the story, the excess energy sent her into a very quiet internal state. With her eyes closed, she had an image of her spiritual teacher. The teacher had so much bliss she said. I asked her to notice the shape of the teacher, and then to notice the empty space the teacher was floating in. I then asked her to see the emptiness and the teacher as the same substance. The emptiness and the teacher (symbol) disappeared, and she felt bliss. Stated another way, she had a tendency to project her bliss on a teacher rather than "own" her own bliss. To appreciate this standard dissociated hypnotic approach of creating symbols, we must understand that hypnosis, which uses symbolic representations, has its roots in pain control. Erickson was a master of pain control. To use symbols as a *first step* and as a *temporary* medium to create dissociation through the use of symbols is a *step* and one I employed in *Trances People Live*. However, like the map is not the territory, *the symbol is not the creator of the symbol*. For this reason, to discover who you are, symbolic representations which can be used as *temporary dissociators* can be used initially to *cope* with trauma. Ultimately, however, to fully process and complete the trauma so that it can no longer hold the observer's attention, the trauma must be explored *directly*. The use of symbolic de-sensitizers which create a counter trance to the trauma keeps the trauma in place and adds another layer of dissociation to the created trances. Therapists need to know that trances must go, not new trances of symbols used to create further dissociation from traumatic experiences. This is why reframing is a form of resistance. Why? Because we reframe experiences in order to avoid feeling what is really there. For example, for years I used Ericksonian approaches to hypnosis and psychotherapy with people suffering from issues of incest. The client always felt better at the end of the session and for a few days. Why? Hypnosis is for *pain control*, not for processing trauma and discovering who you are. Consequently, a client would leave and "feel better" because they were *not feeling* and *dissociating*. We all need to understand that if we enter into the Quantum Approach the focus is to find out *who you are*. The purpose is not to feel better right now because you might not, although ultimately you will. For now, however, it can be said that the clinical use of hypnosis with incest survivors is a *temporary* step to coping. It is not a long-term cure, because trances are being added on the trauma so the client cannot *feel it*. But the trauma will rear its ugly head either directly or in sublimated ways until the trauma is confronted. Why? Because the stored-up excess energy will pull and fixate the attention of the observer. It is only through working with the trauma that the excess energy of the observer is released, so that the observer no longer uses the trauma as a *window* from which to view present time reality.

Psychological Health

The first step in psychological health in the *Tao of Chaos* can be viewed in this way: *The willingness to experience anything*. This does not mean, "Far-out, I want to get punched in the face." It does mean, however, that I am willing to experience whatever is going on with me in my internal subjective inner world. This willingness is the *Tao of Chaos*.

Highlighted Case Example

Therapist: How are you doing after the divorce?

Client: I feel like I have lost my I-dentity since Ted and I broke up. Like now what do I do? In the past, I would always go along with what Ted wanted, so I am confused as to who I am, but I am trying to ignore that and get busy with my life.

> ### Therapeutic Note
>
> A sudden divorce after so many years of marriage is a shock to the system and carries grief. Grief is a biological process not a psychological one. In this sense, the grief and shock must be handled first, before she can make any life decisions.

Therapist: What are you feeling right now?

Client: Confused.

Therapist: Where do you feel the confusion in your body?

Client: In my face.

Therapist: Create the confusion in your face.

Client: I can't create it, it is already there.

Therapist: Okay, make a xerox copy of the confusion.

Client: Okay.

Therapist: Make three more xerox copies of the confusion.

Client: Okay.

Therapist: Now, let go of the copies.

Client: Okay.

Therapist: Now notice the shape of the confusion.

Client: Okay.

Therapist: Now merge with the confusion 100 percent.

Client: Okay.

Therapist: Now intentionally choose for the confusion to be there.

Client: Okay.

Therapist: Now experience the confusion as energy.[1]

---

[1] For further details on seeing states of consciousness and emotions as energy, see *Quantum Consciousness: Volume I*, Chapter 4.

Client: Okay.
Therapist: How are you doing?
Client: Clearer.

Therapeutic Note
Here we are encountering the first trance of confusion. She has been resisting being confused by trying to "get clear." Hence, I ask her to create the trance *knowingly* with awareness—that which she has been creating *unknowingly* without awareness.

Therapist: What are you feeling right now?
Client: Numb.
Therapist: Where do you feel the numbness in your body?
Client: My heart.
Therapist: What is the size and shape of the numbness?
Client: Like a round cocoon.
Therapist: Make several xerox copies of the cocoon.
Client: Okay.
Therapist: Now, let the copies go and merge with the numbness of the cocoon.
Client: Okay.
Therapist: Can you experience the numbness of the cocoon as slow moving energy?
Client: Okay.

Therapeutic Note
Once again to emphasize, the trances of confusion and numbness protected Barbara from experiencing her biological grief. Furthermore, the trances are held in place by a cognitive distortion, i.e., the grief of this divorce *must not* be allowed.

Therapist: What are you feeling right now?
Client: (she begins to sob) Overwhelming pain and grief.

Therapist: Feel the grief.

Client: I am.

(After several minutes pass)

Therapist: What's happening now?

Client: I feel like I have a hole in my heart.

Therapist: Peel back the hole and what is there?

Client: I feel like going to sleep.

Therapist: Create the feeling of sleep as a very slow moving energy and merge with that energy.

Client: Okay.

Therapeutic Note

Here we have a layer of unconsciousness (sleep) that stands in front of the passageway to Essence and which is representative of the #9 fixation of attention.

Therapist: How do you feel right now?

Client: Relaxed but present.

Therapist: Peel back the relaxed feeling and tell me what is there.

Client: Empty space.

Therapist: Enter into the empty space and tell me what you feel.

Client: Peaceful, calm, like I'm home.

Therapist: Now, move forward and feel the grief.

(once again she sobs for a few minutes)

Therapist: Now, move back into the emptiness.

Client: That feels better.

Therapist: Now move into the grief.

Client: Okay.

Therapist: Now move back into the emptiness.

Client: Okay.

Therapist: How are you doing?

Client: Better, but I still don't know what I'm going to do?

Therapist: This week for homework I would like you to practice moving from the empty space to the grief and from the grief to the empty space until you feel okay and willing to feel the grief.

Client: I'll try, but I'm afraid of being overwhelmed.

Therapist: Practice this week feeling just a little grief, and if the grief becomes to much, go back into the empty space.

Client: That I can do.

Therapeutic Note

This is a good place to leave the work. Grief is biological and as such needs time to work itself out. For this reason, I wanted to give her a taste of the grief and a full course meal of the Essence. As she was a beginner in therapy, it was important to let her know that there is Essence and order beyond the chaos of grief. In this way, she can begin to allow her biological grief while simultaneously she begins her relationship to her essential self, which she said she doesn't know.

Conclusion

To conclude, this fixation and this section I would like to reiterate we are not one character type or one fixation of attention. The universe is in constant motion. Therefore we are a combination of character types and fixations of attention. Furthermore, we move from one fixation to another in a very specific pattern. Therefore, temporarily know and process your fixations and move on to the next one. Realize that there is probably *one* that will take a long time to get to know. In this knowing and familiarity, awareness will build and freedom will come from the effects of the fixation and the trauma of loss of being explored. This will ultimately lead to cutting the chains of personality or in its yoga terms, loosening the knot of the heart.

ADVANCED ATTENTION TRAINING

Attention: "The concentration of the mind on an object." (American College Dictionary, p. 80)

A-tension is where the observer/personality over fixates its a-tension to overcompensate for its weakness or feeling of lack. For this reason, tension is felt around specific areas where a *lack* is perceived.

In the last chapter we looked at the observer/personality dyad and how it fixates its attention and uses a particular strategy to resist the trauma of the loss of being and the perception of inner emptiness as a *lack* of something. Then we looked at the Identities or clusters of Identities of the observer/personality dyad. We explored how each I-dentity is facing forward or outward in search of itself or its Essence. Unfortunately, as we have discovered, the observer/personality dyad is "looking for itself in all the wrong places."

To more deeply appreciate and take apart I-dentities, it is important to dive more deeply in the area of attention, and how it works. In *Trances People Live: Healing Approaches in Quantum Psychology*, I spoke of a trance being created by *a fixation* or a shrinking of the focus of attention. Once that attention is shrunken and fixated on an object, a person, or an event, the observer goes into a trance, blocking out all other resources. In *The Dark Side of the Inner Child* the observer fixates its attention on the child and uses that created child state as a *window* from which to see the world. We must understand that although we think we see external reality, the fixated attention of the observer limits our view of reality, and hence we see only that which our subjective trances allow. Unfortunately, this fixation of attention becomes so habitual that the observer's attention remains "fixated" and we habitually see in one way, have one world view, or one view of self.

Attention, therefore, becomes a primary source of interest, because it is through the medium of attention that an observer limits their awareness and thus creates their subjective experience.

In the last Chapter we shifted the observer's fixated attention by asking the observer to break the habit of facing outward and to return to Essence; to turn toward Essence; and shift its fixation of attention *inward*. This inward shift of the observer to see the world from Essence rather than through an apparent outward fixation of attention through personality type is the therapy. Our next step is to move even farther beyond the enneagramic observer/personality dyad by first working with the letting go of the observer and secondly exploring how the observer utilizes its attention.

The Observer Is A Trance

We have explored that the observer fixates its attention using a particular fixation strategy to avoid the pain of the loss of Being. The observer, as mentioned earlier, is arguably a *higher function* of personality. The observer is, however, personality, not Essence. The observer observes erecting an object through the act of observation. Essence is observation with no object or G. I. Gurdjieff's Objective Consciousness. To go beyond the observer and experience objective consciousness, we must recognize that the observer is a trance, or a *frozen* position in consciousness that develops to varying degrees during the growth and development of the personality. This appears to be contradictory. The observer is an I-dentity, and yet we want to enter objective consciousness; isn't there an observer in objective consciousness? No, an observer observes and there is a subject (observer) object (observed). In objective consciousness, beyond the observer, the observer and observer are seen as one. At that junction, the observer observed dyad disappears. Here there is observation with no object. The ordinary observer is a trance because it is frozen, has no motion, and consists of a separate fixation. As mentioned in *Quantum Consciousness: Volume I*, there are an infinite number of observers each with different created observations.

Both psychological and spiritual systems have been developed to access this observer quality as a step in consciousness. However, to go beyond the personality and make Essence a *station*, we must dismantle the observer as a fixation, a contraction, or a condensation of undifferentiated consciousness. Stated another way, when undifferentiated consciousness condenses, it becomes self-consciousness and the subject/object observer, which *is* a "higher function" of personality arises, but is still in duality and hence is personality. As a note, the final state of Raja Yoga, translated as The King of Yogas, Yoga being defined as Union, is Samadhi. Samadhi means no me—hence no observer/observed, just pure awareness with no object.

To do this we will explore the observer as a trance that fixates and becomes what it observes. Next we will dismantle the observer trance so that observation with no object or objective consciousness which is our nature can naturally emerge.

Characteristics of Attention and Observation

Let us begin by looking at how attention works. Noted Sufi Master Idries Shah states: "It is most important that individuals realize:

1. That this attention factor is operating in virtually all transactions.

2. That the apparent motivation of transactions may be other than it really is. And that it is often generated by the need or desire for attention activity (giving, receiving, exchanging).

3. The attention activity, like any other demand for food, warmth, etc. when placed under *volitional* control, must result in increased scope for the human being who would then *not* be at the mercy of random sources of attention...." (*Learning How to Learn*, Idries Shah, p. 85)

Here Idries Shah is saying that the observer and I-dentities have three primary strategies in relating. One, they can give attention to a person, object or event. Second, they can receive attention from a person, object or event; or third, they can exchange attention with a person, object, or event.

"Confusion is caused by the fact that the object of attention can be a person, a cult, an object, an idea, interest, etc. Because the foci of attention can be so diverse people have not yet identified the common factor - the *desire for attention.*" (*Learning How to Learn*, Idries Shah, p. 87)

Here Shah is designating that the desire of an observer for attention is the underlying motivation for the observer's interactions both internally with thoughts and emotions and externally with people, objects, or events.

Therefore, for us to be able to notice the underlying modus operandi of an observer and how the observer uses attention allows us to take apart and move beyond our identification with the old habitual fixated pattern of the observer. For example, if I, as an observer, had always given my attention to a dysfunctional parent and gave myself up, that habitual pattern of the observer to give attention to others and disregard my own wishes becomes an automatic pattern of attention. The observer creates an age-regressed I-dentity which continues to re-enact that fixation of attention in present time through trance-ference with authority figures.

Therefore, the first step in Advanced Attention Training is to dismantle attention patterns so that an observer is not continually looking through the same window of reality.

Advanced Attention Training, Part I

Tao of Chaos Exercise #47

Step I   Notice a thought.

Step II   Is the observer giving attention to the thought, receiving attention from the thought, or exchanging attention with a thought?

Tao of Chaos Exercise #48

Step I   Notice an emotion.

Step II   Is the observer giving attention to the emotion, receiving attention from the emotion, or exchanging attention with an emotion?

Tao of Chaos Exercise #49

Step I   Notice an object.

Step II   Is the observer giving attention to the object, receiving attention from the object, or exchanging attention with an object?

Tao of Chaos Exercise #50

Step I   Notice a person.

Step II   Is the observer giving attention to the person, receiving attention from the person, or exchanging attention with the person?

Notice with each circumstance if there is a giving, receiving or exchanging of attention.

Advanced Attention Training, Part II

This first step enables us to explore how the observer uses attention in relationship to the observed, i.e., thought, feeling, event, or another person.

We can notice that not only do we as observers place attention on a thought, an object, or a person, but the thought or internal image demands attention in the same way.

Idries Shah says it this way. "People demand attention. The right kind of attention at suitable times leads to the maintenance of a thriving individual. Ignorance of the *attention-need* leads to too much or too little intake of attention.

Ignorance of the attention factor, too, leads to mistaking attention demand for something else. This something else is the social, psychological, or other ritual which people think is the essential reason for human contact. In fact, it is only one ingredient of human contact and interchange.

It is a basic error to imagine that only a human being can be involved in the attention situation. Some of the most important attention situations concern real or imagined sources of attention other than human ones." (*Reflections: Fables in the Sufi Tradition*, Idries Shah, Penguin Books, Inc., Maryland, 1971, p.14)

What Shah is suggesting here is that an internal image, thought or emotion is an alive energy that wants attention. For example, if the observer fixates on a trauma and the energy is not released, the observer probably will create a trance such as dissociating or negative hallucination to "not see" the trauma. The thoughts, emotions, images, and excess energy bound up in the trauma seek the attention of an observer. For that reason experiment with the following exercises.

Tao of Chaos Exercise #51

Step I   Notice an image.

Step II   Is the image giving attention to the observer, receiving attention from the observer, or exchanging attention with the observer?

Notice with each circumstance if there is a giving, receiving or exchanging of attention.

Tao of Chaos Exercise #52

Step I   Notice a thought you are having.

Step II   Is the thought giving attention to the observer, taking attention from the observer, or exchanging attention with the observer?

Tao of Chaos Exercise #53

Step I   Notice an emotion you are having.

Step II   Is the emotion giving attention to the observer, taking attention from the observer, or exchanging attention with the observer?

Tao of Chaos Exercise #54

Step I   Notice an object you are having.

Step II   Is the object giving attention to the observer, taking attention from the observer, or exchanging attention with the observer?

Tao of Chaos Exercise #54

Step I   Notice a person.

Step II   Is the person giving attention to the observer, taking attention from the observer, or exchanging attention with the observer?

Tao of Chaos Exercise #55

Step I   Notice an image you are having.

Step II   Is the image giving attention to the observer, taking attention from the observer, or exchanging attention with the observer?

Advanced Attention Training, Part III

The Knower Aspect of the Observer

In *Quantum Consciousness: Volume I* we emphasized that the observer also has a creative aspect. The observer creates what it is observing. The observer also has a *knowing* aspect, which means that the observer has knowledge about what it creates. For example, an observer creates the thought, "I like myself" and the observer also knows the thought "I like myself" and what it is and means. In this way the observer is also a knower, or better said, the observer possesses the knowledge of what it creates.

The knower is the knowing at the level of Essence in *Quantum Consciousness: Volume I*. In this way, we explored that the observer/knower is the known. More simply put, the observer and the observed are one unit, and are made of the same substance. This is a major quantum jump of understanding because experience can only occur if the observer/knower of the experience and the observed/known are seen as different.

Normally we experience one observer watching or witnessing the observables like, "I love myself" or "I hate myself" or images from the past coming and going. It appears as though there is one observer/knower. However, with each known, i.e., "I love myself" or "I hate myself", there is a different and new observer/knower which arises and subsides as a unit with each observed/known.

The Knower/Observer

To understand the knower/observer and its impact on attention and experiences, let us imagine a wall with 10 different portholes (like portholes of a ship). In each porthole there is a different knower/observer which sees a different version of reality. For example, let's imagine you are in a relationship and your partner shows up 10 minutes late for lunch. If you look through porthole #1, the observer sees an inconsiderate person leaving you waiting. If you look through porthole #2, the observer sees a partner who is always late for appointments. The observer in porthole #3 experiences fear that possibly there was some accident or mishap. If you look through porthole #4, the observer sees a partner who is probably taking care of an errand that you didn't want to do and so you feel relieved. In each porthole a different "view" and hence a different perception of reality.

What becomes obvious is that each porthole has a different observer/knower which will provide that limited experience of reality. The appearance is that there is a single knower/observer that is looking through all these different portholes. The *subtle* fact is that each porthole has *a different knower/observer*. Simply stated, there appears to be one knower/observer you probably call "yourself" which knows all these different portholes. The fact is that there is a *different knower/observer for each porthole*. Each knower/observer can only observe and know its particular *knowingness* (perception of reality and experience). This illusion of one knower/observer is a major problem in the area of chaos. People have resistance to not having one stable, localized, unchanging knower/observer; that resistance causes trauma. In psychotherapy for example, we can understand that there are different parts of ourselves with different perceptions and experiences. Obviously, a little girl/boy part of ourselves wants different things than an adult part of ourselves. The attempt by psychotherapy to integrate all of the parts into one unified whole is a basic assumption that causes trauma. *Each part of ourselves has a different knower/observer of the part and hence has limited knowledge.* This means that the knower/observer of, "I like myself" only knows that knowledge called "I like myself." A different knower/observer knows and observes "I don't like myself." With the confines of the knower/know ("I like myself") there is no knowledge of "I don't like myself." Likewise the knower that has the knowledge of "I don't like myself" has only the "I don't like myself knowledge", not the "I like myself" knowledge.

This is why a knower of "I like myself" cannot know the knowing of "I don't like myself," and the knower of "I don't like myself" cannot know "I like myself." For this reason when a knower of "I don't like myself" appears, the knowledge of 1 hour ago "I liked myself" cannot be available. Simply put, each knower has specific and limited knowledge. To go further one must go beyond the observer and the knower to pure knowing with no object.

Let's go back to our porthole metaphor. It appears as though there is *one* knower that opens each porthole, looks through the porthole, and sees and experiences a particular reality. Actually *there are numerous knowers which appear and disappear each having different knowledge or knowing.* And each knower has different knowing and hence thoughts, feelings, emotions, memories and associations. For example, lets say you are in a Mom I-dentity. That I-dentity and the observer of that Mom I-dentity have certain memories, associations, and skills. Simply put, the observer *and* the observed are one unit and arise and subside together.

Why Chaos?

By imagining there is one *organizing knower or observer* which looks through portholes of reality resists the chaos of disappearance. Actually, numerous knowers with their knowing appear and disappear, as a unit. These knowers with their knowing appear and disappear just as what you call *you*, appears and disappears.

Consciousness

What gives us this illusion of one permanent knower? *Consciousness.* Consciousness is that subtle substance that makes and tells us what reality is and isn't. This is not to be confused with undifferentiated consciousness which is emptiness/fullness. This is differentiated consciousness. Years ago while in India, I worked with my teacher, Nisargadatta Maharaj. One day a psychiatrist and his wife came and asked him this very long question about good actions, bad actions, past lives, future lives, etc. He responded, "Who told you that you exist?" When no answer came from the two questioners he said,

"Consciousness tells you that you exist, and you believe it, if you understand just this, it is enough."

What he was saying was that each knower and the knowing it has, is the same consciousness knowing itself. Consciousness tells you there is a subject called a knower and an object called a known. More simply put, a stable subject observer that sees "the inconsiderate partner is late." Consciousness gives the illusion that the knower of "inconsiderate partner" and the knowledge called "inconsiderate partner" are different. Actually *consciousness is both the knower and the knowledge. Trauma occurs when the knower resists its own disappearance* by imagining it (the knower) and the known are made of different substances—not the *same consciousness.* Stated another way, if the knower understands that it and the knowing are the same consciousness, then the knower and the known (I-dentity) disappear, because there can only be a knower and an I-dentity as long as there is a subject/object relationship or contrasts.

Advanced Attention Training, Part IV

Tao of Chaos Exercise #56

Inner World

Step I   Notice a thought.

Step II   Notice the observer of the thought.

Step III   Is the observer giving attention to the thought, receiving attention from the thought, or exchanging attention with the thought?

Step IV See the observer and the thought as being made of the same consciousness.

Tao of Chaos Exercise #57

Step I Notice a memory.

Step II Notice the observer of the memory.

Step III Is the observer giving attention to the thought, receiving attention from the thought, or exchanging attention with the thought?

Step IV See the observer and the memory as being made of the same consciousness.

Tao of Chaos Exercise #58

Step I Notice an emotion.

Step II Notice the observer of the emotion.

Step III Is the observer giving attention to the emotion, receiving attention from the emotion, or exchanging attention with the emotion?

Step IV See the observer and the emotion as being made of the same consciousness.

Tao of Chaos Exercise #59

Step I Notice an internal image.

Step II Notice the observer of the internal image.

Step III Is the observer giving attention to the internal image, receiving attention from the internal image, or exchanging attention with the internal image?

Step IV See the observer and the internal image as being made of the same consciousness.

Tao of Chaos Exercise #60

Step I   Notice a person.

Step II   Notice the observer of the person.

Step III   Is the observer giving attention to the person, receiving attention from the person, or exchanging attention with the person?

Step IV   See the observer and the person as being made of the same consciousness.

Tao of Chaos Exercise #61

Step I   Notice a thought.

Step II   Notice the observer of the thought.

Step III   Is the thought giving attention to the observer, taking attention from the observer, or exchanging attention with the observer?

Step IV   See the observer of the thought and the thought as being made of the same consciousness.

Tao of Chaos Exercise #62

Step I   Notice an emotion.

Step II   Notice the observer of the emotion.

Step III   Is the emotion giving attention to the observer, taking attention from the observer, or exchanging attention with the observer?

Step IV   See the observer of the emotion and the emotion as being made of the same consciousness.

Tao of Chaos Exercise #63

Step I   Notice an internal image.

Step II   Notice the observer of the internal image.

Step III   Is the internal image giving attention to the observer, taking attention from the observer, or exchanging attention with the observer?

Step IV   See the observer of the internal image and the internal image as being made of the same consciousness.

Tao of Chaos Exercise #64

Step I   Notice a person.

Step II   Notice the observer of the person.

Step III   Is the person giving attention to the observer, taking attention from the observer, or exchanging attention with the observer?

Step IV   See the observer of the person and the person as being made of the same consciousness.

Tao of Chaos Exercise #65

Step I   Notice an object.

Step II   Notice the observer of the object.

Step III   Is the object giving attention to the observer, taking attention from the observer, or exchanging attention with the observer?

Step IV   See the observer of the object and the object as being made of the same consciousness.

Advanced Attention Training, Part V
The Cliff Notes

Knowingness

What does this leave us with? Knowingness, with no object, awareness with no object, no individual consciousness, and hence no subject/object. Knowingness is pure isness, yet the paradox of knowingness is that you can never know it. Why? Because in pure knowingness there is no subject/object consciousness, therefore you can just *BE* knowingness.

All states of consciousness only exist because consciousness says they do. Actually, the state of consciousness and the knower of the state of consciousness are the same consciousness. Someone once asked Nisargadatta Maharaj, "Are you in samadhi?" (a no me state of consciousness). He replied, "No, samadhi is a state, I am not in any state." Pure knowingness is no-state and is not knowable because there is no knower. If there is no knower there is no state. Therefore, there is just knowingness with no subject/object.

The Cliff Notes

No matter what experience you are having ask yourself, "What knower or observer is observing that?" Notice what happens.

Tao of Chaos Exercise #66

Step I	Notice an internal state of consciousness that you are in, i.e., confusion, anger, neutral, etc.
Step II	Ask yourself, "What knower knows this state?"
Step III	Notice what occurs when you look for and question "Who is the knower?"

Tao of Chaos Exercise #67

Step I   Notice a perception of an object, i.e., a chair, a bed, a couch, etc.

Step II   Ask yourself, "What knower knows this object?"

Step III   Notice what occurs when you look for the knower.

Tao of Chaos Exercise #68

Step I   Notice an internal image, impression, or memory.

Step II   Ask yourself, "What knower knows this impression?"

Step III   Notice what occurs when you look for the knower.

Tao of Chaos Exercise #69

Step I   Notice a thought.

Step II   Ask yourself, "What knower knows this thought?"

Step III   Notice what occurs when you look for the knower.

Tao of Chaos Exercise #70

Step I   Notice a feeling.

Step II   Ask yourself, "What knower knows this feeling?"

Step III   Notice what happens when you look for the knower.

Tao of Chaos Exercise #71

Step I   Notice a perception of the world.

Step II   Ask yourself, "What knower knows this perception?"

Step III Notice what happens to the perception when you look for the knower.

In order for us to move along we must look at the attention an observer exerts on an idea, emotion, memory, object, or person.

Review

1. The I-dentity either gives, receives, or exchanges attention with thought, emotions, memories, objects, people, etc.

2. Each I-dentity possess different memories, associations, reactions, perceptions, etc.

3. There are many knowers/observers.

4. Each knower has an I-dentity which is a unit of Knower/I-dentity.

5. Each Knower/I-dentity unit arises and subsides together.

6. The Knower and the I-dentity are made of the same substance.

Advanced Attention Training Part VI
Attention and the Knower-I-dentity Unit

It is often difficult to let go of a tightly knit Knower/I-dentity unit. Why? Because the knower gives, receives, or exchanges attention with the thought, emotion, memory, object or person. This attention exchange is the glue that holds them together and gives them the appearance they are made of a different substance. Therefore to move beyond this Knower/I-dentity unit, the a-tension between them must be experienced and acknowledged.

Tao of Chaos Exercise #72

Inner World

Step I   Notice a thought.

Step II   Notice the observer observing the thought.

Step III Ask the observer, "Are you (the observer) giving attention to the thought, receiving attention from the thought, or exchanging attention with the thought?" *Wait for a response from the observer.*

Step IV   Now see the observer and thought as the same substance.

Step V   Notice what happens.

Tao of Chaos Exercise #73

Step I   Notice an emotion.

Step II   Notice the observer observing the emotion.

Step III Ask the observer, "Are you (the observer) giving attention to the emotion, receiving attention from the emotion, or exchanging attention with the emotion?" *Wait for a response from the observer.*

Step IV   Now see the observer and emotion as the same substance.

Step V   Notice what happens.

Tao of Chaos Exercise #74

Step I   Notice a memory.

Step II   Notice the observer observing the memory.

Step III   Ask the observer, "Are you (the observer) giving attention to the memory, receiving attention from the memory, or exchanging attention with the memory?" *Wait for a response from the observer.*

Step IV   Now see the observer and memory as the same substance.

Step V   Notice what happens.

Tao of Chaos Exercise #75

Step I   Notice an object.

Step II   Notice the observer observing the object.

Step III   Ask the observer, "Are you (the observer) giving attention to the object, receiving attention from the object, or exchanging attention with the object?" *Wait for a response from the observer.*

Step IV   Now see the observer and object as the same substance.

Step V   Notice what happens.

Tao of Chaos Exercise #76

Step I Notice a person.

Step II Notice the observer observing the person.

Step III Ask the observer, "Are you (the observer) giving attention to the person, receiving attention from the person, or exchanging attention with the person?" *Wait for a response from the observer.*

Step IV Now see the observer and person as the same substance.

Step V Notice what happens.

Conclusion

The Cliff Notes of Advanced Attention Training

When this becomes clearer and you find yourself in any state ask; *What observer is observing that?* This can move you beyond the observer/observed dyad very rapidly and into objective consciousness.

These exercises are designed to free you from the observer I-dentity unit so that you can *be awareness* with no object.

Why is this beyond the fixations of attention? The fixation of attention is a strategy that the observer uses to fixate attention and hence resist the loss of Essence. The observer *is* the knower and part of the personality and keeps the observer/personality dyad type there through the use of attention. Since we can be aware of the observer, it can be said that the observer is a "higher" function of personality, and yet is made of the same substance as personality. Once the observer/observed disappears we are left with G. I. Gurdjieff's "objective consciousness" or consciousness with no object. This was also called the I I by Ramana Maharishi.

In the final analysis, each knower has different knowing. Trauma is formed because we resist the experience that there is not one stable knower but rather many knowers that have motion; i.e., which appear and disappear. If we allow the appearance and disappearance to naturally occur without the assumption that we have a *definite* location and have always been here (the illusion of time), there is no internal experience of trauma. If we resist and insist that we are in a particular location and are this one stable organizing knower, we will know TRAUMA. In the no-state of objective consciousness, the issue of chaos and order never arises.

This understanding of the appearance and disappearance of different knowers and knowings as a unit which are both made of consciousness is something that may not occur overnight. To give up the knower/knowledge observer/observed unit which holds the knowledge of location, and to take apart the attention between the observer/ observed dyad along with the knower that knows the knowledge of duration (time), is to master the *Tao of Chaos*.

In January of 1979 I was visiting Nisargadatta Maharaj. He was talking about birth and death, and I began seeing past images of when I was a client in therapy, seeing births and deaths. He said to me, "Who is the *knower* of the knowledge of your birth?" I thought to myself, "Who is the knower of the knowledge of my birth," scratching my head. Later that day, when I returned to see him I said, "I have a knower of the knowledge of my birth, so there is a knower while I was born and a knower will be there when I die. There are many different knowers." He nodded and said, "Of course." It wasn't for many years until I realized that each knower has different knowing; one which knows my birth, one which knows my death. Each knower appeared and will disappear and I am beyond any knower/known or observer/observed dyad. It is this resistance to letting go of the knower-known dyad, which you call yourself, that freezes chaos. This is why it takes time to integrate the no-state state of the non-Being Being which is prior to the consciousness of differences and is the *Tao of Chaos*.

THE YIN AND YANG OF CHAOS

As we look back over our sojourn in the world of chaos; Yin and Yang are the perfect metaphors. Throughout *Quantum Consciousness: Volume I*, we talked about form being condensed emptiness and emptiness being thinned-out form. The Yin and Yang symbol, because of it's lack of apparent movement, being in a picture, looks as if emptiness is immoveable, boundaried, and separate from form which also appears as solid. This does not encompass the true meaning of Yin and Yang.

Yang, the active or solid principle, Yin, the passive empty principle, are not two boundaried distinct principles. Rather, the emptiness of Yin condenses down forming the solidness of Yang, and the solid Yang thins out, becoming the emptiness of Yin. This can be easily demonstrated if you close your eyes and catch a thought passing through the empty space. It appears as though the thought (Yang) appeared in the empty space of Yin. After the thought leaves, the Yin or empty space is left. Because of the nature of the *Embodied Mind*, they seem separate, as if the Yin (the emptiness) is separate from the Yang (the thought), and the Yang (the thought) is separate form the Yin (the emptiness). Nothing could be further from the truth. Actually what occurs is that the emptiness of Yin becomes the thought which is Yang, and the thought which is Yang becomes the emptiness of Yin.

Watching the process, they seem separate and boundaried when actually the Yin becomes the Yang and the Yang becomes the Yin; or emptiness becomes form, form becomes emptiness. In the Yoga tradition they would say, Shiva the Yin becomes Shakti the Yang. However, just as you cannot separate the sun from its rays, you cannot separate the Yin from the Yang.

In the land of physics, David Bohm would say the explicate of energy, space, mass, and time (the Yang) enfolds to become the implicate (the Yin), and the implicate (Yin) unfolds to become the explicate of energy, space, mass, and time (the Yang). The Yin and the Yang of the implicate and explicate orders are in one constant *movement*, in a beautiful pulsation, or as called in Sanskrit, spanda, or divine throb.

Where does chaos ultimately fit in? Chaos is a *description of the movements* of Yang becoming Yin and Yin becoming Yang. Stated in the language of Quantum, *chaos is the description of the process* that the explicate appears to be going through to reach the order which is Yin, and Chaos is the process that Yin goes through to be Yang.

What appears as Chaos is not chaos at all. Chaos is the dynamic nature and movement from chaos (Yang) to order (Yin) and from order (Yin) to chaos (Yang).

Intermittently, it can be said that the Yang of chaos, becomes the Yin of Order and the Yin of Order becomes the Yang of chaos. Ultimately, as we continue to see the order in what appears to us subjectively as chaos, and the chaos in the order we realize that as Yin cannot be separated from Yang; so chaos and order are inseparable. In this way, we are left with the late David Bohm's "unbroken wholeness" beyond the no-state state, to the non-ordered order of the non-chaotic chaos, that is Quantum Consciousness.

With love,
Your brother,
Stephen

THE CLIFF NOTES OF
THE TAO OF CHAOS

1. All psychological systems are born out of resistance to chaos or an attempt to order chaos.

2. Include—allow—expand.

3. Allow chaos to order itself.

4. Discover the movement of emptiness becoming form and form becoming emptiness by going into chaos.

5. Become your own energetic generators at the level of Essence.

6. Question everything; see its fundamental presupposition, lie, and self-deception, and then give it up.

7. Eliminate the illusion of location.

8. Give up the mechanistic view that somehow the world is held together and that someone or something is in charge.

9. Be willing to experience not knowing, confusion, overwhelmed, and out-of-control.

10. Expressing feelings is not feeling feelings. Feeling feelings is feeling feelings.

11. Live without intention.

12. See everything as made of the same substance.

13. Experience the growing inner emptiness inside your body as your *Essence* or *Real Self.*

14. Know that although you experience your inner emptiness as separate from everyone else's inner emptiness— THERE IS ONLY ONE EMPTINESS.

15. Know that your inner emptiness is a passage to the great void of the underlying unity which is Quantum Consciousness.

SECTION IV

STREAMS OF CONSCIOUSNESS

TWENTY FOUR · COMPASSION, JUDGMENT, AND SELF-DECEPTION

Compassion has been held in high esteem for years both in psychological as well as spiritual disciplines. Compassion can be seen as an empathic understanding of another's plight. Compassion is not pejorative. It is not an intellectual process; nor is it a created response. All too often, compassion becomes "looking compassionate," "saying compassionate things," or "a supportive hug of understanding." This is *not* compassion, but one person's idea of what compassion looks like, acts like, or sounds like. Compassion is a feeling sense that takes place in the body that brings forth a sense of humanity and connection. I notice, for example, when I "feel compassion," it is a present-time *body* sense, a felt presence, a relationship in present time of being to being that feels connected.

In "spiritual" circles the body is seen as an *obstacle*. In psychological circles the body is often neglected in favor of the mind. Body therapies like Feldenkrais, Rolfing, Bio-energetics emphasize the body with the experience of being grounded in one's body. Or stated more exactly, embodying one's body. Embodying one's body is a major step. The next step, however, is beyond being grounded in one's body, and is spiritual in the true sense of the word. Spiritual, as discussed in *The Dark Side* *of the Inner Child* is the recognition of the underlying unity. This *includes the body*. The final understanding in spiritual disciplines is Tat Tvam Asi. I AM THAT. This *includes* the body as *THAT*. This means that since everything is one indivisible substance, the body too is *THAT* same substance.*

The quantum jump is moving from being grounded and embodying one's body to including the underlying unity with the body and the psychological. In this way, the body is experienced as *THAT* one indivisible substance.

In my case, I dissociated as a child because of sexual abuse and thought I was "spiritual" by leaving my body. Furthermore, I reinforced this dysfunction by involving myself with certain yoga traditions which said, *you are not the body*. After years of body therapies, i.e., Rolfing, Feldenkrais, Reichian Therapy, Bioenergetics, etc., I got grounded in my body. The next step, which was not planned, occurred when I experienced my body as made of the same substance as the air, the couch, the ground, and everything. This is Tat Tvam Asi; everything *included* experientially and recognized as being made of the same one substance. This is the root of compassion.

Compassion is a felt sense of that oneness, with the understanding that whatever occurred to "someone else," could have happened to "me." This brings us to the old saying, "There but for the Grace of God go I," or stated another way, "There but for the grace of the *emptiness* goes the I." This felt knowingness that whatever occurred, did not happen to you but could have, or simply stated; *Shit Happens*. This is compassion. Most psychological and spiritual traditions ask, call for, or hold compassion as a quality of consciousness to be sought after, cultivated, and developed. Compassion, however, is the root of I, the body, and everything all of which is made of the same undifferentiated substance.

---

*The topic of embodiment, body trances, and the Real Self in relation to the body will be the focus of my forthcoming book; *The Way of the Human*.

What might be explored is what stands in the way of *compassion* since compassion is a synonym for *connection*. Connection is always there, yet goes unnoticed because of psychological and emotional defenses and trances which prevent us from experiencing this compassion/connection. Compassion is not an outward cultivation like *learning* to listen, *learning* to be understanding, or *learning* to appreciate another. Compassion is in our body and is our ground of being. Compassion is who we are already. Compassion is a quality of Essence. If we create and learn "how to be compassionate, look compassionate, act compassionate, or say compassionate things," we feel separate from the person we are being compassionate to or for. In other words, in an attempt to "act compassionate" we are concerned with how we look to another, and there is a subtle sense of I am better than they are.

This often occurs because we imagine that people create their intrapsychic problem or physical illness. In actuality, it could have happened to anyone; "There but for the grace of the emptiness goes the I." Let us now explore the ways that prevent us from knowing the body felt compassion of *The Essence* of our *Real Self.*

Judgement

Most forms of psychology and spirituality would say that judgement of another or oneself is something to be gotten rid of, or certainly something you should stop doing. I had a girlfriend in college who broke up with me. In my pain I continued calling her, wanting her back. She said, "You should judge less and understand more." This lofty statement, although it was a nice cliche' was judgemental in itself. After all, I *should* be better than I was if I *judged* her less for leaving me and *understood* her position. The problem here was that I was suffering and wanted her back. Years later I began to understand that feelings, emotions, or thoughts are always being judged by a person as good, bad, or indifferent. For example, if I felt angry, I might judge myself bad, or if I felt caring I might judge myself good. What I noticed with myself and with others was that judging was a way I resisted experiencing things.

For example, in the case of my college girlfriend breaking up with me, I *was* judging her and having an outward focus of my attention on her rather than noticing what I was unwilling to experience within myself, which is an inward focus of attention on myself. It became clearer to me that it was because I was resisting experiencing my own suffering and pain that I was judging her. Simply put, by keeping my attention focused on her injustice to me, I was resisting *feeling* my pain. Why did I not just feel the pain? Because it was *painful* and I would feel *vulnerable*, if I felt it.

Vulnerability is a two-edged sword; we seek it in relationship as an important vehicle to feeling connected, and we run from it simultaneously by focusing our attention outward and judging. Try this exercise for a moment; whenever you are feeling judgemental of yourself or another simply ask yourself, "By being judgmental what am I resisting experiencing?" When you have the answer, become willing to experience what it is. You might be surprised to find out that vulnerability is a *must* if you want to feel the connected and compassionate aspects of Essence which *is humanity and The Way of the Human.*

Self-Deception

One of the most important ingredients to the lack of compassion in our society is self-deception. Lying to oneself about our motives, justifying our own actions with rationalizations, and pretending to be better than we are. These are the symptoms of self-deception. *When we deceive ourselves by lying to ourselves about what we have done, what our motives or intentions really are; we objectify others.* This means that if we lie to ourselves about a quality we have within ourselves, such as stealing, we will intensely criticize those who steal. The degree to which we criticize another, is the degree to which we deny in ourselves the same quality. The old saying, "We criticize most in others that which we see in ourselves" remains the truth in the understanding of allowing our true nature of compassion to emerge. For example, recently I found myself very angry and critical of fellow professionals who were making grandiose claims of how their procedures could and have cured *everything*. I began to objectify my colleagues, judging them as "bad," and certainly not as good as me. When I turned my attention around and began to look at my lies, i.e., how I had lied to others about my successes in therapy, or my claims and success stories, I could see that I, too, was a practitioner of this grandiosity. My self-deception was not admitting to myself that I had done things, or certainly thought about doing things, that were similar to what I was complaining about others doing. When you deceive yourself you must objectify and dehumanize the other you are criticizing. This objectification and dehumanizing, which is initiated by self-deception, forces us to lose our humanity, our humanness, and hence our connection to our body which is the root of compassion. In other words, when you resist experiencing something, deny an unwanted quality within yourself you will probably objectify others, dehumanize them, deny in yourself the same quality they have, and lose the connection to your own body which is the vehicle of compassion. Often as a practise for myself, I just sit with people and *see* them as human beings; not objectifying them. Rather, I just appreciate that next to me is a person with a whole universe of thought, feelings, sensations, fantasies, broken dreams, etc. right in front of me. Experiencing this allows me to *not objectify*, but to connect and appreciate in an entirely different and deeper way both their and my humanness.

Lies and Self-Hatred

Every time we tell a lie to ourself or another we are demonstrating self-hatred. For example, if I lie to myself about my inabilities, I am denying my lack of ability. If I lie to you about who I am, I am saying at some level that I hate who I am, and I want to convince you through my lying that I am not the way I really am.

The simple solution to lying to another is to ask yourself, "By telling this lie, what am I resisting or hating about myself?" Becoming aware of the I-dentity that hates itself for being a certain way allows us to see how we over-compensate by presenting an image that is acceptable. For example, if I see myself as selfish, and deny its existence, I judge it bad or wrong. I will then probably present an image of generosity to another as a way of defending and compensating for the self-hatred. To take apart judgement, we must first confront our lies, self-deceptions, overcompensations, and criticisms of others.

Judgement = Envy

Often times we find ourselves criticizing others when in fact we are envious of others. For example, recently a client of mine told me that when she was young she was highly critical of wealthy business people. Years later, as an attorney, she became exactly like the wealthy business people she was so critical and judgemental about. What I realized was that her judgementalness toward this group of wealthy business people was the way she disguised her envy. In other words, she was judgemental because she wanted to have what they had. I asked her, "By being judgemental, what are you resisting knowing about yourself?" Eventually she went beyond envy to the experience that if they had something she wanted and didn't have, she would feel her own lack, as if she were less for not having what others had. When I pursued this, she said that she judged others so that she didn't have to feel her own *emptiness*, which she had decided was a lack within herself.

Ah yes, the resistance to emptiness again!!!

Dispelling the Myth

When something "bad" or unpleasant happens to ourselves and our friends we tend to get angry, judgemental, and lose our affinity. It seems we all hold a *myth* that somehow we would not, could not, or would *never* have done such a thing. This self-deceptive myth disconnects us from our total quantum self and hence disconnects us from our *human*-ity and compassion. Recently, I uncovered "my lie" about a business situation I had deceived myself about for seven years. My inability to "see" myself was wrapped up in my rationalization of who I was. In other words, my created self-image would not allow me to believe I would have acted unethically. Consequently, I would get angry at everyone else's lack of ethics by judging them and objectifying them. The outcome of this self-deception, i.e., that *I* was capable of the lack of ethics and hence accused others, led to anger and disconnection. A small price to pay for keeping my lie and image going. As soon as I realized my lie, I felt an overwhelming vulnerability, connection, and compassion for everyone. Why? For two reasons. First, to lie takes energy; and second, because I was no longer lying to myself which created boundaries to protect my self image from the vulnerability of my *humanness*, my essential connection to humanity. I am human and so is everyone else. If I could deceive myself, so could others. I was no better, worse, or different than everyone else. *I felt vulnerable, compassionate, connected, and human.*

The myth that "I would not do that"...fill in the blank...is really more than a myth, it is a *lie*.

Judgement and Boundaries

Another reason we judge others is because it seems to be the only way we can remain separate as an individual self. We judge others or ourselves as bad or different not only because we don't want to be like another, or don't want to admit we are like another, but because it is the only way we can be different. We judge others as a way to stay separate and, hence, maintain our boundaries.

I truly do not believe in racism or sexism. I believe that people judge anything that is different from them as bad so as to maintain individuality. Race, sex, and religious discrimination are only the symptoms of deep fear. In short, we judge others because there is a deep belief that if we didn't, we would merge, disappear, and never appear again. This can be a new view not of racism or sexism but what I call *differentism*. The individual self's survival is dependent on feeling *special* or *different* than others. Therefore, we feel fear as though our survival is threatened when we meet people who are different. Unfortunately people who discriminate turn the inward fear into outward anger and seek to destroy that which they were afraid of. For example, Nazi's had a feeling of envy and fear of the wealthy Jews in Germany. Rather than acknowledge their fear and envy which triggered their own sense of lack and fear which would have been an inward focus, they turned their inner lack and fear into anger. This movement turning unacknowledged lack and fear into outward anger, rage, and blame is at the core of racial, sexual, and religious discrimination.

A Psychology of Similarities

Quantum Psychology is a psychology of similarities. It emphasizes that we are all the same, all share the same emptiness, all are emanations of the one emptiness, and are made of the same substance. The psychology of similarities asks us to acknowledge that we are made of energy, space, mass, and time, are made of the same consciousness, and have the same mother and father—The Emptiness.

Compassion: The Ground of Essence: Releasing Self-Deception

My next step was to explore how to release my own lie and self-deception so that I could be more vulnerable. This required a willingness to return to my *body and to Essence: the ground of compassion*, the body-felt sense of interconnection. What I began to do was change my focus from outward to inward. To do this I began to notice whenever I was judgemental and critical of others' actions. I then took that outward energy and utilized it, looking within myself to discover if I had the quality that I was criticizing another for having. Asking myself, "Do I have this inside of me, or, have I ever done something like this and not acknowledged it?" More often than not, I did, and became willing to acknowledge my lie along with experiencing my pain, shame, or whatever was associated with this quality. To my surprise, I felt connected and compassionate to others as I saw the existence of, or even a possibility of its existence within myself.

One of the most powerful experiences of humanness and humanity I ever had was when I went to Incest Survivors Anonymous for the first time. There I was, sharing with everyone else my incest story. The energy it took to deny the incest was removed and the energy it took to maintain the images of nonincest were removed. All that energy that was placed on lying to myself and others was gone, and suddenly, I felt "true humanness and true spirituality"—the underlying body felt connection to all of humanity.

This approach to utilizing the *defensive* energy going outward to *judge* and objectify as a way of defending my inward lie became a way of going deeper within myself and feeling the delicious vulnerability of compassionate humanity. To my surprise, my college girlfriend of 22 years ago was right; "Judge less and understand more." I would say, use the outward defense of judging which you use to resist knowing your lie and feeling your resisted experiences; and *understand* you have the same capacity for the quality you are judging others for. R. D. Laing said it this way:

> All in All
> Each man (woman) in all men (women)
> all men (women) in each man (woman)
>
> All Being in each being
> each being in all being
>
> All in Each
> Each in All
>
> All distinctions are mind, by mind, in mind, of mind.
> No distinctions, no mind to distinguish.
> (*Knots*, R.D. Laing, Vintage Books, Random House, N.Y., 1970)

On Feelings
Expression—Repression—Feeling

Since the advent of the human potential movement over the last 30 years or so, feelings have played a major role in psychotherapy. In the 1960's until present time, people have moved from one side of the continuum called repression to the other side of the continuum called expression. Between these two extremes there was being willing to acknowledge feelings and have feelings.

In the 1990s it is time for us to move to yet another level; that level neither represses feelings nor expresses feelings.

This level *feels feelings*. In the repression of anger, for instance, many therapies would target how the repressed energy of anger seeks feeling through expression. Expression, however, which can be attested to by many people, keeps the reliving and redramatization experience alive. In other words, continued expression only brings on more of the same expression. Why? Because there is a belief in expressive therapies (which, by the way, I advocate as a step beyond repression) that if you somehow express your feelings, then you will be done with them and can move on.

Most of us have seen the fallacy of the little-questioned thesis of psychotherapy. Expression though a step to freedom, begets more expression. Furthermore, expression can be a clever way to resist feeling. In other words, to avoid feeling inward feelings, turn outward and express. Therefore, expressing feelings is not necessarily feeling feelings. Expressing feelings is often a way to *avoid* feeling feelings. Simply put, *expressing feelings is expressing feelings—feeling feelings is feeling feelings*. To move through feelings expression is a step—*feeling feelings is its completion*.

Feeling Feelings

Let me begin by saying first that you have to be willing to acknowledge and express and be willing to have feelings before you can feel feelings. *Feeling feelings* without judgement, evaluation, or significance is elaborated in detail in Chapter 4 of *Quantum Consciousness, Volume I*. However, through workshop presentations around the country, it has become apparent that this is a more crucial point than I realized before. To do this we must go through repression and expression. But to be willing to be your feelings 100 percent, merge with them 100 percent, have them 100 percent as energy is the process.

What then are the ingredients that enable us to move beyond the repression—expression continuum into feeling *feelings*?

1. Being willing to acknowledge there are feelings.
2. Being willing to have feelings.
3. Being willing to make them more intense.
4. Being able to remove the judgement, evaluation, or significance of the feelings; or what they mean about you as a person.
5. Being willing to *BE* the feeling 100 percent.
6. Being able to notice where in your body they are.
7. Being able to de-label feelings and feel them as energy.
8. Being willing to feel feelings as energy with *no intention of getting rid of the feeling*. No intention is crucial! If you are working with feelings in the attempt that through repression or expression they will go away, you are *resisting* the feeling and creating them again.
9. Being willing to not have the feeling. Freedom is the freedom to pick up or put down feelings at choice. The final step is to ask yourself "Am I free to have the feeling, am I free to not have the feeling?" If you are free to not have the feeling or have the feeling you have moved off of the repression—expression continuum.

The No-Solution Solution

Feel your feelings as energy. Just do it to do it without any goal or purpose. This is the no-solution solution.

Living With No Intention

To live with no intention or goal, to do, and be, just to do and be, is the no-intention intention. This requires feeling feelings as energy without being distracted by thoughts, stories, or reasons why. Better yet, see the thoughts, stories, impressions, and associations as energy.

Being willing to feel feelings as energy and living without intention is the *Tao of Chaos*.

TWENTY FIVE • FELDENKRAIS: THE BRAIN AND THE ORDERING OF CHAOS

Carl Ginsburg, Ph.D.
International Feldenkrias Trainer
Editor of The Master Moves and
Author of Medicine Journey's: Ten Stories

I was visiting a friend and he asked me to look at a print that he had hung on the wall of his study. My first impression was that it was some sort of abstraction for there seemed to be only a confusion in front of me of different shadings and subtle shifts of color. On closer inspection I began to see that the print was made up of tiny little squares that were either differently shaded or black or open. At first these seemed to be completely randomly located. Again closer inspection revealed some sort of repeat in the pattern, but it was not exact and did not appear to depict anything that I could see as *something*. My friend asked me to look at the print by looking at my own image, faint as it was, in the glass covering the print. At first I did not see anything different. Then, with extreme suddenness, I saw a three dimensional scene with a canyon, a jagged ridge in the foreground and the image of a bird like creature flying over the canyon. Just as suddenly with a shift in the way I was using my eyes, the print returned to what I had seen originally, a confusion of shadings and subtle shifts of color. I now tried to get back the three dimensional picture. It was not easy. Perhaps I tried too hard. But when it reappeared again, it did so with the same suddenness and disappeared in the same way. I realized then that the print was computer generated and that it contained some sort of shift in the pattern of squares that had the potential to elicit from my brain an organization that would be experienced as the three dimensional scene that I saw, because surely no one could see such a scene in examining the print in detail.

Two characteristics could be noted at this point. The first is that I either saw the three dimensional scene, or the flat abstract print of shadings. There was no in between and no seeing the two together. Trying to see the abstract while seeing the three dimensional scene immediately brought back the abstract print. There was no way to analyze or look for the scene. It either appeared or didn't. In other words there was no process of inference, that I know of, that brought about the scene. It was there to my experience or it wasn't there.

I am reminded of an experiment suggested by John Lilly some years ago. You need an old reel to reel tape recorder. You make a loop of tape so that the loop can run continuously through the machine. You then record a word, he suggested the word, cogitate, on the tape. Playing back the recorded word so that you hear the word repeated again and again becomes a strange experience. For the first few minutes you hear the word that you recorded. But then you begin to hear different words. When I did the experiment, I heard, at different times, five differing words as distinctly as I had heard the original cogitate. Again I heard either one word or another. The shift was always instantaneous. There was no direct relation of the sounds of these differing words to the original cogitate. Lilly reports in his book, *The Center of the Cyclone*, that in an experiment with three hundred subjects, three hundred different dictionary words and two thousand word like sounds were generated.

These experiences are highly suggestive of a strange idea. That contrary to the notion that our brains register sense data from out there in the world, our brains are *generating the organizations* that we take for things in the world. I am not saying that reality is merely created in the mind. What I will try to elucidate is the notion that there is no given raw sense data that makes sense, and that making sense requires the ordering of what initially is a chaotic jumble.

We have to ask the question, what is it to see, or hear, or feel, something as some particular thing that we know? The neurologist, Oliver Sacks, in an article in the *New Yorker* (To See and Not See, May 10, 1993) tells the fascinating story of a fifty year old man, Virgil, who regained his sight through surgery after having lost his vision in early childhood. This "miracle" of regaining sight was not what one would anticipate. Virgil was able to see colors and movement but could not identify objects or shapes. He could not fixate his eyes on a particular target, but made random movements with his eyes. To quote Sacks, "Sometimes surfaces or objects would seem to loom, to be on top of him, when they were quite a distance away; sometimes he would get confused by his own shadow—the whole concept of shadows, of objects blocking light, was puzzling to him—and would come to a stop, or trip, or try to step over it. Steps, in particular, posed a special hazard, because all he could see was a confusion, a flat surface, of parallel and crisscrossing lines; he could not see them (although he knew them) as solid objects going up or coming down in three dimensional space." He had a terrible time discerning the cat from the dog and had to repeatedly examine the cat, for example, which he recognized by touch, or be told again and again that he was seeing the cat. Sacks reports that Virgil felt more disabled five weeks after the operation than he had when he was sightless.

Notice that it is not just the organization of perceptual seeing that is lacking for Virgil but also the ability to organize his eye movements. It is, I believe, impossible to see in a *functional way*, i.e., to perceive objects and space, without *organizing one's movements and that perception and movement ability arise simultaneously.* In any case without the ability of the *nervous system to create such organization*, one is faced with again, *chaos.*

I tried to imagine what it was to be in Virgil's situation, and I found a parallel in my first experiences in France. Although I had studied French in school, and I had some vocabulary and could read and understand many words and sentences, I could understand nothing when I heard French spoken. Worse, I could not hear separate words; I could not tell where one word ended and another began. I also could not detect sound differences such as the difference between dessous and dessus, a simple task for a native speaker. Nor could I produce those sound differences in pronouncing the two words. When I began to be able to hear a little, I would find myself beginning to strain and then lose it again. I discovered that French, unlike English, is spoken without any emphasis on given syllables. What I needed to organize to hear and speak French was different than what I had learned to organize for English. And the hearing coincided with the increasing ability to speak and be involved in communication with people. I am still improving slowly as these skills are far easier to organize before adulthood.

You can see from these examples that nothing is initially given from the world. What is a word, an object, a thing to my experience has *no existence for me independent of my perceiving it.* And my perceiving of it requires an active interaction with the world, including other humans. In the case of language we live in communities of perceivers such as French speakers or English speakers, but each person's nervous system has to organize French or English for the person both as spoken and understood (heard) language. The organization happens through the characteristics of the nervous system, and the action of the person in a community of speakers to begin to communicate with others and be communicated with. Without this active process, which must include *movement* in and interaction with a world, there is no world as such and both the nervous system and "world" remain in *chaos*.

I am suggesting a circularity here, a strange loop in which what we call the world, or reality, is constructed and specified by each growing human being, through the interaction of that being with its environment. For each being at the same time that environment has no structure until there is *interaction*, and this structure changes as the person grows. Because this notion is strange and nonhabitual I have said it in different ways. The evidence for it is clear enough, nevertheless hard to accept, for our constructions have such permanence and stability in our ordinary lives, and such usefulness in getting around in the world that we attach ourselves strongly to them and project them outward to say this is the world, this is reality. It is only in mindfulness and openness to exploration of ourselves as in *Quantum Psychology* that we can find the edges of how we are enclosed.

What is true for perception is also so for that more basic organization process, the organization of our action and movement. In my professional work as a *Feldenkrais movement teacher*, I have had the occasion to work with small children with developmental difficulties usually related to neurological problems. These children move themselves either *chaotically* or with such *stereotyped patterns* that they can not do any action they may want for themselves. For example, they may not be able to reach, lift their head to look around, or roll themselves over, let alone sit up or crawl. What I do is to create some conditions for the child that I know have the potential to allow their nervous systems to do what any child's *nervous system* can do; and that is to *organize the chaos of the movements* into actions that satisfy the child's desire to direct him or herself. The child desires to act in the world, and indeed must do so in order to survive. This is not the place to describe the whole process, but one condition that seems essentially important is to create an environment of safety for the child so that the child knows experientially, through touch, etc., that he will not get hurt. When you see the new organization appear for the child, it seems to come from nowhere. I do not teach movements or corrections of movements to the child. But you may suddenly see a child lift the head and be able to look around when lying prone. Of course he also organizes to use the arms and elbows at the same time. A particular four year old child I worked with who could not even hold her head up properly in sitting on her mother's lap appeared at first completely listless, uncommunicative and uninterested in anything around herself. When she gained for herself the organization necessary to hold her head and look around she became a different person. She made eye contact and looked at people. She began to use words and smiled and interacted with both her parents and other people around her. She became alive and intentional.

As much as we have learned about psychology, the nervous system, cognition, and related topics in the age of science, we know next to nothing about the *organizational abilities of the nervous system to create order*. The Nobel Prize winning biologist, Gerald Edelman, has noted in his book, *Neural Darwinism*, that modern neuroscience has not been able to explain how "neural structure and function can result in pattern recognition or perceptual categorization with generalization." He charges that the critical difficulties and contradictions have been evaded or obscured. The point is that science also includes a created world view that directs the attention to parts and mechanisms, and away from seeing how the *observer* is part of the data or how we must use the sense of the whole to work with any problem of living systems. Yet the ability of our nervous system to make order is so omnipresent to our lives that we normally fail to notice it. It is an elusive obvious. Nevertheless a number of scientists over the past thirty years have been creating a revolution in biology, neuroscience, and the science of complex systems that at least give a hint as to how to answer our question. What we are after then is *how does a nervous system create order out of chaos?* Even to ask this question is to put us into another strange loop. For whatever we evolve as an answer is based on the cognitions that we create as a result of the very system we are examining. It is within this understanding, however, that an answer becomes possible.

There are four streams of thinking that converge on the question at hand. From the practical side there is the thinking of Dr. Moshe Feldenkrais, who was my mentor and teacher. Dr. Feldenkrais developed a methodology for human growth and improvement based on a kinesthetic self awareness and a keen observation of how human beings developed their most basic capabilities, such as the ability to erect themselves in gravity, walk on two legs, and speak. These capabilities, he noted, were organized and therefore learned without the benefit of instruction. In fact instruction could only in the end be detrimental to the process. It would seem that one would have to conclude that the basic human capabilities are self organized through the activity of the person. *The most direct path to the nervous system, then, is through awareness and movement, and the very best we can do is to support and evoke the self organizing abilities of the system. It was no wonder that Dr. Feldenkrais saw the primary function of the nervous system as organizing chaos.* Here we have the observation of self organization, but no theory of how it is possible.

Three recent scientific revolutions direct us to how self organization is not only possible, but inevitable. The first, and closest to the views I have expressed, stems from systems biology and cybernetics and is most cogently developed in the work of the Chilean biologists Humberto Maturana and

Francisco Varela. The second is based on what happens to systems at conditions far from equilibrium and the study of such systems thermodynamically. Nobel prize winner, Ilya Prigogine, has been instrumental in this area. The third stream comes from the study of complex systems at the edge of chaos, and what happens when iteration is present in the system. Collectively the work of the Santa Fe institute has been most significant here with regard to living systems.

We now come to the common feature of all these approaches. And that is the discovery that in a system where the output of the system is fed back into the system, an emerging order or pattern appears as a consequence in the form of some sort of quasi stable structure. The process of feeding back something into the system repeatedly is called *iteration in chaos theory*. With regard to the nervous system, Gerald Edelman uses the term reentrant signalling. Maturana and Varela speak of recursion. This discovery of *order emerging from chaos*, however, is something novel to the sciences that previously had only considered linear chains of events and systems at or near equilibrium. Previously the sciences could only deal with systems that were totally ordered or totally random in a precise way. Complex systems were treated by analogy to what was known. The appearance of emergent properties of a system were not considered. This is why, for example in psychology, it was assumed for many years that it was the environment that organized the nervous system. The process of self organization turns the tables around and we can begin to see that it is life that organizes the environment. We can understand this internally in that the features we take to be the external environment are the consequence of the internal processes of our nervous system that lead to perception and understanding. But living creatures also literally change and organize the external environment by creating, building, designing, etc. In other words perception is not some arbitrary construction of the nervous system. It enables the person to function in the world.

Maturana and Varela in *The Tree of Knowledge* present the most cogent and complete view of living beings from a systems perspective. Already with the single cell life is a process of creating order. A living cell separates itself as a unity from the rest of the universe by creating a membrane. Within the membrane the processes of the cell are such that the end product is itself. Thus in the very essence of life we have the appearance of a strange loop. And although the cell takes in nutrients and energy, and eliminates waste, nothing on the outside effects or changes the basic loop or cyclic organization of processes within the cell as long as the cell stays alive. In other words the *cell is closed to information from the outside*. Darwin actually first proposed this notion when he declared that a new organism could not inherit acquired characteristics. How then does a living cell do the things we observe about its behavior? In response to perturbations from outside the cell, the cell modifies its structure to maintain the organization of processes and its internal set of relationships. This is a basic law of biology according to Maturana, that *for a living system to stay alive it must maintain its organization of processes.*

The beauty of this approach is that it generalizes to all aspects of living organization. Thus *the nervous system is organized also as a closed loop*. This seems a very radical stance to take. How can we say that a nervous system does not input or output information? We know now that every sensory surface is modified by feedback from the central nervous system. We know that a sensory surface, say the retina of the eye, does not respond to stimulation itself, but to difference. An image fixed on the retina will disappear in a very short time as you can find out by looking at something without moving your eyes. We know that color vision does not have a direct relation to the frequencies of light hitting the retina but to the relation of hues and the incident light. The eye is not like a camera, and the brain is not like a computer where the inputs and outputs are always in relation to the human beings that use them. In this view the nervous system, like the cell, operates to maintain it's organization, and selects structural changes that permit it to continue operating. *It is a plastic system, yet it retains a history of it's interactions through what is formed in it's structures. We call this memory.*

We speak here of a nervous system within itself. We live, however, in interaction and communication with others. Here we come to a present confusion to many people who have investigated thinking and the nervous system. Because we use symbols and representations in our communication, we have too easily assumed that these representations are internalized within the system, and that they are operative within the workings of the system, i.e., that our brain contains a model of reality. If we go back to the examples cited at the beginning of this essay, one can begin to discern that this model of the brain does not fit with what one experiences when a perception shifts. The perception is evoked by interaction with an environment, but the *perception is a structure, a learned organization*, that maintains a compatibility between ourselves and the world.

These are difficult points. They challenge the received views that we get from our education. We need these basics, however, to begin to investigate the more complex matters brought to attention through Quantum Psychology. We are sailing here between two conflicting philosophies: that of idealism and solipsism, that our minds create reality, and realism, that our brains contain representations of a real external material world. There is one further split to confront. And that is the notion that what we call mind and psyche is one realm and what we refer to as body is another.

Earlier in this essay I suggested that the organization of

movement and the organization of perception were interrelated events in the nervous system, that they arise simultaneously. From the perspective of the Feldenkrais work, where there is an emphasis on observing how one organizes oneself to act and function in the world, one begins to notice that what we call *mental functions are never separate from motor functions*. Careful self observation will reveal, for example, that when picturing an object in one's mind's eye with the eyes closed, there is the appearance of tension in the muscles of the eye. Similarly with emotional events, there is a perceived state of the motor system that accompanies what we call the emotion. We can see and recognize the motor attitude of a person and guess as to what that person is feeling. We can feel in ourselves changes in our breathing, our state of tension as we shift feeling states. From this perspective we must contend that what we call *mind and body are not two entities related to each other, but a single unity*. Let us use the word, soma, to refer to this unity. This fits well with the ideas of Maturana and Varela where organization is embodied in the processes of the system.

Given that our systems are fundamentally self referential, that we thereby have the ability to self observe, and through language communicate to ourselves about it, we must open to the possibility of mindfulness as a pathway to knowledge about ourselves. We can explore and separate from the very structures we create for living our lives and find pathways to new patterns and options that give us the flexibility for life for which we are already capable. This is the project of Quantum Psychology as developed by Stephen Wolinsky as well as the Feldenkrais work. Feldenkrais work emphasizes awareness as it is experienced in movement, Quantum Psychology the awareness of the processes as experienced in the psyche. Each work is implicitly and explicitly somatic in its basic thought.

We now speak about more complex structures that are

created in our interactions in the world to *order the chaos* internally and externally, and to create the stability we use in our functioning. As you have explored the exercises in this book and perhaps in the previous *Quantum Consciousness, Volume I* by Stephen Wolinsky, you probably came in contact with certain somatic organizations and structures that were called identities. You may have noted that the state connected to the identity involved particular body feelings and a particular motor attitude. For example, you may have experienced an identity called inner child. In your feeling you may have felt small and vulnerable, you may have experienced your breathing as shallow and noticed a slight collapse in the chest and a rounding of the shoulders. In this state you would have a very difficult time asserting yourself with other people and at the same time you might feel victimized and perhaps persecuted. Now this state, according to our concept of self organization, *was initially organized to maintain our organization and inner relationships in the face of a difficulty in our interaction with others.* We can speak here of structural coupling. In a family this will include the dynamics of interaction with other family members. It may have been that by projecting the attitude of a hurt child, we found that our parents behaved differently to us and gave us comfort. Or perhaps some other response was satisfying in terms that our inner state felt more protected. The state became part of our history.

The beauty of Quantum Psychology or Feldenkrais work is that we have resources to first experience and then observe such a state in such a way that we can realize that the identity is only a construction of our system, and that we have available alternative constructions that may easily serve us better in life. We do not have to identify with an identity or the somatic state that accompanies it. We fear chaos. Yet our system is always capable of continuous transformation that mesh with what is happening in the environment. In one sense we come to life with a jumble of nerve cells with an unlimited number of interconnections, a thoroughly chaotic situation. Because of the self organizing capacity of the system, within a few months that nervous system has formed useful structures that channel the activity of the system into actions. In this sense a living person with his or her brain is the most remarkable organizer of chaos in the universe. As humans with our capacity for self consciousness, and reliance thereby on will power, we tend not to trust our system. By living on the edge of chaos, however, we can find that we have all the capacity we need to deal with it. In this we can live full and creative lives.

For Further Reading

Gerald Edelman, *Mental Darwinism*, Basic Books, 1987

Mose Feldenkrais, *The Elusive Obvious*, Meta Publications, 1981

John Lilly, *The Center of the Cyclone*, Julian Press, 1972

Humberto Maturana & Francisco Varek, *The Tree of Knowledge; The Biological Roots of Human Understanding*, New Science Library, 1987.

Ilya Progogine & Isabelle Stengers, *Order Out of Chaos*, Bantam Books, 1984.

Oliver Sacks, *To See and Not See*, New Yorker, May 10, 1993

Jan H. Sultan,
**Advanced Instructor,
Senior Member of the
Rolf Institute of Structural Integration**

During the 1930s when Dr. Rolf was formulating her ideas and techniques about the way in which the human body could be affected positively through her method of manipulation and education, the dominant scientific paradigm was based on Newtonian mechanics as the accepted description of the laws governing the behavior of material bodies.

If you were interested in health and the function of the body, the operational descriptions of the body were based on the model proposed by Renee Descartes, a French philosopher who wrote in the late 1600s that the human body was "nothing more than a soft machine" incidentally and temporarily inhabited by a soul.

Although Dr. Rolf had an abiding interest in metaphysics which in part shaped her world view, she was a scientist as well. She received a doctorate in biochemistry from Columbia University in 1920. Because of her scientific background and her desire to place her ideas in the mainstream culture, she insisted on describing her approach to the body in the language of anatomy and physics. This, in spite of her understanding of the deeper, and more difficult to validate aspects of her work.

In her writing and speaking *she stressed the physics of the structure as her logical base.* Her descriptions are Newtonian and in truth her physical approach was based on the Cartesian model of the body as a soft machine. Dr. Rolf was also a Darwinist in that she believed in evolution as the progression of development of species over time.

She set out to affect the posture of the body towards a better working arrangement with *gravity* by getting the major weight units of the body better balanced around the central-vertical line of gravity's influence to achieve better balance and better function. *She held that this upright posture was the evolutionary thrust of our human species as a biped,* and that if we took on that project consciously, we would become more human and manifest that higher level of function.

It is at this point that Dr. Rolf's true genius, and the crux of her major contribution to our understanding of the body lies. She stood on the Newtonian-Cartesian-Darwinian ground of her time and saw forward to wholism. She observed that as the people she worked with got more organized, they felt better. they reported less restriction in movement, and that they had more energy. She speculated that as the struggle to stand and move upright in gravity gave way to better balance, the life energy became unbound and available for more creative expression. She believed that a better relationship with the gravity field actually allowed the person to be fed and supported by that field rather than broken down. She underscored the idea that *refinement of the body was a direct route to higher consciousness.*

Over the years, Dr. Rolf saw that it was necessary for the person to "take charge" of their structure as in a Yogic practice. As a result, a certain amount of her therapeutic effort went into education. She was fond of pointing out that the Latin root of the word education was educare, which means "to lead out". She insisted that her manipulative efforts to release the connective tissues involved in the postural adaptations of the individual would allow the emergence of the ideal form. When that form was available, then the person had to follow certain postural directives as a learning process to stabilize the new configuration.

Rolf insisted that the *body* (person) is related to its environment through *gravity*, and that the medium of that relationship in the body was the *connective tissues*. These tissues are collectively based on the collagen molecule, and are seen as a system unto themselves concerned with support, form, and the distribution of adaptations to gravitational stress. With this observation Rolf stepped firmly into wholism as she stopped looking at the parts of the body, and began to look at those parts within the context of the whole in its environment. She saw how adaptation to a local injury or developmental problem soon found its way into the whole. That a neck injury had to effect the ankle, and an ankle injury could throw the whole body off balance. She held that the process of compensation always involved a loss of motion and available length in the structure, and that *the sum total of the adaptations in any individual body could be seen as its aging process!*

It is worth noting that the "modern medicine" of today still rests on largely Newtonian-Cartesian premises with surgery and drugs being applied to cure disease or injury without much thought of the person to which this is happening, or the context of their lives.

The history of Rolfing took a major turn in the late sixties when Dr. Rolf came to Esalen Institute to give treatments to Dr. Fritz Perls who was a psychiatrist in residence there. Dr. Perls had been a student of Sigmund Freud in Vienna, and had become a pioneer in humanistic psychology. Over the years he had developed his own unique brand of psycho-therapy which centered around the idea of Gestalt, which loosely means the "completed whole" from the German. Simply, Perls' theory held that we carry incomplete situations in us that reflect traumas or unresolved conflicts, and that these patterns keep us from acting truly in the present. He held that these time-bound situations color our perception of present experiences and will cause self-defeating and neurotic behaviors.

Perls' therapy was very expressive as he guided his patients to express bound up feeling as a way to contact the unconscious material and bring it into the present. He would have his patients pound pillows, imagine parents or other authority figures in a dialog where the patient would play both themselves and the "other" to contact the underlying time-bound state.

Ida Rolf came to Esalen and worked with Perls to help relieve his painful angina pectoris condition. Perls was impressed and inspired by Rolf's method and message. It was a perfect match! Perls' incomplete situation and Rolf's method of releasing the structure through systematic manipulation. Perls saw in Rolf's method the ideal tool for accessing the unconscious material in the body so it could be felt, expressed, and released into the present.

A marriage was made here of the body and psychotherapy. You might say that Ida Rolf was the *reluctant bride* in this situation. She appreciated the sudden demand for her work and set about launching a program to train practitioners to meet the new demand. She was simultaneously fearful and protective of her brainchild being devoured by the focus on the psychological benefits of her work to the exclusion of the somatic aspects. She went to great lengths to assert that while psychological changes were a useful and interesting by-produce of the Rolfing process, the real job lay in *getting the body organized in gravity*, at which point better mental health was to be expected!

In spite of her reservations, Rolfing was launched in the public culture by the interest in human potential that was born in the crucible of Esalen Institute in the late 60's.

Before the connection with Esalen, Dr. Rolf had focused on teaching her ideas and techniques to Osteopaths and Chiropractors and to a few lay people whose interests leaned toward metaphysics. She was primarily interested in impacting the viewpoint of practitioners of physical medicine with her ideas.

From Esalen forward, she began to train a cadre of practitioners who would practice "pure" Rolfing, but who were interested in human development rather than physical medicine. Their market was driven by the human potential movement.

The Rolfers went to work, and Dr. Rolf dedicated herself more and more to teaching and working on her magnum opus; the book of Rolfing. From about 1970 on, she also trained a handful of teachers as the demand for her classes outstripped her ability to teach them.

Dr. Rolf passed away in 1979, leaving the Rolf Institute as the official organization that carries forward the development of her work and that is responsible for training "certified Rolfers". The work has maintained its identity while undergoing significant changes in its range of application. The original interest of Dr. Rolf to impact on the "modern" beliefs in physical medicine has been carried forward to include the teaching of seminars for physical therapists, chiropractors, and other manual therapists. This goes hand in hand with the less publicized premises of Rolfing as a school of inquiry concerned with questions relating to the nature of human bodily being.

We have grounded and assimilated the changes brought to our view of physical reality and bodily being by advances in science. Consider what Einstein's theory of relativity did to Newtonian mechanics, or what the incursion of ideas about the body from Indian and China (in the form of Vedic and Taoist medicine) have done to our view of the body. To paraphrase noted physicist John A. Wheeler, who writes in "Spacetime and Gravity" that Einstein's theory of relativity tells us that mass and gravity are one. That each mass (body) has its own gravity, and that all physical bodies interact gravitationally. *There is no field of gravity, but only relationship.*

We have also come to terms with Descarte, and hold that the body is so much more than a "soft machine". We see that the body is the seat of being and our vehicle for our experiences to flow through. Our years of working with people have taught us that the *form* is an expression of the whole, and that we cannot always impose a template of order on a person's body to the exclusion of their readiness to move that way. We have learned that sometimes the ideal form can take people away from the real issues they need to face before they can be upright, and that to try and "stand straight" may create disorder for the person in some circumstances. You might say we have grown more flexible in the application of Rolf's idea, and more patient with the process it takes to get there.

In the process of learning more about the medium of the body, our *technical approaches have changed a lot from the direct and forceful method that characterized Rolf's approach.* While we have not completely abandoned those techniques, we have adapted a whole array of more subtle approaches that *respect the intrinsic rhythms of the body, and modulate the rates of charge and discharge that are so characteristic of life systems.* We take care that those energetic processes are given their due and are not overrun in favor of merely straightening and lengthing the body. Many kinds of trauma leave their mark on the body, not as tension and rigidity, but as *resignation and disassociation.* These patterns need to be modulated and reintegrated through the nervous system with *a gentle "following" touch, rather than a forceful push.* As awareness and connection are re-established then the free flow of sensation is restored as in Perls' Gestalt formation.

Our training program today leads the Rolfer to understand the *physical structures as well as the role of the nervous system in the maintenance of form and function*. The techniques vary from the old style to a touch that is *subtle* and *evocative*. Our work includes directives that lead the clients' awareness to the internal states and rhythms that make up both the postural habits and the basic orientation within the body and the world.

We have not abandoned Ida Rolf's visionary line of inquiry nor are we following a dogmatic recipe. We are following the Rolfing road where it leads in a spirit of lively inquiry. When we ask someone to change their form and pattern of movement, there is an implicit directive for them to examine and experience themselves differently. This is the line of inquiry we are following; what does it mean to experience the world differently than before? What is the nature of this transformative attempt? What is the best way to learn through the body to facilitate this process?

In a way the *Rolfing process* can be seen as an accelerated *Yoga course*, in which the Rolfer assists the clients in clearing a certain amount of history from the body to get going, and to begin the process of the linking of body, mind, and spirit into present time and space, which is the ultimate goal of the inquiry.

We as Rolfers do not presume to provide the meaning for the clients' experience, which we see as a misuse of the therapy process, but rather to serve as guides for that portion of the journey that involves working with the patterns in the body that are time-bound and that limit the ability to be here and now. As the body gets more integrated, the flow of sensation and awareness increase to literally bring the person into their body allowing for them to be more able to use themselves and the world in a more kindly and effective way.

BIBLIOGRAPHY

Almaas, A. H. *The Void*. Maine: Samuel Weiser, Inc. 1986.

American College Dictionary. New York: Random House. 1963.

Bennett, J. G. *How We Do What We Do*. West Virginia: Claymont Press.

Bentov, Itzhak. *Stalking the Wild Pendulum: On the Mechanics of Consciousness*. Vermont: Destiny Books. 1977.

Buddhist Text Translation Society. Commentary by Venerable Tripitaka Master Hslian Hua. *Shuranama Sutra*. Sino-America Buddhist Association. Buddhist Text Translation Society. 1977.

Bohm, David. *Quantum Theory*. London: Constable. 1951.

Bohm, David. *Wholeness and the Implicate Order*. London: Ark Paperbacks. 1980.

Bohm, David and Peat, F. David *Science, Order and Creativity*. New York: Bantam Books, 1987.

Bohm, David. *Unfolding Meaning*. London: Ark Paperbacks. 1985.

Briggs, John and Peat, F. David *Looking Glass Universe: The Emerging Science of Wholeness*. New York: Simon & Schuster. 1984.

Brown, G. Spencer *Transcripts Professor Von Meier*, Art 269, March 19, 1973.

Capra, Fritjof. *The Tao of Physics*. New York: Bantam Books. 1976.

Davis, M. Fanning, McKay, M. *Thoughts and Feelings: The Art of Cognitive Stress Intervention*. Calfornia: New Harbinger Press. 1981.

Herbert, Nick. *Quantum Reality: Beyond the New Physics*. New York: Anchor Press. 1985.

Hoffer, Eric. *The True Believer*. New York. Harper and Row. 1951.

Hoffman, Yoel. *The Sound of the One Hand*. New York: Basic Books. 1975.

Hua, Tripitaka Master. *The Heart Sutra and Commentary*. California: Buddhist Text Translation Society. 1980.

Isherwood, Christopher and Prabhavanda, Swami. *How to Know God: The Yoga Aphorisms of Patanjali*. California: New American Library. 1953, p. 121-122.

Korzybski, Alfred. *Science and Sanity: An Introduction to Non-Aristotelian Systems and General Semantics.* International Non-Aristotelian Library Publishing Company. 1933.

Lang, R. D. *Knots*. Vintage Press.

Maharishi Ramana. *The Spiritual Teaching of Ramana Maharshi*. Boulder and London: Shambhala, 1972.

Morrison, Philip and Phylis. *Powers of Ten*. New York: Scientific American Library. 1982.

Muktananda, Swami. *Play of Consciousness*. Ganeshpuri: Shree Gurudev Ashram. 1974.

Naranjo, Claudio. *Enneatype Structures: Self Analysis for the Seeker.* California: Gateways IDHHB, Inc. 1990.

Nisargadatta Maharaj. *I Am That, Volume I*. Bombay: Chetana.1978

Nisargadatta Maharaj. *I Am That, Volume II*. Bombay: Codeine.1978.

Palmer, Helen. *The Enneagram*. California: Harper & Row. 1988.

Peat, F. David *Synchronicity: The Bridge Between Matter and Mind*. New York: Bantam Books. 1987.

Peat, F. David & Briggs, John. *The Turbulent Mirror: An Illustrated Guide to Chaos Theory & the Science of Wholeness*. New York: Harper & Row. 1989.

Peat, F. David *Einstein's Moon: Bell's Theorem and the Curious Quest for Quantum Reality*. Chicago: Contemporary Books. 1990.

Peat, F. David *The Philosophers Stone: Chaos, Synchronicity, and the Hidden Order of the World*. New York: Bantam Books. 1991.

Reich, Wilhelm. *The function of the Orgasm. The Discovery of the Orgone*. New York: World Publishing. 1942.

Riso, Don Richard. *Personality Types: Using the Enneagram for Self-Discovery*. Boston, MA: Houghton Mifflin Company. 1987.

Riso, Richard Don. *Understand the Enneagram*. Massachusetts: Houghton Mifflin Company. 1988.

Russell, Bertrand. *The ABC of Relativity*. Mentor Book. New York: New American Library. 1958.

Shah, Indries. *Learning How to Learn: Psychology and Spiritually in the Sufi Way*. London: Octagon Press. 1978.

Shah, Indries. *The Perfumed Scorpion, The Way to the Way*. San Francisco: Harper & Row. 1978.

Singh Jaideva. *Siva Sutra, The Yoga of Supreme Identity*. Delhi: Motilal Banarsidass. 1979.

Singh Jaideva. *Spanda Karikas*. Delhi: Motilal Banarsidass.1980.

Singh Jaideva. *Pratyabhijnahrdeyam: The Secret of Self Recognition*. Delhi: Motilal Banarsidass. 1963.

Suzuki, Shunru. *Zen Mind, Beginners Mind*. New York: Weatherhill. 1970.

Varela, Francisco, Thompson Evan, Rosch, Eleanor. *The Embodied Mind: Cognitive Science and Human Experience*. Cambridge: MIT Press. 1983.

Venkatesananda, Swami. *The Supreme Yoga*. (2 Volumes) Western Australia: Chiltern Yoga Trust. 1976.

Wilber, Ken. *No Boundary: Eastern and Western Approaches to Personal Growth*. Boulder/London: New Science Library. 1981.

Wilson, Colin. *Gurdjieff: The War Against Sleep*. England: Aquarian Press, England. 1980.

Wolf, Fred. *Parallel Universes: The Search of Other Worlds*. New York: Touchstone, Simon & Schuster, Inc. 1988.

INDEX

A

abreaction 245
Acupuncture 90, 91
advanced attention training 10
appropriate reaction 245

B

Beck, A. 212
Bell, John Stuart 5, 68, 69
Bell's Theorem 5, 69
Bennett, J.G. 49
Bentov, Itzhak 100, 137
bifurcation 40, 77, 79, 84, 90, 91, 92, 98, 117, 148, 149, 206, 229, 246, 250, 251, 253
Bioenergetics 91
Bohm, David 4, 53, 59, 64, 103, 106, 110, 150, 300
Briggs, John 26, 78, 84, 89
Brown, G. Spencer 267
Buddhism 56, 110
Buddhist 1, 3, 37, 38

C

Chakra 91, 92
Chaos Theory 2, 15, 19, 22, 27, 33, 36, 40
chaotic 22
character analysis 10
Ch'i 54, 56
Ch'i Kung 91
Christianity 3, 5, 110

D

DeWitt 47

E

Edelman, Gerald 326, 328
Einstein, Albert 27, 63, 66, 69, 73, 90, 115, 117
Enneagram 10
Erickson, Milton H. 17, 77, 112, 268